Contents

Race and News

The history of American journalism is marked by disturbing representations of people and communities of color, from the disgraceful stereotypes of pre-civil rights America, to the more subtle myths that are reflected in routine coverage by journalists all over the country. *Race and News: Critical Perspectives* aims to examine these journalistic representations of race, and in doing so to question whether or not we are living in a post-racial world. By looking at national coverage of stories like the Don Imus controversy, Hurricane Katrina, Barack Obama's presidential candidacy, and even the Virginia Tech shootings, readers are given an opportunity to gain insight into both subtle and overt forms of racism in the newsroom and in national dialogue.

The book itself is divided into two sections, with the first examining the journalistic routine and the decisions that go into covering a story with, or without, relation to race. The second section, comprised of case studies, explores the coverage of national stories and how they have affected the dialogue on race and racism in the United States. As a whole, the collection of essays and studies also reflects a variety of research approaches. With a goal of contributing to the discussion about race and its place in American journalism, this broad examination makes *Race and News* an ideal text for courses on cultural diversity and the media, as well as making it valuable to professional journalists and journalism students who seek to improve their approach to coverage of diverse communities.

Christopher P. Campbell is Professor and Director of the School of Mass Communication and Journalism at the University of Southern Mississippi. He is the author of *Race, Myth and the News* (Sage, 1995).

Kim M. LeDuff is Associate Professor and Assistant Director at the School of Mass Communication and Journalism at the University of Southern Mississippi.

Cheryl D. Jenkins is Assistant Professor at the School of Mass Communication and Journalism at the University of Southern Mississippi.

Rockell A. Brown is Assistant Professor at the School of Communication at Texas Southern University.

Race and News
Critical Perspectives

**Christopher P. Campbell,
Kim M. LeDuff,
Cheryl D. Jenkins, and
Rockell A. Brown**

 Routledge
Taylor & Francis Group

NEW YORK AND LONDON

First published 2012
by Routledge
270 Madison Avenue, New York, NY 10016

Simultaneously published in the UK
by Routledge
2 Park Square, Milton Park, Abingdon, Oxon OX14 4RN

Routledge is an imprint of the Taylor & Francis Group, an informa business

Library of Congress Cataloging in Publication Data
Race and news : critical perspectives / edited by
    [Christopher P. Campbell ... [et al.].
        p. cm.
    1. Racism in the press–United States. 2. Race relations and the press–United States. 3. African Americans–Press coverage. 4. Mass media and race relations–United States. 5. Television broadcasting of news–Political aspects–United States. 6. Journalism–Political aspects–United States—History–21st century. 7. Journalism–Objectivity–United States. 8. United States–Race relations–Press coverage. 9. United States–Race relations.
    I. Campbell, Christopher P.
    PN4888.R3R33 2010
    070.44'93058--dc22   2010029021

ISBN13: 978-0-415-80096-9 (hbk)
ISBN13: 978-0-415-80097-6 (pbk)
ISBN13: 978-0-203-87685-5 (ebk)

Typeset in Minion by Glyph International Ltd.
Printed and bound in the United States of America on acid-free paper by Edwards Brothers, Inc.

Figures and Tables

Foreword

In the final chapter of his 2009 examination of race and economics, *More Than Just Race: Being Black and Poor in the Inner City*, sociologist William Julius Wilson explains how he arrived at a sort of epiphany regarding America's dialogue on race and poverty. In his earlier work (he is the author or editor of a dozen books on the topic), he had argued that a color-blind approach to public policy would be the most effective way to bring about social change. That is, because so many Americans hold fervent mis-perceptions about the relationship between race and poverty—especially that black and Latino Americans are solely responsible for the dreadful economic conditions that affect them at a far greater rate than white Americans—Wilson once believed that it would be more effective to emphasize the impact of social, political and economic policies on *all* poor Americans, rather than on their disproportionate effect on minority communities. He explains his new position:

> In framing public policy we should not shy away from an ex-plicit discussion of the specific issues of race and poverty; on the contrary, we should highlight them in our attempt to convince the nation that these problems should be seriously confronted and that there is an urgent need to address them. The issues of race and poverty should be framed in such a way that not only is a sense of fairness and justice to combat inequality generated, but also people are made aware that our country would be better off if these problems were seriously addressed and eradicated.
>
> (pp. 141–142)

In authoring a book about race and news, we find ourselves in complete agreement with the approach that Wilson now advocates. First, we hope that this book will encourage discussions about race that will lead to a broader understanding of the complex ways that skin color continues to affect American attitudes and public policy. Second, we hope that our analyses of race and news will have an impact on how journalists frame issues of race in the hope that news organizations will eventually provide audiences with coverage that conveys the sense of urgency that will be required to affect public policy and finally move America beyond its racist legacy.

We admit to being baffled by the discussions of American society as "post racial" that surfaced with Barack Obama's candidacy for the presidency of the United States. It's a comforting thought to believe that our country has moved beyond its racist past and that his election is evidence of racial harmony. But there is little evidence to support that belief. Americans who don't happen to be white are far more likely to live in poverty, to receive a second-class education, to have inadequate health care and to be victims of racial discrimination. Our concern is that journalism routinely overlooks the impact of race and racism and has contributed to the notion that we are actually living in a post-racial world.

Our approach to the analysis of news coverage is largely rooted in a body of critical and cultural media studies that was influenced by Stuart Hall and other British Cultural Studies scholars, who believed in closely examining media *texts*—advertisements, television programs, news stories, etc.—to ascertain the meaning of those texts in the context of a broader cultural sense. That is, Hall and his colleagues believed that beneath the surface of the intended (or "preferred") meaning of a media text was the subtle influence of political, social and economic power (Hall, 1982). A news story about a murder, for instance, might be viewed simply as a news organization's routine coverage of violent crime. But for critical and cultural studies scholars, a story about a murder can also carry connotations about racial bias, about economic power, about social history, about political will, and so on. While most of our research is in the form of qualitative *textual analysis*—an approach best suited for answering *how* and *why* questions—a few chapters use quantitative data to answer questions like *who* and *how many*.

Our goal is not to empirically determine the amount or cause of journalism that has a racial context, but to contribute to a dialogue about race and news that we believe is too uncommon; we don't pretend to have a solution to many of the problems that we identify. We do hope to get students, scholars and journalists to consider the issues that we raise, and we believe that it will take that kind of dialogue to arrive at solutions.

While the dominant theoretical paradigm that drives the research in this book is rooted in the work of British Cultural Studies, we've also been heavily influenced by American research on contemporary racism. Among the "types" of racism we examine are "modern," "symbolic" and "everyday" racism; these are ways of identifying the more subtle ways that racism surfaces in American culture in the early twenty-first century. Although America is not devoid of the kind of racism that marked the pre-Civil Rights era, blatant white supremacist attitudes are relatively rare. We are more concerned about the more pernicious and subtle ways in which contemporary racist attitudes can affect the social, political and economic landscape. We also cite the work of Critical Race Theory scholars, who move the discussion of race from ethnic minorities as *Others*, to the analysis of *whiteness* and the examination of how white privilege affects people's attitudes and their support of ill-considered public policy.

This book examines issues related to African Americans more than other ethnic minorities. This is a result of the research interests of the authors, but also speaks to the enormity of the black–white dichotomy in American culture. W. E. B. DuBois wrote more than 100 years ago in *The Souls of Black Folk* (1903) that "the problem of the Twentieth Century is the problem of the color line." We believe that the problem has not been resolved, and that racism remains the problem of the Twenty-First Century. Some of our analyses address coverage related to discrimination against Hispanic, Arab or Asian Americans, providing evidence that the color line that DuBois described is more complicated than ever. We hope that this book will inspire more analysis of the many ways that race plays out in America's increasingly multicultural society.

Indeed, our main goal for pursuing this research is to provoke discussion and to expand the ongoing dialogue about journalism and its potential to provide audiences with coverage that is free of racial stereotypes and offers useful insight into the complicated ways that race affects our world. After each chapter, we've provided a series of discussion questions and assignments that are designed to facilitate the discussion. We've also included lists of places to go for further information about each chapter, including links to Web sites where the dialogue is the most current.

The first part of this book, *Race and the Journalistic Routine*, examines the way that news organizations rely on conventions that dictate coverage that results in predictable but, often, misleading representations of ethnic minorities. Chapter 1, "Yes We Did?: *Race, Myth and the News* Revisited," examines the persistence of myths about race that were first identified in Christopher Campbell's 1995 book, *Race, Myth and the News*. The chapter looks at local television news coverage of the Martin Luther King, Jr. holiday in 2009, and it argues that the coverage is consistent with the problematic representations that Campbell identified in his 1995 study. The chapter argues that coverage of King Day in 2009, which occurred the day before the inauguration of President Barack Obama, dramatically reinforced the "myth of assimilation," which provides audiences with a sense of America's triumph over racism despite overwhelming evidence that American racism is alive and healthy.

Chapter 2, "Newsroom Diversity and Representations of Race," provides a critical examination of how the newspaper industry has handled the coverage of complex topics that deal with issues like race with limited insight from a diverse workforce. Data shows that newsroom employment diversity declined in the early 2000s at most daily newspapers in the United States. This is problematic as recent U.S. Census figures show that mainstream media now covers and serves a more diverse population. The lack of cultural and historical perspective from members of the media creates routine journalism that in many instances ends up reflecting the "preferred meanings" of a still dominant white society. And, even though the physical numbers of the population indicate a shift downward in the proportionate number of whites in this country, the reality is that from a hegemonic standpoint the values of this group constitute the dominant ideology in the newsroom. The implications of having limited diversity in newsrooms and the effect that it has on news content and how media are viewed in society was apparent in the coverage of remarks made by Senator Harry Reid in 2008 about President Barack Obama's lighter skin tone and lack of "negro" dialect helping his chances of winning the democratic nomination. Known to forgo traditional notions of objective news reporting in favor of a more reflective, interpretive approach, black newspapers were able to reflect on the systemic and structural inequalities that continue to exist in this country and included the influence of race on the discussion about Reid's remarks. This chapter argues that such context is often missing from mainstream news reporting, particularly when it comes to covering sensitive matters like race. Mainstream journalists tend to take an episodic rather than a thematic perspective towards the events they cover which leaves out valuable information for interpretation and reflection. This chapter argues that this shortcoming of the American mass media makes it important to take stock of whether or not this institution has figured out a way to meet the challenges of serving a more diverse population.

Chapter 3, "National News Coverage of Race in the Era of Obama," takes a critical look at major news stories involving race that rose to prominence between the summers of 2008 and 2009. The election of the first

African-American president in the U.S. might suggest a post-racial America, but this study questions that notion in light of other news stories during that year. This critique positions Parts I and II of CNN's *Black in America* series as virtual bookends for a year that not only included Obama's election, but racially charged "tea party" and town hall meetings, the arrest of African-American scholar Henry Louis Gates, Jr. at his own home, and a group of minority students being ejected from a Philadelphia country club pool. The chapter suggests that the U.S. still has work to do in regards to race relations.

Chapter 4, "'New' News, Hegemony and Representations of Black Male Athletes," examines the intersection of race, sex and mass media through an interpretive textual analysis of mediated representations of black male athletes involved in controversies concerning sex and white women. Based in Critical Mixed Race Theory, the chapter analyzes several modern examples to illustrate this intersection by examining the hegemonic racial codes and mythmaking that surface in media coverage of black male athletes. Athletes featured in the analysis include Terrell Owens, LeBron James and Tiger Woods. The analysis suggests that issues of race (particularly racism) are stereotypically represented in U.S. contemporary news coverage as there remains a tendency for media organizations to fall back on the familiar common-sense way of portraying black males as hypersexual beasts.

Chapter 5, "From the Water Cooler to the World Wide Web: Race and Audience Commentary on News Stories On-line," examines user posts on newspaper Web sites in response to news stories where race and ethnicity were prominent factors. The results suggest that audiences feel comfortable expressing rude and often racist comments in the usually anonymous on-line environment. The results also indicate that story topics may play a role in whether users post comments related to actual stories or choose to discuss other community issues that are of greater concern. The chapter suggests that perhaps in this era of new media, the audience will play a greater role in setting the media's agenda by posting the issues that they deem most salient.

Chapter 6, "Ethnic News Media and Marginalization: African-American Newspaper Coverage of the AIDS Crisis," examines ethnic media and how the black press covered HIV and AIDS; the chapter also examines author Cathy Cohen's suggestion that "secondary marginalization" may be a factor with regard to HIV and AIDS and the African-American community. Specifically, the chapter examines black newspaper coverage of HIV and AIDS from 1991 through 2001 to better understand how HIV and AIDS information was disseminated, characterized and framed during that crucial second decade of the epidemic with special attention given to coverage of people with AIDS. The chapter argues that it is important to have an understanding of how the news media frame complex issues, especially those pertaining to health, because the characterization or presentation of the information may influence or affect individuals' choices regarding health as well as public policy decisions. The findings indicate that some of the popular African-American newspapers have done only a mediocre job in their coverage of AIDS, even as it specifically pertains to African Americans and, perhaps unintentionally, contributed to the crisis during a critical period as AIDS spread in the black community.

The second part of the book, *Covering Race: Contemporary Case Studies*, examines news coverage of events from the first decade of the twenty-first century that included problematic representations of race. Chapter 7, "Simple Incivility or Outright Racism? How Newspapers Covered Joe Wilson's Outburst during Obama's Congressional Health Care Address," examines newspaper coverage after September 9, 2009, when President Obama addressed Congress about his plan for health care reform. During the speech he was interrupted with a boisterous "You lie!" from Republican Representative Joe Wilson of South Carolina. That incident brought into question whether or not the action was indicative of a clear lack of respect for the president or if it might have more to do with the president's race. This chapter is a critical analysis of newspaper coverage following Obama's speech and Wilson's outburst. Three publications were examined: *The Chicago Tribune*, *The State* (of Columbia, South Carolina) and the *Atlanta Journal Constitution*. The chapter examines the difference in how the events were covered regionally.

Chapter 8, "The Real Price of Oppression: Fox News Coverage of the Virginia Tech Shooter," looks at one particular Fox News special, *Crime Scene: The Virginia Tech Massacre*, as an example of how national news coverage might be used to empower audiences and improve society rather than simply reporting the facts. Local newscasts and even national evening newscasts are severely limited by the length of the broadcasts. As a result, audiences are given headlines, as opposed to in-depth reporting that not only reports the facts but the social effects and the possible solutions. Long-form news reports like the one examined in this study have an advantage. There is more time to tell the story and include important details such as background and future social implications that are left out of short reports. But, unfortunately, as this chapter argues, sometimes these long-form reports fall short of their potential.

Chapter 9, "'Nappy-Headed Hos': Media Framing, Blame Shifting and the Controversy over Don Imus' Pejorative Language," examines how the media covered the events that encompassed the 2007 Don Imus controversy and the shift from focusing on Imus' controversial statements and subsequent repercussions to that of the tribulations of the hip hop culture and the use of misogynistic language in song lyrics by rap artists. The chapter argues that Imus' obvious use of "blame shifting" in this controversy and the media's framing of this incident to validate that shift is a palpable case of image restoration and the ideological constructions of reality. The subsequent framing of the Imus controversy by the media and the dual role this powerful cultural industry takes on in this controversy subtly undergirds the notion that the media became a "target audience" that was manipulated into constructing a reality that Imus' racist language was a part of a bigger problem in the African-American community's sub-culture known as hip hop. Imus used the news media to defend his image by shifting the blame away from his racist, sexist remarks and redirecting the controversy to a mediated discourse on the "in group" language of the hip hop culture; the media in turn create momentum not necessarily about Imus' comments, but follow the blame to the hip hop community.

Chapter 10, "Recoding New Orleans: Race, News, Representation and Spike Lee's *When the Levees Broke*," examines national coverage of events in New Orleans shortly after the city flooded when the city's levees failed during Hurricane Katrina. It contrasts that coverage, which depicted much of the city's African-American population as primitive and criminal, with the representations of the same population in Spike Lee's documentary about the events. The chapter notes the significant difference between deadline-driven daily news coverage and the more reflective approach of documentary production, but it argues that daily journalists could learn something from Lee's more thoughtful, more accurate and less stereotypical examination of the New Orleanians who were victimized by the flooding that inundated the city after Katrina.

Chapter 11, "Localizing Terror, Creating Fear in Post 9/11 Local TV News," examines data that was collected at a time when America was consumed by the terrorist attacks and the possibility of waging war on those believed to be responsible. In the spring of 2003 as the U.S. engaged in war with Iraq, many local TV news stations across the country thought it might be useful to look into possible terrorist connections in their respective cities. A series of reports on one local station in Indianapolis, Indiana, exemplified how the media perpetuated unnecessary and unwarranted fear in viewers. This chapter argues that while people of Middle Eastern descent were once largely absent in the American media, news coverage of this group post 9/11 stereotypes them by oversimplifying their religion, ethnicity and culture and often equates them with terrorism. This is dangerous for members of this group as well as Americans who passively accept these stereotypes.

Chapter 12, "Race and Objectivity: Toward a Critical Approach to News Consumption," examines the fundamental notion that how journalists are traditionally trained to report news stories—"objectively"—may be problematic when those stories deal with a complex issue like race. Using the examples of the media's coverage of the Don Imus controversy and Hurricane Katrina, the chapter argues that when covering complex topics that involve issues of race, ethnicity and culture, taking an interpretive approach to news coverage can provide a more "truthful, comprehensive, and intelligent account of the day's events in a context which gives them meaning" than the traditional idea of reporting in "an unbiased and objective way," or reporting free of interpretation. The benefits of news being reported and interpreted for clarity, value and cultural significance may be a more useful tool for journalists than just repeating facts that have no intrinsic meaning or value to everyday citizens. This chapter argues that the interpretive approach allows journalists to look at the news through the eyes of those who are covered—those who are a part *of* the story. By explaining news developments in the context within which they are created, journalists are able to go beyond traditional news reporting and provide more critical evaluation and meaning.

The book's Afterword, "Re-thinking the News: How American Journalism Can Improve Coverage of Race and Racism," offers a general discussion of the issues that we've examined with an eye toward how news organizations might provide coverage that will contribute to a healthier dialogue on race and race relations. But we don't see the Afterword as the final word, and we hope that our readers—students, teachers, scholars, journalists—will continue to discuss these issues and to contribute to a dialogue that will result in improved news coverage of minority communities and matters of race. Indeed, we hope that our readers will use our analyses as models for their own projects, and we hope those projects will provide additional insight to a dialogue that we believe is of paramount significance.

References

DuBois, W. E. B. (1903). *The souls of black folk*. Chicago: A. C. McClurg & Co.

Hall, S. (1982). Encoding/decoding. In S. Hall, D. Hobson, A. Lowe, & P. Wills (Eds.), *Culture, media, language* (pp. 128–138). London: Hutchinson.

Wilson, W. J. (2009). *More than just race: Being black and poor in the inner city*. New York: W. W. Norton & Company.

PART 1

Race and the Journalistic Routine

CHAPTER 1

Yes We Did?

Race, Myth and the News Revisited

CHRISTOPHER P. CAMPBELL, KIM M. LEDUFF AND
ROCKELL A. BROWN

The editorial cartoon in the January 19, 2009, edition of *The Clarion-Ledger*, the daily newspaper in Jackson, Mississippi, featured a drawing of "History's Calendar," with Monday, January 19, identified as Martin Luther King, Jr. Day and these words: "Yes we can." Tuesday, January 20, was identified as Inauguration Day and read, "Yes we did." The cartoon was drawn by Pulitzer Prize-nominee Marshall Ramsey, whose common-sense understanding of the inauguration of Barack Obama as the 44th president of the United States was reflected in news coverage from all over the country that day: That the inauguration of the country's first African-American president was evidence of the fulfillment of Dr. King's dream.

Such "common sense" has been evident in news coverage of King Day ever since 1986, when the third Monday in January was first celebrated as a national holiday. Christopher Campbell, whose 1995 book *Race, Myth and the News* examined coverage of the holiday in 29 American cities, described the typical coverage of King Day as a reflection of a "myth of assimilation." He argued:

> The ultimate message of nearly all of the coverage of the King holiday ... was that American racism was a thing of the past. The occasional contradiction of that notion was overshadowed by the dominant theme of storytelling and imagery that testified to America as a melting pot. In its coverage of King Day, local television journalism constructed a world in which The American

Dream lives, a parallel world to that of nightly network sitcoms, the world of the (*Cosby Show*'s) Huxtable family.

(p. 111)

That cartoonist Marshall Ramsey, as well as journalists all over the country, would use the inauguration of President Obama to illustrate the country's triumph over racism is precisely consistent with the message that Campbell identified in 1995 and that the authors of this chapter recognized when they examined coverage of the holiday a decade later (Brown, Campbell, & LeDuff, 2005). Did the election of Barack Obama mean that American racism was a thing of the past? Consider this: Only 11 percent of the white voters in Mississippi backed Obama (Tilove, November 8, 2008). That's the same state in which Ramsey's cartoon declared the triumph of racial harmony in the state's largest newspaper. Next door, only 10 percent of Alabama's white voters supported Obama. To the west, 14 percent of white Louisianians voted Obama. A common argument from Southern whites after the election was that many white voters opposed Obama because of his politics, not because of his race. However, Democratic presidential candidates John Kerry in 2004 and Al Gore in 2000 won more than twice as many white votes as Obama in their election bids in those states. Whites were willing to support the politics of Kerry and Gore, but their politics somehow changed when confronted with a black Democratic candidate. *Yes we did*? Maybe not.

The *myth of assimilation* lingers when it comes to news coverage of King Day and other events that news organizations use to demonstrate American racial harmony. We believe that that myth and others that Campbell identified in his examination of local television news remain a significant part of American culture. In this chapter, we will revisit the myths that he described in 1995 in the context of news coverage that aired on the Martin Luther King, Jr. holiday in 2009.

In his 1995 study, Campbell identified patterns of stories in local television news coverage that reinforced three cultural myths. In identifying a "myth of marginality," he argued that people of color are ignored and therefore less significant and *marginalized* in news coverage. He first cited the general "invisibility" of people of color in the news, noting the under-representation of minority news sources and the lack of coverage of minority communities in the newscasts he reviewed, including newscasts from cities with large minority populations. Additionally, he cited other studies (including Entman, 1990, 1992; Gist, 1990; Pease, 1989) that provided evidence of the under-representation and stereotypical portrayal of minorities in all forms of daily news coverage. Campbell also analyzed coverage from two cities that he argued provided evidence of lingering "traditional" or "old fashioned" racism—the kind of racism that most Americans believe to be a thing of the past. The first analysis, in which a TV station in Hattiesburg, Mississippi, followed a brief story on the local celebration of the Martin Luther King, Jr. Holiday with a more detailed story about a local tribute to Robert E. Lee, questioned the curious juxtaposition of the stories as well as the symbolic nature of that juxtaposition. He also examined a story from Minneapolis about a fishing rights controversy that pitted white sportsmen against a regional Indian tribe; the coverage was dominated by the opinions of the sportsmen (led by Minnesota sports legend Bud Grant) and failed to include the perception of the tribe. Campbell argued that the two stories represented "a persistence of racial insensitivity that—when compounded by the news media's general under-representation of minority life—can contribute to a dangerous ignorance about people of color and a continuance of discrimination and injustice" (p. 57).

Second, he identified a "myth of difference," arguing that in local TV newscasts people of color are routinely portrayed, in a number of ways, *differently* than white people. He argued that many stories on local television news continued to reinforce historical stereotypes about people of color, including "positive" (his quotation marks) stereotypes of successful African-American athletes and entertainers as well as the negative stereotypes of people of color (especially African-American and Hispanic men) as violent criminals. Campbell cited other studies (most importantly Gray, 1991) that also found such stereotypes to be the dominant representation of African-American men in mainstream media. Campbell closely analyzed several stories that reflected a pattern of subtle racial biases in the newsroom, and he argued that "however well intended they might be, journalists (and audience members) are likely unaware of the biases and stereotypical thinking that are deeply rooted" in the cognitive and cultural processes in a society that is dominated by white, middle-class perceptions (p. 82).

Finally, Campbell identified a "myth of assimilation." In his analysis of local television news coverage of Martin Luther King, Jr. Day, he described a cherished newsroom myth that portrays people of color, especially African Americans, as having overcome racism and fully assimilated into the American mainstream, where equality has been achieved. Campbell found that stories about the King holiday were dominated by a theme of racial harmony, despite the evidence of lingering racial hostility in many of the cities that adopted that theme. As he wrote:

> That King Day was covered the way it was is not surprising. The social and professional processes that dictate how news is covered

are based on an implicit common sense, a common sense that may have more to do with stereotyped notions about the world than with a true understanding of it. Most Americans would like to believe that their country is a tolerant and fair one, that discrimination does not exist, that equal opportunity is there for all. But what we would like to believe and what actually exists are clearly at odds.

(p. 111)

Campbell expressed specific concern about news organizations creating a mythical world in which racial harmony is the norm when seen in the broader context of newscasts that routinely include images of people of color as suspects in stories related to violent crime. In reflecting on the work of Gray (1986, 1991) and Jhally and Lewis (1992), Campbell expressed this concern: "If our society is the just and fair one that was portrayed on King Day, the constant barrage of menacing images of minorities that more commonly appear on local TV news will undoubtedly fuel racist attitudes" (p. 111).

Since the publication of *Race, Myth and the News* in 1995, researchers have continued to identify problems with the portrayal of race in the news media. Some of that research argues that journalism often misrepresents crime as a larger problem than it actually is, with people of color as the most common perpetrators (Dixon 2004; Dixon & Linz, 2000). Heider (2002) found that outside of prime-time programming, people of color were most often seen on television in the context of news reports about crime. When it comes to images of African Americans in violent crimes, most (Dixon & Linz, 2000; Entman & Rojecki, 2000; Gilliam & Iyengar, 2000; Romer et al., 1998) found that African Americans are shown more often than whites as suspects. Dixon (2004) found that African Americans were more likely to appear as perpetrators than as anchors and reporters, but the opposite was true for whites. Dixon (2004) argued that in local television news "the message here appears to be whites are the authoritative voice of reason, whereas blacks are the source of crime and chaos" (p. 137). LeDuff (2009), who examined newscasts in Indianapolis and New Orleans, found that there was an over-emphasis in those cities on blacks as criminal suspects and that African-American murder was over-reported when compared to local police crime reports.

Although the United States elected an African-American president in 2008, we remain concerned that mythological notions about race in news coverage persist. Next, we will consider that persistence as we examine coverage from King Day, 2009, the day that preceded Barack Obama's inauguration.

Analyzing News as Myth

In his seminal work *Mythologies* (1957/1972), Roland Barthes described his efforts to examine French popular culture through the prism of cultural myths:

> The starting point of these reflections was usually a feeling of impatience at the sight of the "naturalness" with which newspapers, art and common sense constantly dress up a reality which, even though it is the one we live in, is undoubtedly determined by history. … I hate seeing Nature and History confused at every turn, and I wanted to track down, in the decorative display of *what-goes-without-saying*, the ideological abuse which, in my view, is hidden there.
>
> (p. 11)

Barthes was concerned with the way artifacts of popular culture—advertising, photojournalism, studio wrestling and others—can reflect a kind of groupthink that doesn't allow for more complicated interpretations of events. Similarly, the work of cultural anthropologist Clifford Geertz, especially his essay "Common Sense as a Cultural System," is often cited in critical examinations of journalism. Geertz (1983) argued,

> As a frame for thought, and a species of it, common sense is as totalizing as any other: no religion is more dogmatic, no science more ambitious, no philosophy more general. Its tonalities are different, and so are the arguments to which it appeals, but like them—and like art and like ideology—it pretends to reach past illusion to truth, to, as we say, things as they are.
>
> (p. 84)

News coverage routinely reflects mythical *common sense* about the events of the day. Fiske and Hartley (1978) identified "myth chains" as one of the ways in which journalistic storytelling embeds ideological understandings, and they pointed out that "news reporting and fiction use similar signs because they naturally refer to the same myths in our culture" (p. 65). Himmelstein (1984) identified the "myth of the puritan ethic" (p. 205) in news coverage that routinely extolled the values of hard work and middle-class life while implicitly questioning the values of the underclass. Richard Campbell (1991a, 1991b) in describing the myth-making capacity of journalism suggested that the notion of "balance" was itself a "code word for … middle American values." He continues,

> These values are encoded into mainstream journalism—how it selects the news, where it places its beat reporters, who and how it promotes, how it critically reports and thereby naively supports government positions.
>
> (Campbell, 1991a, p. 75)

In describing his approach to myth analysis in *Race, Myth and the News*, Campbell wrote, "The danger of the commonsense claim to truth is in its exclusion of those who live outside the familiar world it represents" (1995, p. 18). His study found the racial mythology embedded in broadcasts across the United States represented "a hegemonic consensus about race and class that sustains myths about life outside of white, 'mainstream' America" (p. 132). Do those myths persist in the twenty-first century? The rest of this chapter will examine that question.

Race, Myth and 2009 King Day Coverage

On January 19 and 20 of 2009 (the Martin Luther King, Jr. Holiday and the day after), we examined the Web sites of television news organizations in ten of the cities that Campbell included in his 1995 study: Columbus (Ohio), Detroit, Hattiesburg (Mississippi), Houston, Los Angeles, New Orleans, Norfolk, Phoenix, St. Louis and Syracuse. At those sites, we viewed the top stories that had been posted, stories that had also been broadcast on the day's newscasts. We identified two clear patterns in the coverage, patterns that were similar to the findings in Campbell's 1995 study and to the findings in a follow-up study we completed in 2005 (Brown, Campbell, & LeDuff, 2005). The first pattern was in how coverage of King Day—especially the King Day that coincided with the inauguration of President Barack Obama—continued to mythologize the end of racism and the successful assimilation of African Americans into American society. The second pattern was of the continued obsession of local television news to cover stories that disproportionately portray African-American men as violent criminals.

Those patterns were most clearly apparent in the news carried on Phoenix's KTVK-TV that day in its coverage of the King Day holiday and of a peculiar hostage case in which two black men were arrested. The myth-making at work in those stories was like that in much of the coverage that we observed in the ten cities we observed for this study, not to mention the coverage routinely viewed by local TV news audiences across the U.S. Our concern is that the coverage reinforces common-sense notions about race that are inaccurate and less useful in explaining the complexities of race in America. What follows is a *myth analysis*—similar to qualitative research approaches known as *textual analysis* or *close reading*—that will examine stories that audiences of KTVK viewed on King Day in 2009. The analysis will first examine the coverage at a *denotative* level; that is, we will discuss a first-level reading of the stories and the meanings that were likely intended by the journalists who produced them. Stuart Hall (1980) would describe these as the "preferred" readings. Second, we will examine the coverage from a *connotative* level; that is, we will examine the stories in the larger context of how meanings are culturally generated and interpreted. Hall (1980) would describe this analysis as the "negotiated" or "oppositional" readings. Finally, we will examine the myth-making attributes of the stories and how the coverage contributes to "common sense" understandings and, as Barthes (1957/1972) wrote, "the ideological abuse which … is hidden there" (p. 11). We'll suggest that newsrooms consider new approaches to the routines that dictate traditional local TV news coverage.

"Dreams Can Come True": The Myth of Assimilation and KTVK's King Day Coverage

KTVK's coverage of the 2009 Martin Luther King, Jr. holiday—the day before Barack Obama's inauguration—began with a series of close-up shots of children participating in a King Day march as they sang the gospel song, "This Little Light of Mine," a prominent hymn of the Civil Rights Movement. The story is introduced by a news anchor who tells the audience, "Now on the eve of an historic inauguration, hundreds in the valley celebrated one man's dream while waiting to witness another's." Reporter Kristine Harrington tells the audience, "As Martin Luther King, Jr. Day has great importance every year, but this year especially so, with so many realizing that dreams can come true." Her comments are followed by clips from Dr. King's historic "I Have a Dream" speech. Next the audience sees an interview with one of the marchers, a twenty-something African-American man, who says, "The dream is being realized as we speak." Reporter Harrington explains: "That's the feeling here in Phoenix about one great African-American leader on the eve of another's presidential election." A series of shots follows in which marchers, all but one of them black, make comments like:

- "Barack Obama is actually fulfilling that dream."
- "It's a great day to be an American."
- "Hopefully, there's gonna be less prejudice and racism.
- "It means, basically, no excuses. It's time to move ahead."

One African-American man, holding his young son in his arms, says of the child, "Maybe one day he can be president. He can go and do whatever he wants, go to college and not even worry about it."

Viewers next see a series of shots that focus on marchers' t-shirts that display images of King and Obama. Harrington explains, "Today's celebration of civil rights, while focused on M.L.K., also feature Barack Obama, and not just in fashion." An elderly black man at the march says, "It is a quantum leap forward, but there is still much work to be done." The reporter says, "The president-elect agrees." The audience sees shots of King and hears (and then sees) Obama, at an event in Washington, say, "On a day where we remember not just a dreamer, but a doer, an actor, somebody who dedicated his life to working at the grassroots level on behalf of change." Viewers see a long-shot of the march in Phoenix as Harrington says, "This is a celebration of that change." The audience then hears an unseen marcher say, "This is a beautiful thing." Harrington, now back in the TV station's studio, tells the audience, "Again, while everybody celebrating today acknowledges Barack Obama's historical accomplishment, they realize too that there is much work to be done and are optimistic strides will be made."

The story's "preferred" reading, as Hall (1980) would describe it, is that the march in Phoenix and President Obama's election represent the triumph of King's dream and America's repudiation of its racist past. The anchor, reporter and sources all concur with the notion that, as one says, "Barack Obama is actually fulfilling that dream." The stories' language—both spoken and visual—reinforces the same common-sense notion that dominated virtually all of the coverage of King Day that we observed in 2009, including the Clarion-Ledger cartoon described at the beginning of this chapter: *Yes we did.* The story's conclusion hints at a notion of lingering racism, and the reporter concludes that there is still "much work to be done," but she avers that "strides will be made." Much of the coverage of 2009's King Day included similar, minor references to the persistence of racism, but the overwhelming message consistently remained hopeful and triumphant.

Our concern is that that common-sense understanding is not a particularly accurate one. Hall (1980) describes "negotiated" and "oppositional" readings that call for analyses of media texts that identify the myth-making potential of journalism. In the case of King Day coverage by local television news organizations, such readings reflect the persistence of the "myth of assimilation" that Campbell identified in 1995. In KTVK's coverage, the language used by the anchor, reporter and the sources in the story reifies the coverage's common sense. The anchor tells us that "hundreds in the valley celebrated one man's dream while waiting to witness another's." The reporter opines that King Day is always important, "but this year especially so, with so many realizing that dreams can come true." Interview subjects testify that "Barack Obama is actually fulfilling that dream" and "it's a great day to be an American."

The story's visual language also supports the common-sense theme of America's triumph over racial intolerance. Black and white film footage of King's "I Have a Dream" speech positions intolerance as a remnant of the 1960s and stands in stark contrast to the integrated march that day in Phoenix. The civil rights anthem, "This Little Light of Mine," takes on a new, less confrontational meaning as the audience sees a series of shots of contemporary African Americans in celebratory mode. Images of Obama and King on the marchers' t-shirts reinforce the story's premise that Obama is the realization of King's dream; as one marcher says, "It's a quantum leap forward."

King's dream, of course, was of a day in which people would "not be judged by the color of their skin, but by the content of their character." Did Barack Obama's election actually mean that that day has arrived in America, the premise of virtually all of the coverage of King Day in 2009? Consider some statistics:

- Twenty-three percent of black American families live in poverty; 6 percent of white families live in poverty (U.S. Census Bureau, 2009).
- A typical black family has an income that is only 58 percent of a typical white family (Associated Press, Nov. 13, 2007).
- Over 32 percent of white Americans have college degrees; fewer than 20 percent of African Americans have graduated from college (JBHE.com, 2009).
- Black unemployment is over 13 percent. White unemployment is 7.3 percent (Wickham, March 29, 2009).
- Joblessness among black teenagers is nearly 39 percent; 19 percent of white teenagers are jobless (Wickham, March 29, 2009).
- The unemployment rate for black male college graduates (8.4 percent) is nearly twice that of white male college graduates (4.4 percent) (Luo, Dec. 1, 2009).
- Thirty-seven percent of white children born to middle-class parents advance to a higher income level than their parents; only 17 percent of black children do (Isaacs, 2007).
- African Americans are jailed at a rate of six times the rate of whites (Sentencing Project, Mauer & King 2007).

Yes we did? Maybe not. Undeniably, the United States has made racial progress since the civil rights era. Our concern, however, is that that progress has become mythologized by news organizations that use King Day and other events to highlight that progress without addressing persistent racial inequities.

How might news organizations approach King Day without lapsing into the same celebratory coverage? Perhaps the forementioned statistics might give them some direction. Is it newsworthy that black Americans are four times more likely than whites to grow up in poverty? That whites are far more likely than African Americans to graduate from college? Or that black Americans are six times more likely to go to prison than white Americans? Are these issues worthy of journalistic analysis and explanation? Would King Day be a day on which these issues could be reported? Would audiences be interested in that analysis? We believe that these stories are worthy of attention from news organizations, and that approaching King Day from a different perspective would provide audiences with a less mythological and more accurate sense of race and racism in America. Such an approach is particularly important because of the other myth that news organizations continue to perpetuate, the "myth of difference." After we look at the racial implications of local television news coverage of violent crime, we'll address how these myths may be affecting American racial attitudes and public policy.

"2 accused": The Myth of Difference and Coverage of Violent Crime

Prominently displayed on KTVK's Web site on King Day were the mug shots of two suspects—both black, both shirtless in the photos—in a curious kidnapping story the station covered that day. The headline on the Web site reads, "2 accused of tying and keeping hostages in trunk." The video version of the story that aired on the station's 6 p.m. newscast is a 30-second "reader," a story read by a news anchor over "B-roll," video shot earlier in the day. The audience is told, "And we now know the names of two men kidnapped and held at gunpoint in a valley hotel. Christopher Taylor and Kevin Powell are both from out of state and police tell us Taylor and Powell tried to sell marijuana to a group of guys at a Circle K, but a fight broke out." Viewers see shots of police at the crime scene and a graphic that reads, "Hotel Hostages 91st Ave. & McDowell." The final shot is a close-up of a pair of the bound, shoeless feet of a black man that apparently belong to one of the suspects. The anchor concludes the story: "Keith Mann and Daniel Price allegedly tied up the two and took them back to their hotel near 91st Avenue and McDowell. The victims were not harmed and two suspects were arrested. However, one more suspect is on the loose."

An odd story by any standards, such coverage is not unusual on local TV newscasts. As we viewed coverage from ten cities in January of 2009, we repeatedly saw stories about violent crime of varying degrees of significance. Those stories were typically accompanied by shots of police on the scene and of handcuffed suspects. Like KTVR's Web site, many TV news organizations post mug shots or police sketches of crime suspects prominently on their sites. The "preferred" reading of such stories—the meaning intended by news producers and reporters—is to report criminal activity in the stations' coverage area. For KTVR, this was the story of police resolving a peculiar incident; a video crew was able to attain some footage and police provided the station with mug shots of the suspects. Such crime coverage is a major part of the daily routine of local TV journalists. A story like this one—apparently resolved by the police—gives audiences a sense that the police have effectively done their work. Stories in which suspects are not apprehended give audiences a sense that danger lurks in their communities.

In this case, the suspects—as seen in their videotaped arrest and in the mug shots displayed on the station's Web site—are black men, not an uncommon occurrence in this kind of coverage, a staple of the local TV news business. In his 1995 study, Campbell's "negotiated" or "oppositional" readings of such coverage held that that the coverage reinforced a "myth of difference," in which African Americans (as well as other people of color) are routinely cast as *different*, as dangerous, amoral perpetrators of violent acts. He argued that news organizations habitually relied on stereotyped notions of African Americans in producing stories about crime. "Television news relies on visual imagery for storytelling, even if the images may contribute to the kinds of stereotypical beliefs that advance racism and discrimination," he wrote. "The mug shots that routinely appear on local television newscasts' crime stories carry connotative messages of wrongdoing, of danger, of conviction-before-trial" (p. 71).

As we observed newscasts in 2005 (Brown, Campbell, & LeDuff) and for the research for this chapter in 2009, we saw the same thing that Campbell observed in 1995: Local television news remains obsessed with coverage of violent crimes, and the images now surface on both newscasts and Web sites. Several of the sites from the ten cities that we observed on King Day in 2009 prominently featured mug shots of black criminal suspects. Local TV newsrooms clearly continue to reflect a myth of difference by focusing on minority crime, and that coverage has a clear impact on viewers' attitudes about both crime and race. Our observations are supported by a number of other studies conducted in the last decade. (See, for instance, Dixon, 2008; Gilliam, Valentino & Beckman, 2002;

Johnson & Dixon, 2008; Klein & Naccarato, 2003; Poindexter, Smith, & Heider, 2003.)

We are aware that the rate of violent crime is high in some African-American communities. We are also aware that the national crime rate has generally declined in those communities over the last two decades, something local television news viewers might be surprised to know. For instance, Gallup's annual crime poll in 2009 showed that Americans believe that crime is increasing, a belief that has been reflected routinely in the Gallup poll over the last ten years, a period in which violent crime actually decreased (Jones, 2009, Oct. 14). Meanwhile, Americans persist in believing that violent crime is an enormous and growing national problem in the U.S., especially in urban locations; local television news viewers are especially likely to have unreasonable fears of such crime (Romer, Jamieson, & Aday, 2003).

Campbell observed in 1995 that local television news coverage of crimes contributes to a disturbing mythology that people of color—especially African-American and Hispanic men—are likely to be involved in criminal activity. He was especially concerned about the newsroom routines that dictated *how* crime is covered. He argued that two factors were at work. First, stereotypical cognitive and cultural processes affected journalists' approach to the stories; that is, local television journalists are unaware of how their own racial attitudes affect the coverage. Second, he argued that the news-gathering process itself contributed to myth-making. He cited "on-the-spot interpretation of events and formulaic reporting" in coverage that left "little room for understanding the complexity of the problems that have led to the perpetuation of mythological 'differences' between minority and white America" (p. 83). Coverage that simply focuses on the crime(s)-of-the day and fails to provide any context for the pathological activities reinforces the myth of difference. Without such context, race becomes the de facto explanation for criminal behavior. More than 60 years ago, Robert Parks observed that the common-sense nature of news gave it a falsely historic and scientific air. "News ... deals with isolated events and does not seek to relate them to one another either in the form of causal or in the form of teleological sequences," he wrote. "A reporter ... seeks merely to record each single event as it occurs and is concerned with the past and future only in so far as these throw light on what is actual and present" (1940, p. 675).

How might news organizations approach crime coverage without perpetuating myths about people and communities of color? One approach would be to include coverage of societal dynamics that have led to circumstances in which crime rates are higher in communities that have been victimized by a variety of troubling factors, including economic inequities, substance abuse and an inept system of public education. Would viewers tune into stories that examined the impact of America's racist history on its current economic structure? Could reporters tell compelling stories about drug dealing and the underground economy that thrives in inner cities? About the relationship between criminal activity and drug and alcohol abuse? About the failure of public education to prepare young people for college and for careers in the mainstream economy? Telling such stories would provide audiences with a broader and less mythical perception of the realities that have led to criminal activity that is typically reported without such context. Because of the economics of local television news—which remains a highly profitable venture even in a troubled world economy—it is unlikely that we'll see any major changes anytime soon. Such changes would require journalists to rethink ingrained routines and to push station managers and their corporate owners to consider new approaches. As long as newscasts continue to generate significant advertising profits, managers and owners will be difficult to persuade to make changes.

Conclusion

So why are we so concerned with the persistence of the myths of assimilation and difference in local television newscasts? Let's begin by considering the role that myths play in a society. Historically, grand tales like those of Roman and Greek cultures were adopted as a means of explaining the world, especially concepts like good and evil. More recently, cultural observers like Levi-Strauss (1967), Barthes (1957/1972) and Fiske and Hartley (1978) have identified *cultural myths* as a way of decoding a society's behaviors. They offered a way to examine modern storytelling—including journalism—as a meaning-making process that reflects hidden ideology. The colloquial use of the word myth—as in *urban myth*—is a less useful tool for analysis, though we believe the pejorative nature of this kind of myth is not far removed from our interpretation of the myth-making capacity of local TV news coverage. That is, we believe that the news myths that we've analyzed here contain a dangerous ideological element that reinforces contemporary racist attitudes and contributes to ill-informed political decisions and public policy.

Sociologist Herman Gray (1991), who identified "twin representations" of African-American men on television, contended that there were two dominant representations: First, he identified the "fictional" representation of middle-class success as seen on the remarkably popular situation comedy, *The Cosby Show* (and since that era on virtually every black family sitcom since). The second "non-fictional" representation was that of the dangerous, criminal black man, as seen in a 1985 PBS documentary, *The Vanishing Family: Crisis in Black America* (and in evening news programs throughout TV's history). Gray's concern was that those two representations were not accurate, and that they represented an overly simplified view of black life. He argued,

> Against fictional television representations of gifted and successful individuals, members of the urban under class are deficient. They are unemployed, unskilled, menacing, unmotivated, ruthless and irresponsible. ... At television's preferred level of meaning, these assumptions—like the images they organize and legitimate— occupy our common sense understandings of American racial inequality.
>
> (p. 303)

Local television news coverage on King Day in 2009, like the coverage we've been observing for more than 15 years, included Gray's twin representations side-by-side. The success of Barack Obama, and, as intimated in the coverage, all of black America, was juxtaposed against the pathological black criminal. Gray was concerned that these two dominant images misrepresented the complexity of black life. We share that concern. When audiences are presented with one "reality" in which racial intolerance is a thing of the past (as it is typically portrayed on King Day), and a second "reality" in which black criminal activity appears more rampant than ever, they could easily conclude—as racists do—that skin color is the explanation for the abhorrent behavior. That is, if racism is indeed a thing of the past, then why would African-American communities be more affected by violent crime? Perhaps that's a question that local television journalists might want to pursue. What might they find?

First, that the "reality" of the assimilation of African Americans into mainstream American life is largely a myth that is perpetuated by local TV newscasts (and is overwhelmingly reflected in prime-time fictional television). Second, that the criminal behavior in poor urban communities has far less to do with skin color than with historical disparities that have created a situation in which many African Americans live their lives outside of America's mainstream economic, educational, judicial and health systems. So instead of covering each King Day (and other events that highlight the progress of American minority groups) as a triumph over racism, why not address the enormous opportunity gaps that exist between blacks and whites? Instead of covering the crime(s)-of-the-day, including insignificant and peculiar "kidnapping" arrests like we saw in Phoenix, how about stories that provide us with some sense of *why* criminal behavior in poor urban communities is rampant?

Sociologist William Julius Wilson (2009) argues in *More Than Just Race: Being Black and Poor in the Inner City* that America needs a "change of frame—indeed, a change of mind-set on race and poverty" (p. 142). He argues that the structural and cultural inequities must be addressed before real change will be possible: "The issues of race and poverty should be framed in such a way that not only is a sense of fairness and justice to combat inequality generated, but also people are made aware that our country would be better off if these problems were seriously addressed and eradicated" (pp. 142–143). By avoiding the myths that have come to define so much of local television journalism's representation of race, those newscasts (as well as other forms of journalism) could go a long way toward re-framing political discussions about race.

This chapter has revisited Campbell's 1995 study of race, myth and the news, and, like the findings to a similar study we conducted in 2005 (Brown, Campbell, & LeDuff), we remain concerned that news coverage continues to perpetuate the same myths about race that it has for at least 15 years. In our 2005 study, we noted that the problem seemed to have become exacerbated over the decade as resources for TV newsrooms shrunk under increasing corporate pressure for profits; that is, local TV newsrooms are now operating with fewer journalists and relying increasingly on less costly news stories provided by national news networks and public relations operations. That means that it is possibly less likely than ever that local television news will provide audiences with more accurate and less mythical coverage related to race. While in this chapter we have examined only a relatively small number of newscasts and closely analyzed only two stories, we are certain that they are consistent with the patterns we have observed for years. Campbell attempted to offer a hopeful outlook in concluding his 1995 study:

> If there is reason to be optimistic, it is in the fact that cultural myths are not stagnant: They can change and evolve or be eliminated and forgotten. And the potent myth-making capacity of local television news could be turned on its head to refute the very myths it now sustains. That would be my hope for American journalism and American society—that the myths about race that they cling to will give way to a more accurate, more truthful perception of people of color that will make America more tolerant

of its diversity and become a more equitable place for all of its peoples.

(p. 136)

Fifteen years later, we have observed few changes in how local TV newscasts cover King Day, violent crime or other stories that can have racial implications. Such changes would require a dramatic reinvention of television journalism, an unlikely event, particularly in an era in which the corporate takeover of local television stations makes significant change even more unlikely. At this point, it would require a kind of generational shift that would have young journalists bringing new perspectives to newsrooms that question implicit routines. New technologies and the growth of news on the Internet are generally requiring news organizations to reconsider their approaches, especially as new business models surface. If news organizations determine they can increase profits by providing more insightful, useful coverage, perhaps substantial change might follow. That may be our only reason for optimism.

References

Associated Press. (2007, November 13). Income gap between black, white families grows. *MSNBC.com*. Retrieved Dec. 14, 2009 from: http://www.msnbc.msn.com/id/21759075/.

Barthes, R. (1972). *Mythologies*. (Jonathan Cape Ltd., Trans.). New York: Hill & Wang. (Original work published 1957.)

Brown, R., Campbell, C., & LeDuff, K. (2005). Rebirth of a nation: *Race, myth and the news revisited*. Paper presented at the annual convention of the Association for Education in Journalism and Mass Communication, San Antonio.

Campbell, C. P. (1995). *Race, myth and the news*. Thousand Oaks, CA: Sage Publications.

Campbell, R. (1991a). *60 Minutes and the news: A mythology for Middle America*. Urbana: University of Illinois Press.

Campbell, R. (1991b). Word vs. image: Elitism, popularity and TV news. *Television Quarterly*, *26*(1), 73–81.

Dixon, T. (2004). Racialized portrayals of reporters and criminals on local television news. In R.A. Lind (Ed.), *Race/gender/media: Considering diversity across audiences content and producers* (pp. 132–145). Boston: Pearson.

Dixon, T. L. (2008). Crime news and racialized beliefs: Understanding the relationship between local news viewing and perceptions of African Americans and crime. *Journal of Communication, 58*, 106–125.

Dixon, L. & Linz, D. (2000). Overrepresentation and underrepresentation of African Americans and Latinos as lawbreakers on television news. *Journal of Communication, 50*, 131–154.

Entman, R. M. (1990). Modern racism and the images of blacks in local television news. *Critical Studies in Mass Communication, 7*(4), 332–345.

Entman, R. M. (1992). Blacks in the news: Television, modern racism and cultural change. *Journalism Quarterly, 69*(2), 341–361.

Entman, R. M. & Rojecki, A. (2000). *The black image in the white mind: Media and race in America*. Chicago: University of Chicago Press.

Fiske, J. & Hartley, J. (1978). *Reading television*. London: Methuen.

Geertz, C. (1983). Commmon sense as a cultural system. In *Local knowledge: Further essays in interpretive anthropology*. New York: Basic Books.

Gilliam, Jr., F. D. & Iyengar, S. (2000). Prime suspects: The influence of local television news on the viewing public. *American Journal of Political Science, 44* (3, July) 560–574.

Gilliam, Jr., F. D., Valentino, N. A., & Beckman, M. N. (2002). Where you lived and what you watch: The impact of racial proximity and local television news on attitudes about race and crime. *Political Research Quarterly, 55,* 655–780.

Gist, M. E. (1990). Minorities in media imagery. *Newspaper Research Journal, 11*(3), 52–63.

Gray, H. (1986). Television and the new black man: Black male images in prime-time situation comedy. *Media, Culture and Society, 8,* 223–242.

Gray, H. (1991). Television, black Americans, and the American dream. In R. K. Avery & D. Eason (Eds.), *Critical perspectives on media and society* (pp. 294–305). New York: Guilford.

Hall, S. (1980). Encoding/decoding. In S. Hall, D. Hobson, A. Lowe, & P. Wills (Eds.), *Culture, media, language* (pp. 128–138). London: Hutchinson.

Himmelstein, H. (1984). *TV, myth and the American mind.* New York: Praeger.

Isaacs, J. B. (2007). Economic mobility of black and white families. *Brookings Institute.* Retrieved Dec. 14, 2009 from: http://www.brookings.edu/papers/2007/11_blackwhite_isaacs. aspx.

JBHE.com. (2009). More than 4.5 million African Americans now hold four-year college degrees. *The Journal of Blacks in Higher Education.* Retrieved Dec. 14, 2009 from: http://www.jbhe. com/news_views/64_degrees.html.

Jhally, S. & Lewis, J. (1992). *Enlightened racism: The Cosby Show, audiences, and the myth of the American dream.* Boulder: Westview.

Johnson, K. A. & Dixon, T. L. (2008). Change and the illusion of change: Evolving portrayals of crime news and blacks in a major market. *The Howard Journal of Communications, 19,* 125–143.

Jones, J. M. (2009). Americans perceive increased crime in U.S. *Gallup.com.* Retrieved Dec. 21, 2009 from: www.gallup.com/poll/123644/Americans-Perceive-Increased-Crime. aspx.

Klein, R. D. & Naccarato, S. (2003). Broadcast news portrayal of minorities. *American Behavioral Scientist, 46*(12), 1611–1616.

LeDuff, K. (2009). *Tales of two cities: How race and crime intersect on local TV news.* Saarbrücken, Germany: Lambert Academic Publishing.

Levi-Strauss, C. (1967). The structural study of myth. In *Structural anthropology* (C. Jacobson & B. Grundfest Shoef, Trans.). Garden City, NY: Anchor-Doubleday.

Luo, M. (2009, December 1). In job hunt, college degree can't close racial gap. *New York Times.* Retrieved Dec. 14, 2009 from: http://www.nytimes.com/2009/12/01/us/01race. html.

Mauer, M. & King, M. (2007). Uneven justice: State rates of incarceration by race and ethnicity. Sentencing Project. Retrieved Dec. 14, 2009 from: http://www.sentencingproject.org/doc/ publications/rd_stateratesofincbyraceandethnicity.pdf.

Parks, R. (1940). News as a form of knowledge: A chapter in the sociology of knowledge. *The American Journal of Sociology, 45*(5), 669–686.

Pease, E. C. (1989). Kerner plus 20: Minority news coverage in the Columbus Dispatch. *Newspaper Research Journal, 10*(3), 17–38.

Poindexter, P. M., Smith, L., & Heider, D. (2003). Race and ethnicity in local television news: Framing, story assignments, and source selections. *Journal of Broadcasting & Electronic Media, 47*(4), 524–536.

Romer, D., Jamieson, K. H., & Aday, S. (2003). Television news and the cultivation of fear of crime. *Journal of Communication, 53,* 88–104.

Romer, D., Jamieson, K. H., & de Coteau, N. J. (1998). The treatment of persons of color in local television news: Ethnic blame discourse or realistic group conflict? *Communication Research, 25* (3, June), 286–305.

Tilove, J. (2008, November 8) Obama made inroads with white voters except in Deep South. *The Times-Picayune.* Retrieved January 23, 2009 from: http://www.nola.com/news/index. ssf/2008/11/obama_made_inroads_with_white.html.

U.S. Census Bureau. (2009). Historical poverty tables. Retrieved Dec. 14, 2009 from: http://www. census.gov/hhes/www/poverty/histpov/hstpov2.html.

Wickham, D. (2009, March 29). Racial disparities still part of rational debate. *Hattiesburg American*, 4C.

Wilson, W. J. (2009). *More than just race: Being black and poor in the inner city.* New York: W. W. Norton & Company.

Discussion Questions

1. Describe the *myth of assimilation*. Is the coverage of the Martin Luther King, Jr. holiday described in this chapter consistent with local television news coverage that you have observed? Is the myth also perpetuated in prime-time television programs with predominantly African-American casts?

2. Describe the *myth of difference*. Is the crime coverage described in this chapter consistent with local television news coverage that you have observed? Can you think of other ways in which crime stories could be approached by journalists?

3. Does Barack Obama's election as the 44th president of the United States mean that America has overcome its racist history? Is that a consistent theme that you've observed as a news consumer?

4. Do you think that news coverage of President Barack Obama was different from news coverage of his predecessor President George W. Bush? Why or why not? Do you think that the *myth of difference* or *race* play a part?

Chapter Assignments

1. Watch (or view online) your local television news coverage of the Martin Luther King, Jr. holiday. First, describe it at the "denotative" or "preferred" level; that is, how would the journalists covering the story prefer to have it perceived? Second, describe it at "connotative" or "negotiated" level; that is, analyze the *myth-making* capacity of the coverage.

2. Watch (or view online) how your local television news approaches crime coverage, especially coverage that includes minority criminal suspects. First, describe the coverage at the "denotative" or "preferred" level; that is, how would the journalists covering the story prefer to have it perceived? Second, describe it at "connotative" or "negotiated" level; that is, analyze the *myth-making* capacity of the coverage.

3. Compare local television news with local newspaper coverage of the same event/story and in comparing their coverage look to see if

there are any identifiable *myth chains* that reproduce *common-sense* understanding.

Useful Tools on the Web

- Richard Prince's Journalisms, news about diversity in journalism: http://www.mije.org/richardprince.
- The Poynter Institute for Media Studies hosts a dialogue on newsroom ethics and diversity: http://www.poynter.org/subject. asp?id=32.

CHAPTER 2

Newsroom Diversity and Representations of Race

CHERYL D. JENKINS

In 2008 U.S. Senate Majority Leader Harry Reid stated that he expected then presidential nominee Barack Obama to "fare better electorally than previous black presidential aspirants partly because of his lighter skin tone and lack of 'Negro dialect'" (Greenberg, January 10, 2010, n.p.). These comments from the Nevada Democrat caused some members of the Republican Party to call for Reid's resignation and drew comparisons to controversial remarks made by former U.S. Senator Trent Lott in 2002 who praised Strom Thurmond's 1948 presidential candidacy and his support for racial segregation. Reid apologized directly to Obama and the president defended the senator and lauded his record on civil rights, but the firestorm continued to brew. At issue by most accounts in mainstream media was whether Democrats were being hypocritical in their pass of Reid's comments in light of the earlier fallout from Lott's remarks. In other words, the issue was being reported as another dichotomous political battle in which both sides saw an opportunity to score points by feigning outrage.

While mainstream media followed this storyline, members of the black press found a different angle to highlight—one that was often alluded to during the campaign, but quickly brushed aside as America ushered in the so-called "post racial" era following the election. This press, known to incorporate more interpretive and sometimes subjective techniques in reporting, took a critical look at why comments such as Reid's still matter by offering a perspective on whether or not a darker skinned African-American candidate would have been able to capture the hearts, minds, and votes of so many Americans. With references to systemic and structural inequalities that continue to exist in this country, the more critical perspective added context to the overall debate and did not discredit the influence of race on this discussion. Such context is often missing from mainstream news reporting particularly when it comes to covering sensitive matters like race. Further, media scholars have noted that mainstream journalists tend to take an episodic rather than a thematic perspective towards the events they cover. Instead of explaining the general background and implications of issues, news reports emphasize the most recent and attention-getting developments (Price & Tewksbury, 1997). This conclusion, along with the fact that mainstream media now cover and serve a more diverse population, are key reasons that many in the newspaper industry continue the almost half-century push for more diverse newsrooms.

According to a 2005 report by the Knight Foundation, newsroom diversity is below its peak levels at most daily newspapers in the United States. The report, based on a study of newspaper employment from 1990 to 2005, states that "while the newspaper industry may be slowly adding journalists of color overall, the gains have been uneven. The share of journalism jobs held by non-whites has receded from its high-water mark in most newsrooms, large and small" (Dedman & Doig, 2005). These findings were generated three years before the 40th anniversary of the Kerner Commission Report. The report, written in 1968 following more than 150 riots in U.S. cities during the late 1960s, found that the mass media played a role in violence that had erupted during this time. The Knight Foundation findings are also troubling considering the demographic evolution of the American society over the past few decades which show a growing minority population. According to the U.S. Census Bureau's Population Profile of the United States report (between Census Day April 1, 2000 and July 1, 2005), the population of non-Hispanic whites declined as a proportion of the entire population, falling from 70 percent in 2000 to about 67 percent in 2005, and all other racial and Hispanic-origin groups grew faster than the national rate between that same period (U.S. Census Bureau, 2005).

This is problematic as research on the journalistic process or, more specifically, how journalists arrive at the daily news through evaluation of news value, newsroom social forces, journalism education and other factors that contribute to the process of news making, has indicated that the news media serve up a view of the world that may not be representative of the American pluralism (Dates & Barlow, 1990; Campbell, 1995; Wilson, Gutierrez, & Chao, 2003). In fact, the lack of cultural and historical perspective from members of the media creates routine journalistic news that in many instances end up reflecting the "preferred meanings" of a still dominant white society. And, even though the physical numbers of the population indicate a shift downward in the amount of whites in this country, the reality is that from a hegemonic standpoint the values of this group constitute the dominant ideology that functions in our society.

The fact that this ideological reality still exists and its repercussions are expressed in countless scholarly and political examinations of the role of the American mass media makes it important to take stock of whether or not this institution has figured out a way to meet the challenges of serving a more diverse population. The challenge is daunting as many studies indicate that even today mainstream newspapers are primarily concerned with their majority readers who are mainly white (Fleming-Rife & Proffitt, 2004; Wolseley, 1990). And others indicate that many American newsrooms have not diversified their workforces. In light of newsrooms having four decades to institute the guidelines from Kerner and research supporting the fact that the goals of achieving diversity at American newspapers has yet to be reached, this chapter provides a critical examination of how the newspaper industry has handled the coverage of complex topics like race with limited insight from a diverse workforce; the issues of diversity that still exist in these newsrooms, including hiring practices; and the role diversity has played in making news content more inclusive and comprehensive.

In response to the 2004 American Society of Newspaper Editors' diversity study which showed woeful numbers of minorities working in American newsrooms, popular journalism blogger Tim Porter (2004) asked the question, "Why do America's newspapers remain so white despite 25 years of effort to have them be more reflective of the communities they cover?" (n.p.). Five years later, the question remains because those numbers remain dismal. As such, it is significant to examine the implications of having limited diversity in our newsrooms and the effect that aspect has on news content and how media is viewed in society.

Theorizing Diversity

The idea of diversifying newsrooms and covering complex issues with more diverse perspective and insight has been an objective of American media for almost half a century. This aspect of the news organization has theoretical basis and implications. First, the notion of a more complex or inclusive media stems from this institution's historical tendency to portray African Americans and other marginalized groups as either inferior to the dominant class in society or not include their perspectives at all.

According to columnist Lewis Diuguid and scholar Adrienne Rivers (2000), "Dominant media have either excluded African Americans or portrayed them in such a bad light that some black people may have preferred exclusion" (p. 121). They assert that the goal of the Kerner Commission's recommendations to create a more "inclusive" media have yet to be realized. They state:

> The Kerner Commission and others pointed out that the media were viewing the diverse and multicultural news and events in this country through the lens of a monoculture—the culture of white males. What appeared in newspapers, magazines, television, and radio were distorted images of people who were different …
>
> (p. 121)

To further highlight the troubles traditional mainstream newspapers have had in gaining the trust of African-American readers because of this partiality, Andrew Hacker (1994) states:

> African Americans know that the dominant media are white. To their eyes, the mainstream media speak for a white nation, which expects all citizens to conform to its ways. Nor do they see that much has changed since the Kerner Commission remarked, "The media report and write from the standpoint of a white man's world."
>
> (quoted in Diuguid & Rivers, 2000, p. 121)

Since Kerner, many of the efforts made by the media to include more diverse content in their news coverage have been coupled with a tendency by this institution to ignore repeated complaints by scholars, critics, and members of marginalized groups in society that although overt aspects of racism have lessened, facets of institutional racism remain prevalent in news coverage of minorities by the American press. For example, Byerly and Wilson (2009) state that "superficial coverage of minority issues, or the occasional use of a racial minority source, creates what Entman (1990) calls 'enlightened racism,' something more subtle than overt racism but which nonetheless generates animosity among the races and tends to reinforce white resistance to the political demands of blacks and other racial minorities" (pp. 214-215).

This shift to a more "subtle" form of racism has played as important a role in media depictions of minority groups as overt racism did in the past because mass media tend to reflect the ideals of the dominant society. To understand mass media's present influence on racial attitudes, Entman

(2006) posits that racial messages in local news are congruent with the theory of *modern racism*. The concept of modern racism emerged from social scientists' observing the contradiction between white Americans' endorsement of racial equality in the abstract and their often-intense opposition to concrete policies designed to produce more equality. Entman explains:

> Modern racism centrally involves "anti-black effect" combined with attachment to "traditional [American] values." The orientation leads modern racists to express "antagonism toward blacks," "pushing too hard" and moving too fast … resentment toward … racial quotas in jobs or education, excessive access to welfare, [or] special treatment by government … [and] denial of continuing discrimination.
>
> (Sears, quoted in Entman 2006, pp. 206-207)

Further, Entman (1990) posits that local television news and other forms of media promote modern racism even as and particularly because, it delegitimizes old-fashion racism.

> Whites who have modern racist sentiments do not necessarily believe that blacks are inherently inferior or that discrimination should be legal. What many whites with modern racist tendencies do consciously feel is some amalgam of negative effect (especially fear and resentment), rejection of the political agenda commonly endorsed by black leaders, and denial that racism is still a problem.
>
> (p. 207)

Entman's discussion on modern racism and the influence of the American media on this concept provides context for a larger discussion on the high number of crime stories with the subtext of race being reported in the news. A disproportionate number of the victims and defendants in these stories were African American and the "heightened salience and threat seemed to have racial meanings for white Americans" (p. 203). For Entman, the racial messages of the local news coverage he investigated were congruent with the theory of modern racism advanced by David Sears and others. But, diversifying newsrooms alone will not immediately quell the bias in news coverage that includes minorities as the industry itself is still dominated by what Byerly and Wilson (2009) call "white agendas." According to their study, "Journalism as Kerner turns 40," simply changing the faces of journalists isn't likely to bring a shift toward more

enlightened or race-conscious reporting. Specifically, news stories by journalists of all colors may still reflect what cultural scholar Stuart Hall calls the "preferred meanings" of the dominant culture. According to Hall (1980):

> The domains of "preferred meanings" have the whole social order embedded in them as a set of meanings, practices and beliefs: the everyday knowledge of social structures, of "how things work for all practical purposes in this culture," the rank order of power and interest and the structure of legitimations, limits, and sanctions.
> (quoted in Campbell, 1995, p. 2)

In this sense, many journalists may not be aware of the "biases and stereotypical thinking that are deeply rooted in the cultural and cognitive forces of nonminority life" (Campbell, 1995, p. 82). Byerly and Wilson (2009) explain that the aspect of "preferred meanings" in news may be reflected in the "over-emphasis of crimes by blacks and other non-white races, the superficiality of coverage of issues and events that matter to those races, and the elevation of deeds and values of whites" (p. 215). A longitudinal study by Stabile (2006) surmised that the criminalization of African Americans by the news media has been a staple of the news industry since the 1800s. Stabile recommends that journalists "need to break out of the crime news frame altogether, and seek the causes and solutions to such deeply entrenched social problems in places other than the criminal justice system, and offer perspectives that do not merely reproduce the logic of racialized [culture]" (Stabile, 2006, quoted in Byerly & Wilson, 2009, p. 215).

Further, Wilson, Gutierrez, and Chao (2003) state the "minority reporters often find that their ideas are often disregarded because white colleagues define news in terms of the dominant cultural perspective" (p. 128). And, even though many newspapers seek to increase the number of minorities in their newsrooms, "the decision-making continues to reside with white editors who reinforce certain journalistic norms and values" (Nishikawa et al., 2009, p. 244). This often leads to status quo journalism where minority journalists conform to traditional journalistic norms that in most instances leaves little room for perspective or more diverse news content.

Foundations of Diversity

There is historical precedence for this type of examination concerning the role of diversity in the media. The aforementioned Kerner Commission actually challenged the news media to "diversify their workforces, news agendas, and reporting" over 40 years ago. The commission recommended in its extensive report that the news media should "take a leadership role" in helping to reverse the lack of understanding in the general public about the plight of black America during the late 1960s. This, according to the commission, could be accomplished by "news organizations engaging in voluntary self-studies of their own news content, developing sources within the black community, and by assigning regular beat reporting within African American neighborhoods" (Byerly & Wilson, 2009, p. 212).

These suggested changes were also significant because they could possibly prove to members of the African-American community that the news media can be "trusted" to report in a way that is fair and balanced and that encompasses aspects of the entire American population. According to the report:

> The news media had historically neglected the Negro's legitimate expectations to report on the miserable conditions that existed in most African American neighborhoods. Neglect in reporting, as well as distortions and inaccuracy, had left a majority white population with little understanding of both the pervasive nature and the effects of longstanding discrimination on African-American peoples, or the smoldering rage that was building within their communities. Black people distrusted the media, which many referred to as "the white press" … The news media were generally viewed as instruments of the white power structure, as the conduit for police and other (white) authority figures to dominate public opinion, and unfair in their reporting of the black experience.
> (Kerner, quoted in Byerly & Wilson, 2009, p. 212)

Further, the report states that African Americans' "distrust" and dislike of media was mainly directed at newspapers. They expressed that television "at least showed what was going on." This point could also be a factor in low newspaper readership among minority groups in this country (Shosteck, 1969). In fact, the distinction in how different forms of media are viewed by minority groups has been examined in several studies (Allen & Thornton, 1992; Jones, 1990; Mastin, 2000; Shosteck, 1969; Vercellotti & Brewer, 2006), and most have indicated that these groups, African Americans in particular, tend to rely more on television than on newspapers for news from mainstream sources. According to Vercellotti and Brewer (2006), there are variations along demographic lines where this distinction is concerned, particularly when it comes to socioeconomic status; but, by and large, newspapers lagged behind television in news trustworthiness among minorities.

This fact, coupled with the additional reality that many minorities combine their consumption of mainstream news with alternative forms of media, like the black press, to get a more thorough and inclusive view of important events in society, augments the need for more comprehensive reporting in mainstream newspapers. Byerly and Wilson (2009) state that "multi-racial, multi-cultural audiences of today are looking for news that reflects the world they live in, and they seek out the media that provide it … racial minorities use both mainstream and their own specialized news sources but prefer and are more likely to trust the second" (p. 215). This is problematic for mainstream newspapers in a general sense because the industry is in such turmoil economically. And, with newspapers folding and a segment of readers turning to other forms of media to get what they feel is a more "complete" account of the day's events, the call to diversify American newsrooms is an aspect of the news organization that is critical to its survival.

This may be the precise reason that many newsrooms incorporate legitimate aspects of diversity into their news content and newsroom workforce. As recent trends in the newspaper industry show a slow move towards diversifying newsrooms and to understand the practical implications of this move, it's important to note the origins of this aspect of the Kerner Report recommendation. This thorough review of the American media's influence on racial unrest in the U.S. during the 1960s provides the foundation for media diversity today.

The Kerner Report: Furthering Diversity

According to Boger and Wegner (1996), President Lyndon Johnson commissioned two major, interdisciplinary examinations of housing and urban policy in an effort to implement the "war on poverty" in this country during the 1960s. As a result, the National Commission on Urban Problems (Douglas Commission) and the President's Committee on Urban Housing were created. But, when major racial riots tore across the urban landscape during the spring of 1967, President Johnson appointed a third commission, the Kerner Commission, explicitly charged to explore the links between racial discrimination and urban policy (pp. 4-5).

Released in March 1968, the Kerner Commission's report, officially titled the *Report of the National Advisory Commission on Civil Disorders*, addressed the role of mass media in the violence that erupted during more than 150 riots in dozens of U.S. cities the previous year. According to Byerly and Wilson (2009) the commission had studied 24 of those cities, with investigations revealing that in most cases the violence had been committed by "young African-American men between the ages of 15 and 35 … their acts were mostly crimes against property—breaking store windows, looting, setting fire to buildings, engaging in other acts of vandalism, and inciting others to join them" (Kerner Report, 1988, quoted in Byerly & Wilson, 2009, p. 210).

The media, in its "telling" of the incident, seemingly concentrated its efforts on depicting these young men as violent and "aggressive" showing images in newspaper photos and on television highlighting their actions participating in what was described as deviant activity. These images ultimately created distorted views of inner cities in America and suggested to the "uninformed that the nation was suddenly falling apart, had gone mad, or both, and that a particular community of people was at fault" (Byerly & Wilson, 2009, p. 210).

Thornton (1990) asserts that in essence, "the Kerner Commission indicted the media for treating African Americans as invisible people and the profession of journalism for being 'shockingly backward' in not seeking out, hiring, training, and promoting black Americans" (p. 392). To sum up the commission's view on the lack of diverse perspectives in the media, Thornton continues:

> Stating that tokenism was not enough, the panel issued a clear call for change. It said African American editors and commentators were essential to the policy-making process and urged the news media "to do everything possible to train and promote their Negro reporters to positions where those who are qualified can contribute to and have an effect on policy decisions." In the collective mind of the commission there was no split: blacks would do both.
>
> (p. 392)

The commission's recommendations were based on an extensive analysis of how media covered the plight of inner cities. The members pointed out that there was "significant imbalance between what actually happened in our cities and what the newspaper, radio, and television coverage of the riots told us happened." They also cited "gross flaws in the presentation of facts, and sensationalism, as well as the quoting of inexperienced or prejudiced officials without reporters having exercised journalistic judgment or double-checking information they were given" (Kerner Commission report, quoted in Byerly & Wilson, 2009, p. 211). This summation by the commission forced mainstream media to take a hard look at how it dealt with covering such complex issues. And although efforts were made to improve coverage of racial minority communities, there is still significant work left to do.

Further, Boger and Wegner (1996) state that the black-white racial divisions that dominated the Kerner Commission's vision of urban life in 1968 remain sharp today, "although they have been complicated by the emergence of other ethnic groups—Cubans, Puerto Ricans, Mexican Americans, Latinos from Central and South America, Japanese, Chinese, Vietnamese, Cambodians, Thais, Koreans, and others—whose legitimate claims for participation in American urban life make political, social, and economic relationships more challenging" (p. 5). As such, diverse and comprehensive coverage of racial groups in this country has become a critical aspect of a newspaper industry that claims fairness in its reporting.

Present State of Newsroom Diversity

One interesting aspect of the Harry Reid controversy was the almost complete lack of uproar in the African-American community about the senator's comments. As mainstream media used sound bites and quotes from political talking heads to discuss the "shock" of Reid's comments, members of the black press used the incident as an opportunity to point out the "cultural misconceptions that continue to separate black and white Americans." A column in the *Afro-American Red Star* (2010, January 16–22) notes:

> In discussing the "shock" of Reid's assertion of color and diction as justification for candidate Obama's pending acceptance, the realization that such may not necessarily be as shocking or offensive to many African Americans did not appear to be important. No small wonder when, as pointed out by Richard Prince's "Journal-isms" blog, "there were no journalists of color in any of the discussions."
>
> (p. A10)

Instead of focusing on the comments made by Reid, black journalists including Melissa Harris-Lacewell of the *Afro-American Red Star*, Julianne Malveaux of the *Michigan Chronicle*, Herb Boyd of the *New York Amsterdam News*, and Jasmyne Cannick of the *Los Angeles Sentinel*, all point to the "structural biases" that exist in society that do make it difficult for darker-skinned African Americans to attain academic and political accomplishments. In addition, most African Americans aren't quick to assume that only certain political parties were insensitive to issues of race. Harris-Lacewell (2010, January 16–22) wrote in the *Afro-American Star* that the halls of Congress would "echo with utter emptiness" if every political official guilty of racial insensitivity were weeded out: "Any implication that racism is the sole purview of the right obscures the continuing and troubling realities of racism within the Democratic Party and the Progressive political movements" (p. A11). She further states:

> The point is not so much public gaffes as it is the creation, support and maintenance of systemic and structural inequalities. This is why Trent Lott's wistfulness about a Strom Thurmond presidency is in a different class than Reid's comments. Lott was longing for a bygone era when structural barriers and entrenched inequality were the norm. Reid was enthusiastic that the same barriers were lessening and that America was ready ... for a new racial reality.
>
> (p. A11)

A story by Boyd in the *New York Amsterdam News* (2010, January 14–20) quotes civil rights activist the Rev. Al Sharpton as saying:

> To compare what Reid said with Lott ... was outrageous and insulting. Trent Lott commended a Dixiecrat for running for office, who left the Democratic Party to fight integration. How do you compare Trent Lott saying that ... "wish we could have those days where blacks are in the back of the bus" ... to saying why a black could be elected president.
>
> (p. 4)

What the commentary critically suggests is that racism, either overt or subtle, is still an issue in certain aspects of American culture that continually reveals itself. Malveaux (2010, February 3–9) states that the comments made by Reid along with other racially insensitive statements made in recent years "puts to rest any notion that our nation is 'post-racial.' We remain racial, and we are not above using race for political gain" (p. A6). Historically, black newspapers have filled in the gaps on discussions about race that need context and perspective in order to be useful in decision making. And although some minority columnists at mainstream papers have attempted to tackle such a complex topic, particularly when mainstream America is directly affected, these newspapers have fared worse in covering the issues that affect minorities in this country and it's mainly because of the makeup of the newsrooms themselves.

Many scholars link the inadequacy of minority coverage in news to the lack of minority journalists and executives in mainstream newsrooms (Bramlett-Solomon, 1993; Dates & Barlow, 1990; Entman & Rojecki, 2000;

Heider, 2000; Nishikawa et al., 2009). And, as several scholars assert, there has been slow progress in the employment of minority journalists even as the number of racial and ethnic minorities in the United States has grown steadily (Dates & Barlow, 1990; Nishikawa et al., 2009; Weaver & Wilhoit, 1991, 1996).

According to the ASNE survey results of newsroom employment for 2008, only 13.41 percent of the 46,700 full-time journalists were people of color. This is a decline of 0.11 percent from the year before (American Society of Newspaper Editors, 2009). According to Byerly and Wilson (2009), most of those journalists of color were concentrated in large urban areas, leaving small towns and rural communities—many of which are witnessing increases in people of color—with "woefully white reporting staffs" (p. 220). Coupled with these statistics is the fact that American daily newspapers shed 5,900 newsroom jobs last year, which, according to ASNE, reduced their employment of journalists by 11.3 percent, down to the levels of the early 1980s. Of the journalists who departed newsrooms, 854 were minorities, bringing the number of minority journalists down to reported levels in the 1998 census.

Many in the industry are perplexed by the dismal numbers of minority journalists considering some strides that have been made to diversify newsrooms. In his assessment of the ASNE diversity study results from 2004, which were very similar to those reported in 2009, Porter (2004) looked at possible reasons behind the low number of minorities working in American newsrooms. He posits three possible issues that may have an effect on minority hiring: pipeline issues [insufficient minorities in journalism programs], pay issues [minority journalism (and communications) students opting out of journalism at graduation for more lucrative starting positions in other industries], and/or retention issues [minorities leaving newspaper business faster than they can be hired].

Using results from a report gathered by University of Georgia professor Lee Becker who tracks entry-level newspaper hiring to give these issues perspective, Porter surmises that they are not mutually exclusive and that, in some regards, minority applicants have similar issues in the industry as non-minority applicants. There are areas, though, where Becker thinks the industry should be more cognizant. For example, in regard to pipeline issues, Porter states from his interview with Becker on the matter:

> It is a myth that there are not enough minority applicants to alter the face of America's newsrooms. There are more minority students looking for newspaper jobs than are able to get them. So, it's not simply a matter of an inadequate supply. Newspapers reject some minority graduates, though, because they do not meet the

> criteria by which entry-level hires are judged … and as a result white journalism school graduates continue to be hired at a higher rate than minority graduates.
>
> (n.p.)

Becker's opinion stems from the notion that some journalism programs, especially those at small colleges and universities with limited funding for adequate technology and other basic necessities, are not able to provide the training necessary for most entry-level jobs in the industry. Although this aspect is not limited to any particular demographic of students, Porter's overall assessment of diversity issues in American newsrooms shows that many minority students attend smaller programs, "sometimes with weekly or monthly or no newspaper at all through which they can gather clips, and they're not getting the number of internships in those programs they need to be getting" (n.p.). If the industry provided more professional training, many of these aspects could be overcome, but that's not happening in most newsrooms across the country.

Problems with pay and retention were also not found to be necessarily exclusive to just minority job applicants; but Porter does note that a 2003 ASNE study indicated that "lack of professional challenge" and "limited opportunities" were the two primary reasons minority journalists leave newspapers. The study found that "the issue of advancement opportunities proved far more salient to journalists of color than to white journalists. For white journalists, the issue of advancement opportunities ranked last among the reasons they might leave the field" (as quoted in Porter, 2004, n.p.).

An additional aspect that may affect minority hiring and retention in American newsrooms is the newsroom culture itself. According to a study on newspaper culture by Northwestern University's Readership Institute, a division of the school's Media Management Center, most newspapers have "defensive" cultures and are "resistant to change" (Readership Institute, 2001, n.p.). Porter suspects that "a minority reporter in a nearly all-white newsroom, one with a likely even whiter management structure, is by definition change, difference and not the norm." This assessment reaffirms Nishikawa et al.'s (2009) notion that "minority journalists are so constrained by the traditional norms that dominate mainstream newsrooms that they are unable or unwilling to improve the coverage of minorities" (p. 243).

As a result and in this respect, "a diverse newsroom does not always equal better coverage of minorities and stronger readership from a multicultural community"(p. 245). But, the fact that many "racial myths" in mainstream news coverage are driven by "universally recognized" news values and norms makes diversifying newsrooms all the more important. Larger numbers of racially diverse journalists could help to effectively diversify news content than is possible in white-dominant newsrooms (Byerly & Wilson, 2009). Also, more diverse perspectives in newsrooms could help provide context for news issues that have traditionally been framed by mainstream news media in ways that are not always fair to the minority groups they cover.

For example, *Miami Herald* columnist Leonard Pitts, Jr., an African-American Pulitzer Prize winner, joined many of the writers of the black press in their criticism of the lack of black "voices" on the talk show circuit discussing the Harry Reid incident. Pitts argued that journalists of color would have added more insight to the discussion about what comments like Reid's actually mean to the group he supposedly offended. Pitts states:

> They (journalists of color) might have helped frame the one question that has gone conspicuously unaddressed in the loud debate over what Reid said: Was he right? Sure he was. Moreover, there is something unbearably precious in the idea of pundits bypassing that question to debate the existence of colorism and black dialect.
>
> (Pitts, 2010, January 13, n.p.)

In this instance, Pitts is framing the discussion in a way that moves the focus to legitimate issues of race in this country and how these issues fit within the modern constructs of social identity in American society. Pitts posits that the profound impact of colorism and black dialect permeates throughout American culture, and is recognized in and outside of black America; and further, to call Reid out for recognizing such obvious social markers is hypocritical at best. Pitts (2010, January 13) states, "anyone who doubts the existence of a black dialect ... denies self-evident truth. Of course there is, just as there is a Boston Irish dialect, a Southern white dialect, a Midwestern dialect. So what?" (n.p.). In reference to the existence of colorism, Pitts states that the "doll tests" conducted by Dr. Kenneth Clark in the 1930s and 1940s found that colorism is highly pronounced among African Americans. "If colorism is this pronounced among black people—and it is—is anyone naïve enough to believe it has no beachhead among white ones?" (2010, January 13, n.p.).

Pitts and members of the black press were careful to frame the Reid incident in a way that removed it from what these journalists consider real instances of racial insensitivity, most notably the comments of former Senator Lott. Those comments, which suggested a better America if a pro-segregationist had been elected president, were of more concern to members of the African-American community than the "blunt, indecorous, impolitic" (Pitts, 2010, January 13, n.p.) words of Reid. This framing allows readers to make sense of the noted theme highlighted in the black press and often missing in mainstream media which is that often entrenched racial elements that exist in American society have caused darker skinned African Americans with fewer Europeanized features to fare worse than their counterparts.

Further, several studies on the function of news framing, which provides a way to make sense of relevant events and dramatically shapes the way issues are viewed by an audience or reader, have shown a tendency by mainstream news media to use overt racial bias when reporting about segments of the minority community (Entman, 1990; Gross & D'Ambrosio, 2004; Poindexter, Smith, & Heider, 2003; Richardson & Lancendorfer, 2004). The aspect of modern racism is as pervasive in news media as it is in society and media tend to promote aspects of this social condition just as members of society do … in order to delegitimize old-fashion racism (Entman, 1990; Entman & Rojecki, 2000). As Gross and D'Ambrosio (2004) posit, predispositions about certain segments of society have an effect on how mediated frames are understood or viewed by receivers of a message. Without detailed and intelligent background on a topic, which most mainstream media tend to neglect when covering complex topics like ones that may include issues related to race, these "framed" portrayals of minorities or their communities may be construed negatively.

This type of coverage is problematic, particularly if the framing of the news event is racialized in anyway. In this case, the news coverage may enhance a negative attitude among non-minorities about members of different racial groups. As such, the recommendation by the Kerner Commission to include multiple perspectives in newsrooms can also be viewed as a way to limit the effects of ideological restraints and social cues.

By the Numbers

In 2005 the Knight Foundation looked at the trend of newsroom diversity over a 15-year period and found that among the 200 largest newspapers in this country, "73% employed fewer non-whites, as a share of the newsroom jobs, than they did in some earlier year from 1990-2004. Only 27 percent of these large dailies were at their peak as 2005 began" (Dedman & Doig, 2005, n.p.). Claiming to add context to ASNE's annual survey on employment trends in American newsrooms, the Knight Report shows which newspapers are meeting the goals of "parity between newsroom and community," and highlights the year-by-year changes for individual newspapers that take part in the survey. The report prepared by journalists Bill Dedman and Stephen K. Doig traced the historical record of non-white employment at each of 1,410 newspapers surveyed by ASNE, and compared its employment with the circulation area that it serves.

What Dedman and Doig found was that the nation's six largest newspapers had fallen from their peak in diversity hiring: Gannett, the company with the best overall record on diversity, had seen non-white employment at its flagship *USA Today* slide steadily since 1994. *The Wall Street Journal* peaked in the 2000 report, *The New York Times* in 2003, *The Los Angeles Times* in 2000, the *New York Daily News* in 1995, and the *Washington Post* in 2004. Figure 2.1 shows the fall in the number of non-white workers at Gannett's largest newspaper, *USA Today,* during the survey period.

According to the report, another example of a newspaper with sluggish employment of minority journalists is the *Baltimore Sun* (see Figure 2.2): "Draw a line around the *Sun*'s circulation area, and the population was 33.9 percent non-white according to the 2000 Census ... (but) in the *Sun*'s newsroom ... employment of journalists of color peaked back in 1991 at 19.6 percent ... fell to 14.2 percent the next year and struggled back up to 18.0 by 1996, and has drifted lower, settling this year at 15.9 percent of the staff" (n.p.).

On a more positive note, the report indicated that *The Chicago Tribune, Houston Chronicle, The Boston Globe, Arizona Republic* (Phoenix), *The Atlanta Journal-Constitution, Detroit Free Press, The Oregonian* (Portland), *The St. Petersburg Times,* and *The San Diego Union-Tribune* reached their peak of minority employment during the last year of the report's

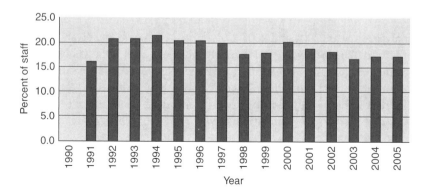

Figure 2.1 Trend in non-whites working in the *USA Today* newsroom.
Source: www.powerreporting.com/knight

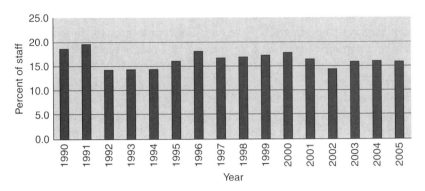

Figure 2.2 Trend in non-whites working in the *Baltimore Sun* newsroom.
Source: www.powerreporting.com/knight

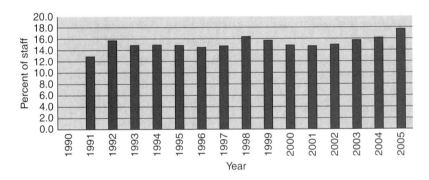

Figure 2.3 Trend in non-whites working in the *Chicago Tribune* newsroom.
Source: www.powerreporting.com/knight

analysis. In years 2004 and 2005 *The Chicago Tribune* had a diversity index of 52 and 62 respectively. The diversity index of 62 is 16 points higher than the median diversity index for all newspapers reporting in the same circulation category of more than 500,000 daily sales (Dedman & Doig, 2005). Figure 2.3 shows the trend of diversity hiring at the *Tribune* during the period of the Knight Foundation survey.

Concluding Thoughts

The American Society of Newspaper Editors' recent data coupled with the Knight Foundation's analysis of newsroom diversity hiring trends shows uneven progress in the Kerner Commission's goal of diversifying newsrooms in this country. The limited amount of diverse voices in newsrooms has proven to not serve journalism well in historical and contemporary examples of complex news coverage. Recent news events like the Jena Six case, the aftermath of Hurricane Katrina, the election of President Barack Obama, and reforms in immigration laws have forced sometimes bitter discussions about issues of race and ethnicity in this country. On the other hand, coverage of the controversial comments made by Senator Harry Reid in 2008 showed mainstream media's shortcomings in providing appropriate context to explain the complexities surrounding issues of race in this country. In short, the media's role in synthesizing and framing these discussions has been questionable. Just as covering the struggles within this country's inner cities during the 1960s required a critical understanding of the conditions of these areas and the sentiments of those who lived there, contemporary issues that involve issues of race, ethnicity and culture need the same comprehensive approach.

Unfortunately, the attempt to reach the goal of having more diverse newsrooms has been hindered by an industry-wide problem to keep newspapers profitable and running. The overall job loss reported in the ASNE 2008 survey was the "largest one-year decline in employment in the history of ASNE census." This issue is as problematic as the former, but some in the industry seem to understand the importance of not neglecting one issue to fix another. Former ASNE president Charlotte Hall stated that, "the loss of journalists is a loss for democracy … the loss of people of color from our newsrooms is especially disturbing because our future depends on our ability to serve multicultural audiences. ASNE is committed to keeping newsroom diversity on the front burner even in tough times" (American Society of Newspaper Editors, 2009, n.p.).

The group reported that in this decade, there has been a net increase of Latino, Asian and Native American journalists and a net decline of African-American journalists (American Society of Newspaper Editors, 2009). This is obviously problematic since members revised its mission statement ten years ago to add, "The percentage of minorities in the newsrooms of the nation's daily papers must be on parity with the percentage of minorities in the general population by 2025 or earlier" (n.p.).

Beyond the social aspects of more diverse newsrooms, there are economic implications as well. According to Gross et al. (2001) newspapers in the new millennium must be more responsive to diverse audiences and advertisers if they are to survive. With the ASNE reports on declining employment rates in the newspaper industry and with newspapers beginning to fold around the county, alienating a segment of readers with limited perspective on complex issues or lack of coverage on topics outside of mainstream ideals and values can be detrimental to the survival of the industry itself.

References

Allen, R. L. & Thornton, M. C. (1992). Social structural factors, Black media, and stereotypical self-characterizations among African-Americans. *National Journal of Sociology*, 6(1), 41–75.

American Society of Newspaper Editors (2009, April 16). *U.S. newsrooms employment declines.* Retrieved from: http://asne.org/article_view/smid/370/articleid/12.aspx.

Boger, J. & Wegner, J. (1996). *Race, poverty and American cities.* Chapel Hill, NC: The University of North Carolina Press.

Bramlett-Solomon, S. (1993). Job appeal and job satisfaction among Hispanic and Black journalists. *Mass Communication Review, 20*, 202–211.

Byerly, C. & Wilson, C. (2009). Journalism as Kerner turns 40: Its multicultural problems and possibilities. *Howard Journal of Communications, 20*, 209–221.

Campbell, C. (1995). *Race, myth and the news.* Thousand Oaks, CA: Sage.

Dates, J. L. & Barlow, W. (1990). *Split image: African Americans in the mass media.* Washington, D.C.: Howard University Press.

Dedman, B. & Doig, S. K. (2005, June 1). Newsroom diversity has passed its peak at most newspapers, 1990–2005 study shows. Retrieved from: http://www.powerreporting.com/knight/.

Diuguid, L. & Rivers, A. (2000). The media and the black response. *Annals of American Academy of Political and Social Science* (The African American Male in American Life and Thought), *569*, 120–134.

Entman, R. (1990). Modern racism and the images of blacks in local television news. *Critical Studies in Mass Communication, 7*, 332–345.

Entman, R. (2006). Blacks in the news: Television, modern racism, and cultural change. In A. Reynolds & B. Barnett (Eds.), *Communication and law: multidisciplinary approaches to research* (pp. 201–207). Mahwah, NJ: Lawrence Erlbaum Associates.

Entman, R. & Rojecki, A. (2000). *The black image in the white mind: Media and race in America.* Chicago: University of Chicago Press.

Fleming-Rife, A. & Proffitt, J. M. (2004). The more public school reform changes, the more it stays the same: A framing newspaper coverage of Brown v. Board of Education. *The Journal of Negro Education, 73*(3), Special Issue: Brown v. Board of Education at 50 (Summer).

Greenberg, D. (2010, January 17). The feigned-outrage game; Reid's is the latest stray remark to stir the phony indignation so common in today's news cycle. *The Baltimore Sun.* Retrieved from: http://www.baltimoresun.com.

Gross, K. & D'Ambrosio, L. (2004). Framing emotional response. *Political Psychology, 25*(1), 1–29.

Gross, R., Curtin, P. A., & Cameron, G. T. (2001). Diversity advances both journalism and business. *Newspaper Research Journal, 22*(2), 14–27.

Hall, S. (1980). Encoding/decoding. In S. Hall, D. Hobson, A. Lowe, & P. Wills (Eds.),*Culture, media, language* (pp. 128–138). London: Hutchinson.

Harris-Lacewell, M. (2010, January 16–22). Harry Reid and racism. *Afro-American Red Star, 118*(23), A11.

Heider, D. (2000). *White news: Why local news programs don't cover people of color.* Mahwah, NJ: Lawrence Erlbaum Associates.

Jones, F. G. (1990). The Black audience and the BET channel. *Journal of Broadcasting and Electronic Media, 34*, 477–486.

Malveaux, J. (2010, February 3–9). On Harry Reid's "light skinned" comment: W. E. B. Du Bois was right. *Michigan Chronicle, 73*(21), A6.

Mastin, T. (2000). Media use and civic participation in the African-American population: Exploring participation among professionals and non-professionals. *Journalism and Mass Communication Quarterly, 77*, 115–127.

Nishikawa, K. A., Towner, T. L., Clawson, R. A., & Waltenburg, E. N. (2009). Interviewing the interviewers: Journalistic norms and racial diversity in the newsroom. *The Howard Journal of Communications*, *20*, 242–259.

Pitts, L. (2010, January 13). Reid got it right. *The Miami Herald*. Retrieved from: http://www.miamiherald.com/2010/01/13.

Poindexter, P. M., Smith, L. K., & Heider, D. (2003). Race and ethnicity in local television news: Framing, story assignments, and source selections. *Journal of Broadcasting & Electronic Media, 47*(4), 524–536.

Porter, T. (2004, April 21). ASNE's diversity study: Looking for answers. Message posted to: http://www.timporter.com/firstdraft/archives/000298.html.

Price, V. & Tewksbury, D. (1997). News values and public opinion: A theoretical account of media priming and framing. *Progress in Communication Sciences*, *13*, 173–212.

Readership Institute (January 2001). Inside newspaper culture. In Impact quick-read summary. Retrieved from: http://www.readership.org/impact/impact_summary.pdf.

Richardson, J. D. & Lancendorfer, K. M. (2004). Framing Affirmative Action: The influence of race on newspaper editorial responses to the University of Michigan cases. *Harvard International Journal of Press/Politics*, *9*(4), 74–94.

Shosteck, H. (1969). Some influence of television on civil unrest. *Journal of Broadcasting & Electronic Media*, *13*(4), 371–379.

Thornton, L. (1990). Broadcast news. In J. L. Dates & W. Barlow (Eds.), *Split image: African Americans in the mass media*. Washington, D.C: Howard University Press.

U.S. Census Bureau (2005, July 1).*Population Profile of the United States*. Retrieved January 1, 2010 from: http://www.census.gov/population/www/popprofile/files/dynamic/RACEHO.pdf.

Vercellotti, T. & Brewer, P. R. (2006). "To plead our own cause": Public opinion toward black and mainstream news media among African Americans. *Journal of Black Studies*, *37*(2), 231–250.

Weaver, D. H. & Wilhoit, G. C. (1991). *The American journalist: A portrait of U.S. news people and their work*. Bloomington, IN: Indiana University Press.

Weaver, D. H. & Wilhoit, G. C. (1996). *The American journalist in the 1990s: U.S. news people at the end of an era*. Mahwah, NJ: Lawrence Erlbaum Associates.

Wilson, C., Gutierrez, F., & Chao, L. M. (2003). *Racism, sexism and the media*. Thousand Oaks, CA: Sage Publications.

Wolseley, R. E. (1990). *The Black Press, U.S.A*. Ames, IA: Iowa State University Press.

Discussion Questions

1. Do you think diversity in American newsrooms is a necessity for journalism to play its role in a democratic society?

2. Do you feel the issues being reported in mainstream newspapers (i.e. *Washington Post, New York Times,* etc.) are reflective of issues that are important to the more diverse population of this country? Explain.

3. Describe the difference in interpretive news reporting and subjective news reporting. Does the work of newspaper columnists enhance the coverage of issues with a racial component?

4. What challenges do you think journalists of color face in today's newsrooms?

5. Describe the community in which you live by using demographic data provided on the U.S. Census Web site. Include the race and ethnicity of the people who live there, their economic status, the educational levels obtained and the ratio of males to females.

Assignments

1. Compare and contrast the top news story of the day in your local newspaper with the top news story on the same day in a newspaper produced by a specific minority group.

2. Interview a journalist of color at your local newspaper. Ask him or her to describe their view of diversity in the newsroom. Also, ask if they feel their race makes a difference in the way they report the news. If the answer is yes, ask him or her to describe how so.

3. Select a news story from any major U.S. newspaper (mainstream) and use its angle as a topic for a round table discussion with your classmates. Compare the points made during the discussion with the points expressed in the news story. Are the views of the sources in the story similar to the views of your classmates? Does the story contain enough background and context for the students to make what they consider to be valid points? What background elements would you add in order to provide more context to the news story?

For Further Study On-line

American Society of Newspaper Editors:
http://www.asne.org

Knight Foundation:
http://www.knightfoundation.org

Power Reporting Resources for Journalists:
http://www.powerreporting.com

UNITY: Journalists of Color:
http://www.unityjournalists.org

Maynard Institute:
http://mije.org/

CHAPTER 3

National News Coverage of Race in the Era of Obama

KIM M. LEDUFF

We have reached an important historical milestone in America—the election of the first African-American president of the United States. And most of America has come to learn about him through what we see on television. Television is a powerful medium that has the potential to inform us and shape our views, especially about those we don't encounter regularly in our daily lives. But what we learn can have a positive or a negative effect on our daily existence depending upon where we choose to get our news. When the issue is race, television appears to have a way to go before it is truly representative of the reality that exists for many minority groups in this country. While it is important to remember that society often plays a part in shaping the news, there are forces that edit, gatekeep, frame and manipulate what American audiences receive as news, often leading to distorted representations. And while it appears that we as a society have made great strides toward improving the minority condition in this country, there have been a number of recent reminders in the news that perhaps we have not overcome racism to the degree that the election of an African-American president might imply.

This analysis begins in the summer of 2008 as Obama campaigned for the presidency and ends during the summer of 2009, once he was elected. This critical analysis of a poignant snapshot in time serves to illustrate the ebb and flow of race relations according to national television news over a one-year period. In the process, I will critically examine specific stories and productions that were part of the national news agenda and deduce possible meanings and interpretations that were likely conjured in the minds of American audiences. The points of demarcation will be a special featured on CNN called *Black in America*. The first segment of the documentary aired during the summer of 2008 and the second segment, *Black in America II*, aired in the summer of 2009. CNN later aired two additional specials, *Latino in America* and *Muslim in America* later in 2009. Needless to say, there are countless stories that could be analyzed if all races in America were incorporated in this particular study. But for the purpose of simplifying what could be an exhaustive critique of racial portrayals of minority groups on national news, this analysis will be limited to issues of race and racism that rose to prominence involving African Americans between the airing of the two CNN productions. But before getting into the analysis of the year in national news, it is important to look at the history of media coverage of African-American life and culture in America.

TV News Coverage of America in Black, White and Color

Stuart Hall (1980) said that "the media are where struggles over meaning and the power to represent it are waged" (p. 10). Nowhere is this more evident than in the battle between the real life experience of black Americans and the depiction of their lives and experience according to television news. According to the Pew Research Center (2004), the Kerner Commission's 1968 Report of the National Advisory Commission on Civil Disorders initialized much of the mass communications research related to race and news.

Historically, television has not been kind in its depiction of the lives and culture of black people. According to Herman Gray (1989), "Although fictional and non-fictional representations of blacks emanate from separate generic quarters of television, they activate meanings for viewers across these boundaries. That is their representations make sense in terms of their intertextuality between and within programs" (p. 378). Dates and Pease (1994) observed that "on a day-to-day basis most viewers of American TV news know black men only as criminals, and people of color as poor, desperate or dangerous" (p. 91). Miller and Wanta (1996), in their research on agenda setting in news, point out the irony is in the fact that "some researchers have held that minorities in the United States, especially African Americans, tend to rely on television as a primary source of information" (p. 914). These negative images surely have an impact on their views about themselves and their place in society.

According to Entman (1994), TV news "paints a picture of blacks as violent and threatening toward whites, self-interested, and demanding toward the body politic–continually causing problems for the law-abiding tax paying majority" (p. 29). In addition, Dixon (2003) says that "the message appears to be whites are the authoritative voice of reason, whereas blacks are the source of crime and chaos" (p. 137). Shaw attributes the problem to the fact that the press covers a much wider range of white life than minority life. He explains, "The press play a significant role in perpetuating ethnic stereotypes, while fueling conflicts that polarize our increasingly multicultural society" (Shaw, 1990 in Shafer, 1993, p. 198). So, besides polarization, which is a major societal issue, what other effects are possible? How do these images and messages impact viewers? Mass communications theorists have examined these effects and have come up with a vast array of possibilities.

What audiences see on the national news may influence what they believe about people with whom they have little or no interaction. Media images may be seen as representations that contribute to the construction of social reality of race in the United States. Representations of race may lead to discussions of social class and structure in the United States. Mass media portrayals construct social reality for individuals and groups. But who is constructing the narratives that tell audiences about minority life in America? Are they qualified to tell the story? Are they capable of telling it fairly? Entman (1994) asked, "Is the journalist's responsibility limited to creating an accurate verbal and visual record in the news text or does it encompass stimulating an accurate mental representation in the audience's mind? " (p. 516). It seems that it should encompass both, but previous studies suggest that is not the case. According to Entman (1994):

> The choices TV journalists make appear to feed racial stereotypes, encouraging white hostility and fear of African Americans. The employment of highly visible black anchors and reporters paradoxically presets white audiences with daily images of black success, messages suggesting that racial discrimination no longer impedes African Americans thereby raising questions as to why crime and demands on the political system persist.
>
> (p. 510)

Dixon (2003) looked at the role of anchors and reporters as positive images and compared them to the negative images of minorities in crime coverage. He found that blacks were more likely to be seen as criminals than reporters, but suggests that:

> Portraying a white person in a positive role interacting with a person of color in a negative role might reinforce stereotypes

of Blacks. … having people of color report on other people of color who committed crimes might decrease stereotyping among viewers by providing white viewers with immediate evidence that "they are not all like that.".… portraying people of color as both reporters and criminals in the same news story could reinforce prejudice. This is because the reporters might be seen as the "exception to the rule" that most blacks are in fact criminals.

(p. 134)

But the negative stories are only one aspect of news coverage. Stories of black success also impact audiences. One would think that seeing someone like Obama doing well would make white audiences more accepting of minorities in the real world. One would think that images and stories of black accomplishment would allow African Americans watching to believe that the American dream is a possibility. But there is stark contrast between news coverage and the reality that those living in America face day-to-day. Media coverage of black life hovers at extremes—extreme success and extreme failure. As social critic and activist, Tim Wise (2008) points out:

If you have been told that everyone has equal opportunity, and yet you see profound inequalities between whites on the one hand and folks of color on the other, how do you resolve the apparent gap between promise and reality? You can either conclude that the ethos is a myth, that things aren't as equal as you've been told or you can decide that there must be something wrong with the people at the bottom. They must be inferior, they must not work as hard, or they must be less intelligent. Their genes or their cultures must be defective.

(p. 64)

National television news has the power to make America aware of the inequality that exists in this country. Instead of only looking at the crisis or the success, the media needs to do a better job of the factors that led to the outcome. Wise notes, "The real question is, how much more successful would persons be (and for that matter how many more Oprahs would there be, figuratively speaking), if racism and white privilege weren't such a problem?" (p. 70).

National News Coverage of Racial Highs and Lows

This study is quite simply a critical analysis of a chronology of events over a one-year period beginning in Summer 2008 and ending in Summer 2009.

The goal of the analysis is to point out the mixed messages and confused depiction of race relations in this country if one were to use national news coverage to gauge the current status of race relations in America. The stories and segments selected for this analysis were chosen because in all cases race was an important element of the media frame.

In the process of this analysis, the goal is to ponder some important questions about national news coverage of race. The first research question is: Does the national coverage included in this snapshot in time offer insight into why black and white America is so divided when it comes to perceptions about race relations? In a 2010 Pew Center survey, it was reported that while some blacks think their status is improving since Obama's election:

> four decades after the turmoil, triumphs and tragedies of the Civil Rights era, most blacks still doubt the basic racial fairness of American society. More than eight-in-ten blacks—compared with just over a third of whites—say the country needs to make more changes to ensure that blacks have equal rights with whites. Blacks also continue to lag behind whites in their satisfaction with their lives and local communities, and most remain skeptical that the police treat blacks and whites equally.
>
> (Pew Research Center, 2010, n.p.)

Perhaps the vast difference in opinion about racial fairness might be partially attributed to the television news coverage that audiences have access to. News organizations often frame stories within the parameters of black success and black failure, black wealth versus black poverty. The race appears to live at extremes. While many black Americans who fall somewhere in between recognize the flawed media image, some white Americans use these extremes to rationalize the black experience as: those who work hard can achieve the American dream and those who don't are simply lazy. This leads to the second research question: In the course of the year examined, do the stories hover at extremes or do we see the diversity of the black experience?

Finally, CNN's attempt to shine a light on race, black life and culture in America, not once but twice, suggests that some in journalism recognize that they are falling short or misrepresenting minority groups. So in their attempt to rectify or least acknowledge the fact that blacks have been poorly represented, how did they do? This leads to the third research question which is: Did the CNN documentaries (*Black in America* and *Black in America II*) offer insight into black life and experience that traditional media coverage leaves out? Or did the coverage contribute to the media's perpetuation of black stereotypes?

As noted earlier, the two bookends for this study are *Black in America* and *Black in America II* which both aired on CNN. The summer of 2008 was a hopeful time in this country for many Americans of all races. The presidential campaign had begun and for the first time there was a viable African-American candidate in the running. In March of 2008 Obama came under scrutiny because of comments made by his church pastor Rev. Jeremiah Wright. There was concern that his affiliation with a pastor who made (what many deemed) anti-white comments might be indicative of his stance on race. In response Obama gave a speech in March of 2008 in which he addressed race relations in this country. It was clear that the candidate was not oblivious or in denial about the reality of race in America:

> Race is an issue that I believe this nation cannot afford to ignore right now. We would be making the same mistake that Reverend Wright made in his offending sermons about America—to simplify and stereotype and amplify the negative to the point that it distorts reality.
>
> The fact is that the comments that have been made and the issues that have surfaced over the last few weeks reflect the complexities of race in this country that we've never really worked through—a part of our union that we have yet to perfect. And if we walk away now, if we simply retreat into our respective corners, we will never be able to come together and solve challenges like health care, or education, or the need to find good jobs for every American.
>
> Understanding this reality requires a reminder of how we arrived at this point. As William Faulkner once wrote, "The past isn't dead and buried. In fact, it isn't even past." We do not need to recite here the history of racial injustice in this country. But we do need to remind ourselves that so many of the disparities that exist in the African-American community today can be directly traced to inequalities passed on from an earlier generation that suffered under the brutal legacy of slavery and Jim Crow.
>
> (Obama, 2008, n.p.)

It was clear from Obama's speech that he had no false impression that his position as a viable presidential candidate meant that racism was a part of the past. He acknowledged that America still had work to do. And it appeared that CNN also realized that in America race relations and media coverage of African-American life and experience were sub-par, so they produced a multi-part national news documentary regarding the subject.

Black in America

CNN shed light on the issues faced specifically by black Americans in a series of reports hosted by Soledad O'Brien. The first of the series aired in July of 2008. The special focused on three major issues: the black woman and family; the struggle of the black man in U.S. society; and the assassination of Martin Luther King, Jr. While the reports were insightful, they still focused on the poverty and crime that black America is always associated with. The coverage of King's assassination investigated the conspiracy theories that existed about the murder. But there was one story that stood out because it looked into an issue that often goes ignored in the media. While there is a general understanding in American society about the politics of blackness and whiteness, the politics of skin color and intra-racial discrimination that often goes uncovered.

One segment of the *Black in America* special was titled "A Tale of Two Brothers." The long form news package examined the story of Rev. Dr. Michael Eric Dyson, a preacher, professor and social critic, and his younger brother Everett, who is in prison for murder. As the story unfolds it becomes clear that the two men grew up in the same household and shared similar experiences. O'Brien questions how they ended up in such widely different situations as adults. Everett attributes much of it to his making bad choices. But Michael argues there is more to it than that. Michael's skin tone is lighter than his brother's. His argument is that because he is light, white America is more accepting of him. Because of that he was given opportunities and encouraged in school in a way that his brother was not. One of the important messages that came out of this story was the recognition that very often people who appear to be the epitome of success in the black community are often closely connected (often by blood) to others who are living in poverty, incarcerated, or lack access to education and opportunity.

This story highlights an example of the underlying social and historical politics that black Americans face even when given circumstances in which theoretically they should succeed. Here audiences see two brothers who were given the same set of circumstances when they were born—but society treated them differently. One was privy to favoritism because his appearance reflected some possible connection to the white norm while the other was often ostracized because his appearance didn't reflect that ancestral connection. It harkens back to the slave days when lighter skinned slaves (often the product of a white slave owner and a female slave who was used for sexual gratification) were allowed to work in the house as opposed to the field. Or when slave mothers or black mistresses negotiated benefits for their mulatto children. It is easy to say that that is ancient history.

But when the media covers stories like this one, a critical audience can't help but wonder if there is not some remnant of hegemonic thinking lurking in society.

A quick glance at audience posts and discussion on the CNN Web site revealed how the documentary was received by some viewers. The reception appeared to be quite mixed. While many people were happy to see that the cable news network focused time and attention on the issues and problems faced by many in the black community, some argued that the report focused too much on the negative aspects of black life in America. Because these posts are anonymous, it was not possible to know who responded or if the interpretations reflected racial polarization. But what was clear was that audiences didn't agree on what the documentary contributed to audiences.

At the time this special aired in the summer of 2008, America was on the verge of something unique and historic. There was the potential for America to elect the very first African-American president. Interestingly enough, his racial classification was a subject for much debate in the media (particularly amongst conservatives). Barack Obama's light brown skin was the result of the union of his parents—he was the son of a Kenyan born father and a white American born mother. Many in the media touted the fact that his ancestry did not include the baggage of slavery. But did his light skin (like Michael Eric Dyson's) afford him greater opportunity and acceptance by whites? Would that potentially lead to his success in his run for the presidency?

Obama

Barack Hussein Obama was indeed the first successful black candidate for the U.S. presidency and he made no effort to deny his heritage (even when it caused some to question his native born status in the U.S.). In his speech on race (referenced earlier in this chapter), then-candidate Obama described his ethnic heritage:

> I am the son of a black man from Kenya and a white woman from Kansas. I was raised with the help of a white grandfather who survived a Depression to serve in Patton's Army during World War II and a white grandmother who worked on a bomber assembly line at Fort Leavenworth while he was overseas. I've gone to some of the best schools in America and lived in one of the world's poorest nations. I am married to a black American who carries within her the blood of slaves and slaveowners—an inheritance we pass

on to our two precious daughters. I have brothers, sisters, nieces, nephews, uncles and cousins, of every race and every hue, scattered across three continents, and for as long as I live, I will never forget that in no other country on Earth is my story even possible.

It's a story that hasn't made me the most conventional candidate. But it is a story that has seared into my genetic makeup the idea that this nation is more than the sum of its parts—that out of many, we are truly one.

(Obama, 2008, n.p.)

This man was the walking definition of America's melting pot. And many questioned whether he should be considered a black candidate or a multiracial candidate. Early on it was clear that Obama had a knack for unifying society. He recognized difference, but at the same time managed to focus on commonalities and how they make America stronger. By June 3, 2008, it was confirmed, Obama was the Democratic presidential candidate. In his speech accepting the nomination he said, "America, this is our moment. This is our time. Our time to turn the page on policies from the past. Our time to bring new energy and new ideas to the challenges we face. Our time to offer a new direction for the country we love" (CNN, 2008, n.p.) And for the first time in a long time it appeared that regardless of race, age, color, or creed, many Americans were coming together in support of a man who was the embodiment of the American Dream. But did his rise to the forefront reflect a post-racial America? In other words, had America moved beyond the constraints of racial classification? Or was this just another example of even the slightest physical reflection of a connection to whiteness resulting in the benefit of privilege?

On November 4, 2008 Barack Obama was elected the 44th President of the United States. On this historic occasion the common story in the national media wasn't just about the election of the first African-American president, but what it meant to African Americans around the country, especially those who lived through segregation and never imagined the day they would see the first black man elected President. According to the national media, the presidential inauguration in January was a symbol of solidarity in this country. Millions of faces of all shades and hues were seen on the mall in Washington D.C. to observe Obama's inauguration first-hand. But national news did not ignore the possibility that this utopian feeling in America would be short-lived.

After the election, results of a study by the Pew Research Center's Project for Excellence in Journalism were released which suggested that overall: "Obama's coverage was somewhat more positive than negative while

McCain's, in contrast, was substantially negative" (Pew Research Center, 2008, n.p.). The study also looked specifically at broadcast networks and found that while the networks (ABC, NBC, CBS) and CNN remained mostly neutral in their coverage of the Democratic and Republican political campaigns, not everyone was fair in their approach. It appeared that MSNBC "stood out for having less negative coverage of Obama than the press generally and for having more negative stories about McCain and Fox News worked in the opposite direction, by being more positive toward McCain" (Pew Research Center, 2008, n.p.). In hindsight, these results are not surprising and further reinforced the reality that where a person watches news may influence what they are made to believe about the president, the political parties and in turn race relations in this country.

By summer 2009, the sense of sense of hope and positivity that had dominated much of the national news coverage of the Obama campaign virtually disappeared. National media reported that Obama's approval rating had dropped according to the polls, and along with that, Obama's new stimulus package and eventually a health care plan would add fuel to the fire that polarized political parties and, in the process, the races. Tea parties, town hall meetings and protests of Obama's plans for the nation filled the newscasts and America was no longer viewing society through rose colored glasses.

Tea Parties

Obama became president at a time when America was in the worst financial crisis since the Great Depression. In an effort to boost the economy he initiated major legislative policy, an economic stimulus package. To protest Obama and the stimulus package, conservatives around the country organized "tea parties" (T.E.A. being an acronym for Taxed Enough Already). While most national news organizations downplayed the events, Fox News took part in the events. In April of 2009, Media Matters for America reported, "Several Fox News hosts will be broadcasting their shows from the protests and have encouraged viewers to attend them" (April 13, 2009). The report also informed audiences that "in its promotion of the forthcoming protests, Fox News repeatedly aired President Obama and the Democrats are socialists, communists, fascists, and thieves" (April 13, 2009, n.p.).

While the reports focused on the political aspect of the tea parties, it was clear from the visuals on most national news reports that these were not events that were heavily attended by African Americans (a quick perusal of national news coverage posted on YouTube will confirm this assessment).

It was also clear that the protests were not only about Obama's being a Democrat. It was a comedian's guest appearance on another national network that honestly addressed the racial reality about the tea parties. Actress and comedian Janeane Garofalo said on Keith Olbermann's MSNBC show (April 2009), "It's not about bashing Democrats. It's not about taxes. They have no idea what the Boston Tea Party was about. They don't know their history at all. This is about hating a black man in the White House. This is racism straight up. That is nothing but a bunch of tea-bagging rednecks" (Elder, 2009, n.p.). The tea parties were the first example of aggressive behavior on behalf of conservatives hidden behind the guise of politics. Garafalo's comments might have been considered offensive to some, but perhaps she was expressing a sentiment that most media organizations would not touch. While unfortunate that the issues had to be addressed by a comedian rather than a serious newsmaker, the comment did open the floodgates for debate. But tea party coverage wasn't the only place this racial and political split were apparent. Town hall meetings were yet another place where Democrats and Republicans (liberals and conservatives, and essentially code for blacks and whites) began to clash.

Town Hall Meetings

Beginning after Obama's election it was not uncommon to see stories that began at the local level reaching national prominence because they were indeed so ugly. Stories of town hall meetings—localized "discussion" about health care reform—where people publicly challenged politicians and violently retaliated against those of other political parties were common in the national news. The situation got so bad that it became a topic of discussion on many network talk shows. Cultural critic and activist Tim Wise was interviewed by CNN's Don Lemon (2009) about the town hall meetings gone awry. Wise explained that, in his opinion, not all who opposed Obama's reform plans were racist. But he offered insight into how race factored into the tea parties and town hall meetings. Wise said that that there is "a background noise of white racial resentment present" (2008, n.p.). He pointed out two examples of what he meant by this. First, he recalled an incident at a recent town hall meeting in Missouri when a white man ripped up a black woman's poster of Rosa Parks and received resounding applause for his actions. Police carted off the woman (even though she was the victim of assault) and in the very same room there were white conservatives who held posters referring to the president as the n-word (September 12, 2009). An example of remnants of America's racist past rearing its ugly head in modern times.

Wise's second example was the impact of right-wing radio talk show hosts like Glen Beck, who suggested that the health care bill was a way for Obama to get reparations for blacks (which inherently suggests that they would have to get sick to reap the benefits); or Rush Limbaugh who stated that Obama hates white people; or Pat Buchanan who said that white men are experiencing exactly what blacks experienced during segregation. Wise argues that when these opinion leaders and others portray Obama as Hitler, "we must remember that Hitler was a racial fascist and white America begins to think—hmmm … I wonder what race he's gonna come for? Ah, yes us!"(2008, n.p.). It generates racial paranoia according to Wise.

In a similar vein, *Atlanta Journal Constitution* staffer and syndicated columnist Cynthia Tucker came under fire for her comments on MSNBC's *Hardball with Chris Matthews*. She made the claim that the real issue is the president's race. She simply verbalized what many were thinking, but few were willing to say out loud. She said that in her estimation "45 to 65 percent of the protestors" who participated in town hall meetings were motivated by racism (Matthews, 2009, n.p.; see also Finkelstein, 2009).

While coverage of these meetings where liberals and conservatives clashed rose to prominence in early 2009 they are nothing new. And over the years the mission of these meetings is usually very clear. Adele Stan of independent on-line news outlet Alternet.com suggests that "the recent spate of town hall dustups may look like an overnight sensation, but they've been years, even decades, in the making. Since the days in the late 1970s, when the New Right began its takeover of the Republican Party, it has cultivated a militia of white people armed with a grudge against those who brought forth the social changes of the '60s" (2009, n.p.).

Wise made similar claims and referenced 40 years of documented history when it comes to conservative white America's acceptance of social programs in this country. He says that the data shows that "whenever we talk about social programs and spending there is a large percentage of white America which hears, blacks, hispanics and illegal immigrants. The implicit suggestion in media coverage is that the government is taking from hard-working white folks and giving to lazy black folks" (2008, p. 70). He says that this type of thinking began after the Civil Rights Movement in the early 70s when the media began to cover poverty in a way that no longer depicted the poor in America as the whites who suffered in the great depression or in Appalachia, but as inner city blacks living below the poverty line in public housing and on public assistance. And conservatives claim that the liberal media is biased and only covering one side of the story. But perhaps that is all part of the plan to sway the beliefs of audiences. Adele Stan (2009) argues that audiences need to think about how conservatives are manipulating the media in this process. She argues that a few wealthy conservatives whose deep pockets may be hit by health care reform are behind the propaganda. She explains:

> Need to make it look like regular Americans oppose the health-insurance reform bills now being considered by Congress? Make sure a handful of those angry white people turn up at the town hall meetings now being conducted by members of Congress through-out the country. Make sure they disrupt the meeting and rattle the congressperson. Capture it all on amateur video and put it up on a faux, amateur-looking Web site, and try to kid the media into thinking there's a widespread rebellion happening. After all, the media are gonna want that dramatic footage.
>
> (Stan, 2009, n.p.)

And if all audiences have to base their decisions on is what is seen in the media, well, national news still does a great job not covering the factions at work in society that lead to inequality and challenge black success, but instead focusing on the crisis situations that ultimately portray blacks as constantly either in need or complaining about unfair treatment. There were two more incidents that occurred in this year of coverage that serve as evidence.

The Pool Incident

In June 2009, an incident reminiscent of pre-civil rights America infiltrated the national news in America. A group of black children attending a summer camp were ejected from a country club pool even though the camp coordinator made arrangements and paid for the campers to use the facility. According to reports on MSNBC on July 10, 2009:

> Alethea Wright, director of Creative Steps, a summer camp for minority children, said the organization paid for weekly swim time at the pool. But during a trip there June 29, (2009) some of the children said they heard people asking what "black kids" were doing at the club …. Wright said she went to talk to a group of members at the top of the hill and heard one woman say she would see to it that the group, made of up of children in kindergarten through seventh grade, did not return.
>
> (MSNBC, 2009, n.p.)

In response the country club sent a statement to a local NBC affiliate reporting that "There was concern that a lot of kids would change the complexion … and the atmosphere of the club" (MSNBC, 7/10/2009). While the country club officials claimed it had more to do with space than race, news reports pointed out the fact that the kids had no reason to lie about the comments they heard.

Coverage of this incident was yet another reminder in the national news that Obama's election was in no way a reflection of the status of race relations in America. If anything, his election and the clashes that have ensued as he attempts to change America's policies don't allow the media to ignore the historical and societal forces at bay any longer. This was a blatant racist incident and the coverage of black children being discriminated against juxtaposed with Democrats and Republicans becoming more polarized showed that even when a minority makes it to the most powerful position in the world he is not always "welcomed by everyone in the pool."

A silver lining to this story that did receive some national media coverage was that African-American actor and director Tyler Perry sent all the kids in the camp to Disney World to at least temporarily help them forget the negative experience. While the trip could not erase the experience of discrimination the kids endured, it did show American audiences that African Americans are not always looking for someone else to handle their burdens as the media sometimes suggests. Hopefully, this story also illustrated to African-American audiences the importance of lifting others who are sometimes held back by forces beyond their control. Within a month of this incident another incident occurred that once again served as a reminder that, no matter how much one achieves, racial profiling is still alive and well in contemporary America.

Dr. Henry Louis Gates, Jr.

In July of 2008, Harvard University professor Henry Louis Gates, Jr., who is African American, was arrested at his own home in Cambridge, Massachusetts, by police officer Jim Crowley, who is white. According to multiple news reports, a neighbor thought she saw someone breaking into Gates' home and called police. When officer Crowley arrived he repeatedly questioned Gates and he reported that in the process Gates became irate after being questioned repeatedly while on his own property. While the officer described Gates as agitated and threatening, multiple national news reports showed Gates' mug shot and explained that the 5'7", 150-pound scholar also walks with a cane. His demeanor could not possibly have been as physically threatening to the officer who was visibly larger and stronger.

In response to the incident and the national coverage, *New York Times* columnist Maureen Dowd wrote: "As the daughter of a police detective, I always prefer to side with police but this time I'm struggling. No matter how odd or confrontational Henry Louis Gates Jr. was that afternoon, he should not have been arrested once Sergeant Crowley ascertained that the Harvard professor was in his own home" (2009, n.p.). In an unrelated event the same week, President Obama held a special address on his health care reform plan. During a question and answer session, he was asked about the Gates incident and in response said that he was indeed biased because he was a friend of Gates. But he added that he felt the Cambridge police "acted stupidly" in arresting someone when it was clear it was his home. The comment infuriated the officer and segments of the American public. Though Obama stood by his comments, to make amends he invited both men (Gates and Crowley) to the White House to discuss the situation over a beer. According to CNN, the goal according to Obama was to turn the event into a "teachable moment" (2009, n.p.).

This incident was discussed all over the national media. It also occurred days before CNN's *Black in America II* aired and therefore became part of the show. The discussion was essentially about the fact that this incident illustrated that in America even an educated black man who has achieved success has the potential to be profiled by police and arrested for no logical reason. It brought into question how stereotypes about the black man (often perpetuated in television news) might have influenced the neighbor's phone call and the police officer making the arrest. As Dowd explained, "Race, class and testosterone will always be a combustible brew" (2009, n.p.). And one could also not help but wonder if George W. Bush (or his father, or any of the past presidents) would have been questioned about the incident in an unrelated news conference and called upon to be a peace maker as Obama (the first black president) was. This incident and the coverage surrounding it once again got America talking—but in a nation that was already split racially and politically, the discussion often led to further polarization.

Clearly as the snapshot of one year in American media coverage was coming to a close, any avid national news viewer was likely dazed and confused about the status of race relations in America. On the one hand things appeared to be getting better, but at the same time news of blatant racial discord as well as racism disguised as politics filled the news. So where does that leave black America? Well, the virtual bookends for this study *Black in America* and *Black in America II* were about as bi-polar as the overall news media in their coverage of black life in America. According to CNN (and most national news coverage according to the literature), if you're black and living in this country you either have lots of money or none; you achieve amazing success or no success at all. The diversity of black life and the existence of the middle class are rarely evident.

Black in America II

Black in America II aired in July 2009. It was clear based on the topics covered that an effort was made to look at more of the positive aspects of African-American life in America. But there were consequences to that approach. There were two stories that stood out in this special. The first was about Malaak Compton Rock, wife of comedian Chris Rock, and her program Journey for Change. Malaak Rock is the wife of a celebrity and clearly is one of the "haves" in society. And her charity gives to those who "have not." While the focus of the story was not the fact that this representation further perpetuates the notion of black Americans living at extremes, one cannot help but note that this is implicit in the message audiences received. On a positive note, this story does show (just as Tyler Perry's actions did) the importance of African Americans not depending solely on mainstream white America to uplift the black community. As part of the program Malaak takes students from Brooklyn, New York, to South Africa. The most poignant part of the documentary was when the kids (who were by all accounts poverty stricken themselves) were given the ability to help others who had even less in South Africa. As they purchased uniforms, shoes and school supplies for others, many felt a sense of empowerment for the first time. The hope is that the lesson for American audiences was that no one wants to be in need, and often the poor are indeed the most charitable because they know what it is like to experience need.

The politics of skin color were implicit in yet another story in the *Black in America* series that resulted in "more of the same" on CNN's behalf. The story was about Steve Perry, an African-American school principal in Hartford Connecticut who makes sure that every graduate of his preparatory school goes on to college. According to the CNN report:

> Perry founded the school with the specific purpose of creating an institution that would serve students with backgrounds similar to his own. Perry was the product of public housing and a teen mother. He recalls, "I had to be a principal at some point, or a prisoner, because I spent more time in the principal's office than the principal."
>
> (O'Brien, July 2008)

And Perry is bi-racial and therefore has a very fair skin tone. Once again, the story features an example of a black male who achieves success possibly because of his perceived connection to whiteness. This is by no means an attempt to suggest that Perry's story is not newsworthy. His effort is commendable. But one of the criticisms of the second half of the *Black in America* series is that most of the people featured who were examples of black success had lighter skin tones, likely the result of white ancestry somewhere in their heritage.

So at the end of the one-year snapshot what can the viewer surmise? It appears that in America, we have a lot to do to improve race relations. In addition it appears that even though media recognize the fact that they perpetuate stereotypes, they don't exactly know how to go about improving the portrayal of African-American life and culture in national news coverage.

The Big Picture

Let's pretend for a moment that you are an alien coming to America and learning about this new-found territory from a device known as a television. What would you learn about the people who inhabit this country if you watch national news between the summer of 2008 and the summer of 2009? The first thing you might notice is that there is a split in society. There is one political party known as Democrats and another known as Republicans. Depending upon which channel you turn to, the perspective you get is quite different. Fox News tells you much more about those Republicans than CNN or other national TV news outlets. It seems that a representative of the Democratic Party has been elected as the leader of this nation, and the fact that his skin color is different from that of any other person who has ever held this position appears to be a cause for celebration. But the celebration doesn't last very long. Some who identify themselves as conservative (which appears to be code for Republican) become unhappy with this leader. They protest him and his plans in large groups, and you notice that most of the faces involved in those groups don't share the same skin tone as the President.

As you learn more about the darker skinned people in America (sometimes called black or African American) from the national news, you find that the images of successful black males look very much like Obama. Steve Perry, Michael Eric Dyson and Henry Louis Gates, Jr. are all educated, successful and doing well. But their fair skin tones suggests a connection somewhere in their lineage to the whites who are incorporated in the majority of images and who appear to have the most power in this country according to television. These men look more like the majority group than the darker skinned children in Philadelphia who were turned away from the country club pool, or the children from Brooklyn that Malaak Compton Rock took to South Africa. What does the future hold for them? According to the news, nothing very positive, unless things change. And your theory about the lighter skinned black men … well, even when one of these men is on the faculty at one of the greatest educational institutions in this country and living in middle-class America, apparently some segments of society still dictate that he can be arrested for entering his own home. After all, he does appear to have some similarities to the white majority, but his skin tone and features make him an official member of the minority group. And based on what you see on television, dark skinned people are usually responsible for crime and corruption. They are also pretty lazy and don't attempt to help themselves. Isn't that why the white majority is protesting the plans of the president? It appears that in America the way of life is to "stick with your own kind." Wouldn't it make sense that if a member of the minority group works his way to a place of power he should do all he can to help his fellow minorities and challenge the majority who once upon a time oppressed his group? That's what the news suggests.

This hypothetical analysis may sound ridiculous, but it isn't far fetched when one looks closely at how this country is depicted in the national television news. This research was approached with a number of research questions. The first was: Does the national coverage included in this snapshot in time offer insight into why black and white America is so divided when it comes to perceptions about race relations? Perhaps this one-year snapshot does offer some insight into why Americans think so differently about race in America. Clearly the national news portrays extremes. And as Tim Wise suggests, when audiences are exposed to a multitude of successful blacks (Obama, Dyson, Gates or Oprah, Bill Cosby and others in entertainment) it gives white audiences the false impression that blacks have an equal opportunity to achieve "the American Dream" and that only the poor and lazy who choose not to work hard get left behind.

The second question was: In the course of the year examined, do the stories hover at extremes or do we see the diversity of the black experience? Because blacks and whites in America essentially live very separately, most whites don't have enough real world examples of the diversity of black America and aren't privy to conversations that suggest that blacks still struggle because of skin color. In some cases it may not be a conscious decision to ignore the black experience, but simply a lack of understanding. African Americans realize that there is work to do in this country and coverage of events like the ones featured in the national news over the course of this year only exacerbate the feelings of unfair treatment amongst blacks.

The final question was: Did the CNN documentaries (*Black in America* and *Black in America II*) offer insight into black life and experience that traditional media coverage leaves out? Or did the coverage contribute to the media's perpetuation of black stereotypes? It seems likely that the title alone made this special more attractive to African Americans than mainstream audiences. Therefore, the majority group who needed the insight was likely watching another network. While the series was a decent attempt at offering insight into black life and culture it also reiterated the stereotypical extremes of black life that are so prevalent in the mass media.

Both parts of the series also incorporated examples of black male success that suggested that in order to be black and successful, skin color may play a role. There are so many newsmakers who fall into this category: Former Secretary of State Colin Powell; Tennessee Congressman Harold Ford, Jr.; Newark Mayor Corey Booker; Urban League President and former New Orleans Mayor Marc Morial. These are just a few examples and many are members of families who have achieved political success in America. It is important to note, this doesn't seem to be as much of an issue for black women. There are many darker skinned black women in the public eye who are examples of success.

So where do we stand in this, the Obama era? Not far from where we stood pre-Obama. American society still has much work to do when it comes to race relations. In addition, the media really has to do a better job of addressing the social and political issues that are fueling unfair treatment of minorities and conservative polarization and strife against the federal government. Much of it has to do with a history of misunderstanding and hegemonic thinking. But until these discussions become a regular part of mainstream television news coverage, we as a society will have a difficult time moving beyond our troubled and often racist past.

References

CNN. (2008). Election center. Retrieved March 3, 2010 from: http://www.cnn.com/ELECTION/2008/.

CNN. (2009, July 31). After beers, professor, officer plan to meet again. Retrieved March 3, 2010 from: http://www.cnn.com/2009/POLITICS/07/30/harvardarrest.beers/index.html#cnnSTCText.

Dates, Jannette L. & Pease, Edward C. (1994). Warping the world—media's mangled images of race. *Media Studies Journal*, 8 (3, Summer), 89–95.

Dixon, Travis. (2003) Racialized portrayals of reporters and criminals on local television news. In: Rebecca Ann Lind (Ed.) *Race/gender/media: Considering diversity across audiences content and producers* (pp. 132–145). Boston: Pearson.

Dowd, M. (2009, July 25). Bite your tongue. *New York Times*. Retrieved January 10, 2010 from: http://www.nytimes.com/2009/07/26/opinion/26dowd.html?_r=1&scp=2&sq=MAUREEN%20DOWD&st=cse.

Elder, L. (2009, April 24). Tea parties: Calling all racists. Creators.com. Retrieved March 6, 2010 from: www.creators.com/opinion/larry-elder/tea-parties-calling-all-racists.html.

Entman, Robert M. (1994). African Americans according to TV news. *Media Studies Journal*, 8 (3, Summer), 29–38.

Finkelstein, M. (2009, August 7). Cynthia Tucker: 45–65% of townhall protesters are racists. Retrieved March 5, 2010 from: http://newsbusters.org/blogs/mark-finkelstein/2009/08/07/cynthia-tucker-45-65-townhall-protesters-are-racists.

Gore, M. (2008, October 30). Suite 101.com. from Obama and MSNBC media bias: Coverage positive towards Democrats, negative towards Republicans. Retrieved March 6, 2010 from: http://us-elections.suite101.com/article.cfm/obama_and_msnbc_media_bias#ixzz0jaZsl1NV.

Gray, Herman. (1989). Television, black Americans, and the American dream. *Critical Studies in Mass Communication, 6* (4, December), 376–386.

Hall, Stuart. (1980). Encoding/decoding. In S. Hall, D. Hobson, A. Lowe, & P. Willis (Eds.), *Culture, media, language.* London: Hutchinson.

Lemon, D. (Host). (September 12, 2009). Tim Wise: Race is a factor. CNN. Atlanta.

Matthews, Chris. (Host). (June 17, 2009). Cynthia Tucker on Hardball with Chris Matthews. MSNBC. New York.

Miller, R. & Wanta, W. (1996). Sources of the public agenda: The president-press-public relationship. *International Journal of Public Opinion* Research, 8(4), 390–402.

Obama race speech: Read the full text. (2008, March 18). Huffington Post. Retrieved January 10, 2010 from: http://www.huffingtonpost.com/2008/03/18/obama-race-speech-read-th_n_92077.html.

O'Brien, S. (Host/Producer). (July 2008). *Black in America: The black woman and family.* CNN. Atlanta.

O'Brien, S. (Host/Producer). (October 2009). *Black in America 2: Tomorrow's leaders, today's pioneers.* CNN. Atlanta.

Olbermann, K. (Host). (April 2009). Janeane Garofalo on Countdown with Keith Olbermann discusses tea parties. MSNBC. New York.

Pew Research Center for the People and the Press. (2004). Media consumption and believability study. Retrieved January 10, 2010 from: http://www.people-press.org.

Pew Research Center. (2008, October 22). How the press reported the 2008 General Election. Retrieved January 10, 2010 from: http://www.journalism.org/node/13307.

Pew Research Center. (2010, January 12). Blacks upbeat about black progress, prospects. Retrieved from: http://pewsocialtrends.org/pubs/749/blacks-upbeat-about-black-progress-obama-election.

Pool denies turning away minority kids Philadelphia swim club says safety, not race, led to cancellation. (2009, July 10). MSNBC.com. Retrieved January 10, 2010 from: http://www.msnbc.msn.com/id/31833602/ns/us_news-race_and_ethnicity/.

Report: emerging culture of paranoia Obama derangement syndrome epidemic on conservative airwaves. (2009, April 13). Media matters for America. Retrieved January 10, 2010 from: http://mediamatters.org/research/200904130024.

Shafer, R. (1993). What minority journalists identify as constraints to full newsroom equality. *Howard Journal of Communication, 4* (3, spring), 195–208.

Stan, Adele. (2009, August 10). Inside story on town hall riots: Right-wing shock troops do corporate America's dirty work. Retrieved March 5, 2010 from: http://www.alternet.org/news/141860/inside_story_on _town_hall_riots:_right-wing_shock_troops_do_corporate_america's_dirty_work/.

Wise, Tim. (2008). *White like me.* Brooklyn: Soft Skull Press.

Discussion Questions

1. Do you remember Obama's acceptance speech on the night of his election? How would you describe "the feeling in the air" in your home? Your school? In the nation, according to the media?

2. What recent stories regarding race have been covered in the news? Does the coverage appear to be covered fairly on all broadcast news and cable networks in your opinion?

3. The passing of Obama's health care plan (which happened after this study was conducted) resulted in lots of protest and even acts of violence. What did you think of the coverage? Was it in line with the coverage examined in this chapter? Or, did the media incorporate new perspectives?

Assignments

1. Pick one of the stories addressed in this chapter (Obama's election, inauguration, the Philadelphia pool incident, Henry Louis Gates' arrest) and look for coverage of it on CNN.com, Fox.com and MSNBC.com. In an essay compare and contrast the differences in coverage. Who are the sources incorporated? Are they liberal or conservative? What is the angle of the story? What does the coverage tell audiences about race?

2. In small groups or individually, do a quick straw poll on your campus of 20 people. On your survey ask people where they get their news (TV, newspaper, web, etc.), what TV or cable networks they trust for news, and get demographic information, including: age, race, and political party. As a class, discuss your findings. This is very similar to the process news organizations use to create the polls featured in their newscasts. Does this seem like a trustworthy or accurate method of judging public sentiment about issues? Why or why not?

For Further Study

Blacks Upbeat about Black Progress, Prospects A Year After Obama's Election: http://pewsocialtrends.org/pubs/749/blacks-upbeat-about-black-progress-obama-election.
A report on how Americans feel about race in America after BarackObama's election to the presidency.

Online coverage of *Black in America*:
http://www.cnn.com/SPECIALS/2009/black.in.america/?iref=allsearch.

An article from Time magazine about the politics of skin color.
The politics of perceiving skin color, http://wellness.blogs.time.com/2009/11/23/the-politics-of-skin-color-perception.

CHAPTER 4

"New" News, Hegemony and Representations of Black Male Athletes

ROCKELL A. BROWN, REYNALDO ANDERSON AND JASON THOMPSON

Racist ideology served to justify domestic repression, domination, and enslavement of African Americans for more than 250 years and legalized segregation for an additional 100 years. As such, it must be acknowledged that some of the remnants from that legacy remain a part of the collective conscious and continue to influence the cultural landscape. In essence, although segregation is no longer the law of the land and overt racist policies have for the most part diminished, "the culture still accepts or promotes voluntary behavior such as living in racially segregated communities and marrying within color lines, rejuvenating the artificial distinction of race, which continues to impose burdens on both groups" according to Entman and Rojecki (2000, p. 206). In short, racist ideology continues to prevail in American society.

According to Stuart Hall (2003), ideology does not consist of isolated and separate concepts, but in the articulation of different elements into a distinctive set or chain of meanings. The mass media, according to Hall, are among the apparatuses that generate and circulate ideologies and thus reproduce stereotypes and myths that serve to reinforce white supremacy. Like other major societal institutions, the mass media possess the unique ability to produce, reproduce and transform ideology. In doing so, it reinforces its hegemonic representations of the social world. Thus, in this three-pronged process, it manages to provide audiences with "representations of the social world, images, descriptions, explanations and frames for understanding how the world is and why it works as it is said and shown to work" (Hall, 2003, p. 91). Other scholars (e.g., Foss, 2004) have taken this a step further by arguing that some ideologies are "privileged" and these ideologies influence the way members of society see the world. As Foss explained, "Some ideologies are privileged over others in a culture ... the result is a dominant way of seeing the world or the development of a hegemonic ideology in certain domains" (p. 242).

Historically, the media have served the function of defining race, the meanings associated with its imagery as well as how problems concerning race should be understood, according to Hall (2003). He suggests that the media are a prevailing disseminator of ideas about race and it is the location for articulating, working on, transforming and elaborating on those ideas. The mass media have provided us with a grammar of race, which teaches and conveys meaning of and about race to audiences. This grammar is ancient, yet it remains in use because it is easy to understand. It aids in characterizing and describing individuals that are considered to be "other." This is especially true of black men. As indicated by Collins (2005):

> Historically, African-American men were depicted primarily as bodies ruled by brute strength and natural instincts, characteristics that allegedly fostered deviant behaviors of promiscuity and violence ... The buck, brute, the rapist, and similar controlling images routinely applied to African-American men all worked to deny Black men the work of the mind that routinely translates into wealth and power. Instead, relegating Black men to work of the body was designed to keep them poor and powerless.
>
> (p. 153)

Lasting beliefs and notions about African Americans include the idea that they are physically strong but mentally weak and lacking self control or restraint (Collins, 2005). For example, as it pertains to African-American men, historical representations have characterized and depicted them and their bodies "as inherently violent, hypersexual, and in need of discipline. This controlling image of Black men as criminal or as deviant beings encapsulates this perception of Black men as inherently violent and/or hyper-heterosexual" (Collins, 2005, p. 158). These images have been prevalent and a part of popular culture and mass media since the days of the colonial press, minstrel shows of the eighteenth and nineteenth century, the first feature length film, *Birth of a Nation*, and continue today with news and media coverage of professional African-American male athletes (Powell, 2008). Collins (2005) indicates that one way to understand how racial ideologies are created and disseminated is by examining and recognizing the significance of the scene in *Birth of a Nation* in which Gus, the freed slave (a white actor in black face), was depicted as yearning for the white daughter of a well-known Southern family. In this scene, rather than giving in to Gus' advances, she kills herself by jumping off a cliff in order to protect her honor. Mythically, black men were often depicted as rapists as well as potentially violent, especially toward white men as a means of retaliation. Collins (2005) contends,

> According to this controlling image, Black men were naturally sexually violent, primarily through the potential use of the penis as a weapon of violence against White women. African American men were simultaneously accused of having a natural sexual desire for White women that grew in part from their now untamed buck status as sexual animals, and in part from ideas about White womanhood as beautiful, the most desirable and irresistible women, lacking agency in sexual matters, and in need of White male protection from dangerous "free" Black men.
>
> (p. 64)

Campbell (1995) cites Wilson and Gutierrez (1985) and West (1993) in discussing stereotypes concerning African-American sexuality. They observe that African Americans are characterized as sexually promiscuous or like an exotic *other*—as the exotic other they are depicted as lacking intelligence and driven by innate sexual desires. Other enduring stereotypes of African Americans include the noble savage, savage brute, as well as the savage-sambo. In these instances the term "savage" is a synonym for sexual prowess, dangerousness and impulsiveness. Most of these images emerged during the minstrel era; however, into the twenty-first century minstrelsy continues to manifest in popular entertainment via sports and music programming as well as in film and television artifacts.

The purpose of this chapter is to examine the intersection of race, sex, news and African-American male athletes through an interpretive textual analysis of mediated representations of designated professional African-American athletes that have been involved in controversies concerning sexuality and white women. Using Critical Mixed Race Theory we draw on several modern examples to illustrate this intersection by examining the racial codes and mythmaking that surface in news and infotainment coverage of black male athletes. In the following, we highlight previous findings as well as examples that illustrate the manner in which today's "new" news infotainment outlets perpetuate the myth of difference as described by Campbell (1995) thus further laying the groundwork for the present analysis. Examples featured in the analysis include the LeBron James/Gisele Bundchen tandem which appeared on the cover of *Vogue* magazine in March 2008; the Terrell Owens/Nicollette Sheridan skit which opened one of ABC's many *Monday Night Football* telecasts; and the February 2010 Tiger Woods *Vanity Fair* magazine cover and feature article.

Old News vs. New News: The Infotainment Phenomena

The concept of "New News" as introduced by *Rolling Stone* media critic Jon Katz describes the phenomenon of blending information and entertainment. This style or format is becoming more popular because "Old News" formats (conventional journalism) are not as much a part of people's daily lives as they once were (Katz, 1992; Severin & Tankard, 2001). In essence, evolving lifestyles have been impacted by emerging technologies which have further fueled media convergence. Thus, as evidenced in other chapters of this book, people receive their news from a variety of sources and their understanding of various issues are shaped by more than traditional Old News sources such as newspapers and network and local TV news.

In today's celebrity crazed environment, which is infused with technology, the lines have become more blurred when trying to define or identify what is "news". The definition of journalism and the role of journalists are shifting as well with the emergence of bloggers and commentators or special contributors who do not have journalistic training. As audiences have become more segmented and the lives of celebrities become more newsworthy, conventional journalism is no longer the standard or rule; rather, it has become the exception. To this end, the analyses discussed here show how even though the method and format may be different (i.e. the Internet, newspapers, magazines or television) the meanings and messages really do not change as illustrated by the two examples highlighted here in popular magazines. Historically, the magazine is older than the newspaper and it has played a central part in the social and cultural lives of Americans (Campbell, Martin, & Fabos, 2009) and it is suggested that it was the outlet looked to most for information of the day concerning war, education, slavery, etc. "Like newspapers, radio, movies, and television, magazines reflect and construct portraits of American life. They are catalogues for daily events and experiences … We read magazines to learn something about our community, our nation, our world and ourselves," according to Campbell, Martin, and Fabos (p. 283). For example, according to its online media kit, *Vanity Fair* characterizes and describes itself in the following way:

> From entertainment to world affairs, business to style, design to society, Vanity Fair is a cultural catalyst—a magazine that provokes and drives the popular dialogue. With its unique mix of stunning photography, in-depth reportage, and social commentary, Vanity Fair accelerates ideas and images to center stage. Each month, Vanity Fair is an unrivaled media event that reaches millions of modern, sophisticated consumers who create demand for your brand.
>
> (Vanity Fair, 2010)

Thus, it partly defines itself as a source of news with its in-depth reportage.

Critical Mixed Race Theory

Critical Mixed Race Theory operates from a standpoint that intersects theories of race and sexuality and delineates a general economy of racialization, a theory rooted in historical representations of race (Sexton, 2008). For example, previous legal restrictions of interracial marriage were rationalized to protect the idea or purity of white womanhood and maintain white supremacy. Precisely put, anti-miscegenation historically legitimized the political economy whereby the production and maintenance of a "Color Line" played a functional role in the broader society with the notion or representation of "blackness" as the bottom of the racial hierarchy. However, contemporary multiracial discourse claiming to be an extension of the Civil Rights Movement is actually an extension of the ideological reactionary conservative movement and is complicit with white supremacy and mistakenly regards itself as avant-garde and is sometimes contradictory in its aims, according to Sexton (2008). For example, when Tiger Woods first emerged on the national scene he embraced the legacy of Lee Elder, a noted African-American golfer, and the groundbreaking legacy of Jackie Robinson, an African-American baseball legend, yet, he referred to himself in an interview as a "cablanasian" distancing himself from the African-American community. Sexton maintains that Critical Mixed Race Theory engages the historical formation of regulations surrounding interracial sexuality and the contemporary discourse surrounding the politics of multiracialism in the post-civil rights era. He suggests, for example, that the fear of miscegenation operates in the interest of white supremacy, anti-blackness, and is important to the construction of whiteness in the

United States; this gives cover to a deeper psychic fear of contradictory desire for equality, repressed same sex desire, disavowal of common humanity that if eroded would undermine the racial order.

The present analysis addresses hegemony, race, sex, and news. Thus, it is necessary to critique media technologies as well as explicitly examine the cultural tensions that permeate the image of black sexuality of black male athletes operating freely in a sphere of white institutional racism (Sexton, 2008). Sexton further indicates that the politics surrounding racial formation, interracial sexuality and news is foundational for racial difference in relation to its *containment, contestation* and *production*.

For example, in regard to *containment*, the liberal mainstream society vis-à-vis media and news promotes a discourse and image that has a two-fold strategy, explicitly encouraging equality and opportunity towards blacks, and implicitly continuing to encourage the economic and socio-political isolation of blacks. *Contestation* is concerned with the struggle over representations of interracial sexuality and multiracial identity in contrast with the discrepancies with the contemporary links with power, coercion, consent, pleasure and sexuality and gaps in historical memory that help to reinforce the idea of black males as the primary contemporary threat to women and men; finally, *production* is focused on the production and reproduction of anti-blackness by institutionally racist organizations and individuals that respond to phobias towards the black body, population and males utilizing a "multiracial" discourse to escape critique (Sexton, 2008).

Sex and Mediated Representations of Black Males

The mass media produces, reproduces and disseminates images and representations of African-American men and their bodies as "sites of inherent deviance" (Collins, 2005, p. 161). In her analysis of images of black men in *Hustler* magazine, Dines (1998) points out sufficient representations of promiscuity by black males and she argues that the focus of the camera and plot in both film and magazines is usually "on the size of the Black penis and on Black men's allegedly insatiable sexual appetite for White women" (p. 161). These types of mediated images have served to shape societal beliefs, perceptions and expectations regarding black men. Black male athletes are particularly more prone to be perceived in this manner as well as be depicted in ways that reflect this line of thinking because their bodies on and off the field of play are often described in terms of their physical attributes.

Mediated representations of interracial intimate relationships remain rare. This is likely because historically the issue has been taboo in that it is not accepted within the larger society. The savage ways in which black men have been characterized and depicted in popular culture have further fueled anxieties regarding their desire for white women. Interracial relationships have long been taboo in much of society. Furthermore, where mass media is concerned, there have been more attempts to explore the idea through the film apparatus compared with television. Thus, it is not surprising that evidence suggests that prime-time television entertainment rarely shows black men and white women in inter-gender relationships (Entman & Rojecki, 2000). Additionally, by the end of the twentieth century, no network broadcast television commercial had ever featured a black adult character interacting romantically with a white character. This further illustrates the lack of social acceptance of interracial intimate relationships as well as the lack of acceptance of "genuine equality embedded within the culture" (Entman & Rojecki, 2000, p. 169). Interracial romantic relationships continue to lag behind in gaining social acceptance. As Entman and Rojecki (2000) explain:

> Nearly four hundred years after Blacks and Whites began living together in America, cultural taboos against interracial romance and sexuality remained strong enough that no major Hollywood film by century's end had yet paired first-rank Black and White stars as a maturely sexual, long term couple … When interracial relationships were featured, on-screen sexuality was virtually always toned down.
>
> (pp. 206–207)

In many regards, not portraying interracial relationships serves the ideological function of marginalizing interethnic and interracial couples as well as their offspring. It is as if they do not exist and, worse, it implies that there is something wrong or immoral about those relationships. In fact, it is as taboo a subject matter for media as homosexuality. However, more recently, television programming has begun to feature more gay and lesbian characters. Entman and Rojecki (2000) indicate that the media functions as a gauge of cultural integration and as a potential accelerator either to cohesion or to further fuel cultural separation and political conflict. In some instances, the media have served to bring society closer together, but more often than not, the media frame issues as "us" vs. "them." This has been especially true with regard to matters involving race and interracial relationships.

Media Coverage and Depiction of Black Male Athletes

The chronicle of sports in America is a long and celebrated one (Eitzen, 2001; Eitzen & Sage, 2003). This can be seen in the coverage of sports by the mainstream media. The media have presented images of athletes soaring in the air for a dunk, running at top speed for game-winning touchdown and celebrating with their teammates after breaking a world record. In short, the media's coverage of sports has entertained and captivated Americans for many years. This, however, is only part of the story. At first glance it may appear that the media's coverage of sports has been entirely utopian, yet, when a closer look is taken, there are noticeable inequalities present within this coverage (Coventry, 2004; Kahn, 1991). More specifically, the unfair treatment of black male athletes in sports, based primarily on their racial/ethnic identity, has been widespread (Eastman & Billings, 2001). Apparent racism and discrimination in sports media coverage has cast a dark cloud on an otherwise innocent and wholesome American pastime.

Moffitt (2001) found that black male athletes were depicted more positively than previous studies reported in her analysis of black male athletes in British and American newspapers. She indicated that both positive and negative images were present; however, she states, "Those images of a negative nature suggest that the sports media may still serve as a keeper and maintainer of the hegemonic structure manifested within the sports world" (p. vii). In his examination of the 2004 disruption of the NBA's Detroit Pistons and Indianapolis Pacers basketball game, also described as the "malice in the palace" or the "brawl," Frederick (2007) found that the frame that was adopted to tell this story was the one advanced by David Stern, the NBA commissioner. For the most part, journalists followed Stern's lead in assessing the situation and delineating blame. Thus, Stern spread the blame around, with most of it levied at the Pacers' Ron Artest, who ended up serving one of the longest suspensions in NBA league history (a total of 86 games).

Frederick suggests that Stern came down hard on Artest to satisfy growing concern among the league's corporate sponsors and white fan base that the league was becoming too thuggish and too heavily influenced by hip hop culture. For many sports fans, the image of Ron Artest going into the stands will forever be ingrained in their minds because for weeks following the incident that image was endlessly replayed by the media. According to Frederick (2007), this imagery served to reinforce Stern's framing of Artest as being an out of control employee deserving severe punishment like that of a disobedient child or, worse, slave. He concluded,

The racial implications of this legacy are profound: Artest appears as the out-of-control black athlete that threatens white suburban audiences and Stern appears to be the white disciplinarian who restores order and punishes him. White sportswriters appear to be complicit in this framing because of their reliance on direct quotes from the few authoritative figures in the NBA: Stern, and to a lesser extent, the head coaches involved.

(p. iv)

This example further illustrates the ongoing patterns of hegemonic control via mediated images. The entire incident conjures up images of wild, unruly, savage black men, further advancing and supporting this mythical common sense understanding of black men and their inclination to be violent.

Over the years many researchers have discussed how black athletes have been stereotyped in sports (Eastman & Billings, 2001; Hoberman, 1997; Lapchick, 1991, 2000; Sailes, 1996). For example, black athletes are typically described as having tremendous physical ability and only a modicum of intellectual ability. In contrast, white athletes are commonly described as possessing greater intellectual aptitude and mental astuteness (Davis, 1990; Lapchick, 1991; Woodward, 2004). It has been suggested that white athletes know how to "think the game" and that black athletes rely more on advanced physical attributes in order to find success in sports. Eitzen and Sage (2003) explained the prevailing stereotypes of blacks in the sport of basketball. These scholars highlighted how blacks and whites are described differently in the sport. They stated: "[Blacks] tend to be more aggressive, better jumpers and rebounders, better at playing close to the basket, better at individual moves, and more flamboyant. Whites, on the other hand, tend to be more disciplined and better grounded in the fundamentals" (p. 297). The difference in language used to portray black basketball players and white basketball players is glaringly evident. Simply put, the implication is that black players are not as smart as white players, and, instead, black players solely rely on their physical gifts in order to thrive in the game of basketball. White players are "more grounded in the fundamentals," which means that they know how to think through the intricacies of the game. Conversely, black players do not think but instead only react.

Bigler and Jefferies (2008) took this a step further by exploring a different context. These scholars examined sports publications to explore how NFL draft experts evaluate black college quarterbacks. They discovered that, indeed, racial stereotypes played a part in the experts' evaluations of the athletes as they rated African-American athletes higher in physical abilities but rated them lower in cognitive areas, thus implying that they hold poor mental skills. According to the researchers, this type of occurrence "can have lasting effects, perpetuating the myth that Blacks aren't smart enough to play quarterback or that they do not possess the leadership qualities necessary to excel at the position [which] can instill in white athletes a false sense of superiority that can manifest itself in ways that could have enormous consequences for race relations" (p. 139). In fact, it is common for Blacks to be steered away from the quarterback position based on the aforementioned stereotype that they lack the mental ability to perform at this position. Not only is it common for blacks to be steered away from the quarterback position, but they are directed away from any position in sports that requires significant mental capabilities. Again, because black athletes are believed to have extraordinary physical ability while concomitantly lacking intellect, they are usually steered away from positions that require cerebral skills (i.e., central positions) and instead are encouraged to play positions that rely more heavily on agility, aggressiveness, physical strength and power (i.e., non-central positions) (Eitzen & Sage, 2003). In this case, positional segregation is based on aligning itself with existing racial/ethnic stereotypes and it helps to perpetuate these stereotypes.

For the purposes of the present analysis, the relevance here lies in the evaluation of the physical abilities of the athletes. Thus, as long as the "black" athlete is using his physical strength on the court or the playing field, it is okay, but once removed from the competition the black athlete must remember his "place," which is subordinate to their white male counterparts. They must learn to exhibit discipline and restraint especially where (white) women are concerned.

Research finds that athletic ability and physical attributes continue to be the leading descriptors of African-American athletes used by announcers and commentators of athletic competitions who remain largely white (Coventry, 2004; Rada & Wulfemeyer, 2005). Coventry (2004) completed a study that examined commentators in the television sports broadcasting industry. Coventry discovered that white people were more often play-by-play announcers. A play-by-play announcer is a position of power and prestige given that they are featured during sports contests and they guide viewers (gaze) and listeners throughout the entire game. Play-by-play announcers have the most control of the air-time, while also controlling language that is used to describe the athletes in the contest. For that reason, a white play-by-play announcer may frame a black athlete in a way that calls attention to the black athlete's physical attributes in lieu of mental capability. This is merely another example of the legacy of the ideological function of the grammar of race that has constructed ideas about race as well as served a hegemonic role of subordinating African Americans.

Some contend that sports reporters and announcers in many ways represent the white supremacists' capitalist patriarchal power structure of sports (Rada & Wulfemeyer, 2005) because they are able to frame and interpret events instantaneously for audiences. In their study examining racial descriptors in television coverage of intercollegiate sports, Rada and Wulfemeyer found that disparities still exist when it comes to racial bias in televised sports coverage. Their findings were similar to previous studies which determined that announcers continue to discuss and describe African-American athletes as "physical specimens using their God-given ability compared to white athletes who are characterized as hard working and intelligent" (p. 81). They admit that, over time, images of African Americans in sports have improved. Thus, they contend that African Americans are accepted today as athletes; however, "should African Americans endeavor to journey beyond the field or court, they are then typecast into the same stereotype-ridden portrayals that have been found in other venues of television programming" (p. 81).

News Coverage: Race, Sex and Black Male Athletes

According to Entman and Rojecki (2000), "The predominant imagery of Blacks on television oscillates between the supremely gifted, virtuous and successful and the corrupt, criminal and dangerous (with some Black athletes a bit of both), much more than does with Whites" (p. 207). In other words, the range of images and depictions of African Americans in entertainment and popular culture are often limited and stacked in one of three categories noted above because of both the opportunity structure and perceived options of African Americans based on societal reinforcements. According to Hacker (1992), some whites are most comfortable with African Americans serving as their entertainment in the realms of sports, music and comedy, which also impact the images shown. Furthermore, with regard to news images, Campbell (1995) suggests that the bulk of coverage of African Americans in newscasts he examined occurred during the sports report. This is somewhat ironic because initially whites were reluctant to accept blacks on the sports stage, but now the sports arena is one place where whites now more willingly accept blacks.

In the early 1900s, during the days of boxer, Jack Johnson, the media as well as society were more accepting of overt forms of racism and laws or policies (Powell, 2008). Overt racism occurs when open and favorable coverage is given to arguments, positions and spokespersons that elaborate openly racist arguments or advance racist policy (Hall, 2003). Today, there are more (than some openly acknowledge) instances of inferential racism. Hall suggests that these instances, whether "factual" or "fictional," are naturalized representation of events and situations relating to race. Each of these representations has racist premises and propositions inscribed in them as a set of unquestioned assumptions like those revolving around African-American male athletes.

Innuendos about promiscuity and the endowment of the genitalia of black men remain a part of the mythical image of men. Professional black athletes are not exempt from these characterizations which further perpetuate an image of black men as deviant and sexually aggressive. Furthermore, the media has the penchant to devote the bulk of their resources, time, and coverage to the deviant and sexually aggressive behavior of black athletes while concomitantly devoting less resources, time, and coverage to similar behavior showcased by white athletes (King & Springwood, 2001). There are several contemporary examples of black male athletes marked by controversy concerning their character as a result of criminal allegations concerning sex. In her examination of images of black male athletes in British and American newspapers, Moffitt (2001) cites the Mike Tyson rape incident as an example of mediated events and images that served to "validate the perception of a racial ideology that insists that Black men are sexually aggressive. It is assumed that the heightened prowess of these well-endowed men makes it virtually impossible to act civil regarding issues of women and sex" (p. 123).

There are other examples as well of mediated events that seem to serve to validate this perception of black men. For example, we can call attention to the 1994 media coverage of two University of Nebraska-Lincoln football players, Christian Peter and Lawrence Philips, who each were charged with sexually assaulting women (King & Springwood, 2001). Christian Peter is white and Lawrence Philips is black. Although these two athletes were charged with similar crimes and represented the same university, the coverage of Philips' crime seemed to receive significantly more air-time than Peters' crime (King & Springwood, 2001). In fact, Peters' incident did not reach far beyond the campus community. By contrast, Philips' incident had made national news (King & Springwood, 2001). In the case of these two athletes, one may be led to surmise that the difference in the media coverage can be attributed to racial difference.

To further push this point, one only need to briefly compare coverage of the incidents involving Kobe Bryant of the NBA's Los Angeles Lakers and

Ben Rothlisburger of the NFL's Pittsburg Steelers. During the summer of 2003 Bryant was accused of raping a woman who worked at a resort where he was recuperating from off season surgery. Ultimately, Bryant did admit having sex with the woman but he said it was consensual. Following the accusations, Bryant called a press conference and with his wife by his side he admitted committing adultery. During much of the following season, Bryant traveled back and forth between Colorado, Los Angeles and wherever the Lakers were playing for his court dates. However, after 14 months, the case was dismissed because the accuser did not want to proceed. At the time of the allegations, Bryant was a three-time NBA champion, an all star, enormously popular and he had numerous endorsement deals with companies like Ferrero, maker of Nutella chocolate spread, Sprite, and McDonald's, all of which he ended up losing. He has since rehabilitated his image and regained much of his endorsement status.

Next, fast forward six years and Ben Rothlisburger, quarterback for the 2009 Super Bowl Champions Pittsburg Steelers, was accused of sexual assault by a Harrah's Lake Tahoe employee. The differences between the two stories are 1) Rothlisburger was not married and 2) the amount of media coverage pales in comparison to that given to the Bryant incident. Both men are superstars at the top of their game in their respective sports and both are very popular outside of their sport. Both men were accused of sexually assaulting women (violence toward women) which are crimes, but one is black and the other is white. The details are different, of course, but the allegations are similar. While the Bryant case made news and sports headlines, the Rothlisburger case was only covered by sports journalists. Bryant's case was in both news and sports headlines for months while Rothlisburger's incident was barely a topic of discussion in sports for a few weeks. Rothlisburger claimed his innocence and so did Bryant; Rothlisburger was given the benefit of the doubt, but Bryant was not. In one case, there is a black man and a white woman and the other features a white man and a white woman. Although the current analysis is not about Bryant or Rothlisburger, this example is relevant and should not be overlooked.

T.O. and King James

On November 15, 2004, Terrell Owens appeared with TV actress Nicollette Sheridan in a skit which opened ABC's *Monday Night Football* clash between the Philadelphia Eagles and the Dallas Cowboys. In the skit Sheridan surprises Owens by showing up in his locker room before game time. Sheridan, appearing to have just finished taking a shower, is only wearing a bath towel around her body as she stands before Owens.

Owens, dressed in his full football uniform, is visibly surprised when he notices Sheridan. He then proceeds to question why she has appeared in the locker room. Sheridan explains that she wanted to spend time with Owens. Still covered in her towel, she makes an effort to entice Owens to dismiss competing in the game and instead spend the evening with her in the locker room. Sheridan is successful. She accomplishes this by allowing her towel to drop on the floor thus revealing her nude body for Owens to observe. Owens cannot resist this spectacle as he says, "Oh hell, the team is gonna have to win this one without me," Sheridan jumping into his arms in a noticeably sexually suggestive manner. From a critical perspective, the Owens incident touched a silent nerve in the area of *miscegenation*. The image of the white woman cheating on her white man, with a dark athletic stud, fed into the subconscious fear of race mixing and sexual domination by black males.

Fast forward to March of 2008. NBA megastar LeBron James appeared on the cover of *Vogue* magazine with supermodel Gisele Bundchen. James was dressed in a muscle-cut shirt, shorts and a pair of basketball sneakers. In contrast, Bundchen donned a fancy, loosely-fitting, strapless dress along with open-toe shoes. James is clearly much larger than Bundchen as the two of them are situated in an attention-grabbing pose. James is pictured with his mouth wide open signifying that he is yelling. As he yells, his imposing physique is put on display as one can see his muscles rippling and visible veins in his arms, hands and just above the chest. James is also dribbling a basketball with his right hand while concomitantly having his other hand and arm wrapped firmly around Bundchen's waist, signifying an attempt to keep her in his grasp. Bundchen, on the other hand, is pictured with a grin on her face. Her body appears quite relaxed, nonverbally communicating that she feels comfortable, safe and secure in the arms of this physically imposing man. A second photo in the magazine pictures James sitting on a stool. While sitting on the stool, one of his hands is placed on his waist while his left hand and arm are wrapped around the legs of Bundchen. She is standing on two blocks firmly leaning on James for support. James' facial expression is one of a slight smirk as he maintains his pose and posture. Bundchen once again appears quite relaxed, nonverbally communicating that she feels comfortable, safe and secure in the arms of James.

The two previously outlined examples concerning Terrell Owens and LeBron James provide evidence to undergird the assertion that black athletes have been stereotyped in sports by the media (Eastman & Billings, 2001; Hoberman, 1997; Lapchick, 1991, 2000; Sailes, 1996). In fact, these two modern day examples make it evident that the media continue to rhetorically construct negative images of black athletes as womanizers and overly sex driven animals (Collins, 2005; Moffitt, 2001; Powell, 2008), and these images doubtlessly stoke the flames of existing stereotypes about black male athletes. Our concern is that the media continue to depict black male athletes as non-rational animals that lack self control concerning both sex and women (Collins, 2005; Moffitt, 2001). The depiction of both Terrell Owens and LeBron James are particularly strong examples to illustrate how the media do this. Moffitt (2001) contends that mediated images seem to make an attempt to validate this misconception about black males. These images attempt to "validate the perception of a racial ideology that insists that Black men are sexually aggressive. It is assumed that the heightened prowess of these well-endowed men makes it virtually impossible to act civil regarding issues of women and sex" (p. 123).

It must be underscored that in both the case of Owens and James, they appeared with Caucasian females. This depiction by the media subscribes to the Reconstruction era myth that the vulnerable white woman thoroughly desires the strong, virile, sensual black man to please her in a way that her white man cannot (Campbell, 1995; Collins, 2005; West, 1993; Wilson & Gutierrez, 1985). This image also presents these men as being more than willing and able to meet these women at the point of their need. In fact, when we take a closer look at the *Vogue* magazine publication, in particular, James' visage in the second photo, it seems to nonverbally communicate that he has accomplished something meaningful by having a beautiful white woman at his side. The smirk on his face seems to communicate that he is satisfied with having captured her and that he also has plans to be intimate with her. Concerning the cover of the magazine, James' mouth-wide-open countenance is rather disturbing because he resembles a monster. This facial expression, coupled with a dainty damsel in his arm, communicates that he is holding a woman in his possession seeking to have her satisfy him. In fact, the magazine cover photo calls to mind the World War I propaganda poster for enlistment in the U.S. Army. This poster pictured an ape holding a half-naked woman in his arms. The ape is pictured with his mouth wide open and visibly enraged. All of this both supports and perpetuates the myth that black males lack self control and desire to be with white women (Collins, 2005).

The same argument can be made about Terrell Owens in his *Saturday Night Live* appearance with Nicollette Sheridan. Akin to James, Owens is a physically imposing black male athlete while Sheridan is a slender white female with a pretty face. Similar to the *Vogue* magazine coverage, the *Monday Night Football* skit perpetuates no less than two prevailing stereotypes about black men. The first is that black men are sex-crazed creatures. For that reason, the black man will stop at nothing to satisfy his physical urges. The second is that black men are overly attracted to the beauty of white women (Collins, 2005) and wish to be with them sexually. The fact that Owens decided to spend the evening with Sheridan rather than do his job (i.e., perform in the football game) presents the strongest evidence to support the myth that black male athletes will stop at nothing for a sexual tryst with a white woman. Sheridan had little difficulty seducing Owens. In fact, the language that Owens used made him sound like a nineteenth-century black slave when he uttered, "Oh hell, the team is gonna have to win this one without me." Sheridan can easily be perceived as either the white slave master's wife or daughter attempting to have her needs satisfied by the well-endowed black man. Though ABC eventually apologized for airing this skit, the damage had already been done as the skit perpetuated the popular stereotypical myth of black men as sexually aggressive.

Tiger

On November 27, 2009, golfer Tiger Woods was involved in a crash outside his home that purportedly involved his wife smashing a window and dragging him out of the car after a domestic dispute. In the days following the incident the initial report began to unravel into a story involving marital infidelity, a string of mistresses, and a media fascination with the world's most famous athlete, a male of African descent, and the lurid details of sexual trysts with white women. Tiger Woods had risen to the top of his profession financially and athletically based upon a carefully constructed narrative that ostensibly embraced him as a non-stereotypical athlete, the heir of the victory of the Civil Rights Movement, and a glimpse of America's multiracial future. However, in the days following the incident the news and media were to bring into focus the American obsession with the sexual impulses and attraction of the black athlete, critique Wood's access to women, and begin to reproduce a narrative that brought into sharp relief the relationship between a crafted public image and capitalism. Correspondingly, through the lenses of a critical mixed race perspective, Tiger Woods would violate the accommodationist role he had embraced with the broader society in return for his material success and image with his Swedish wife. Although Tiger had broken no laws, he was portrayed in the *Vanity Fair* article as privately vulgar and given over to gross sexual commentary despite the fact he was married to a beautiful Swedish model. The subsequent sensationalized sexual exploits of Tiger would be covered in following weeks depicting him as a sex crazed (darker complexioned in pictures) black male who was out of control and this narrative was re-produced over and over every time a former (alleged) mistress emerged. The news production conditioned the broader society for reprisal against Woods' behavior that resulted in the withdrawal of endorsements and sponsors as he had to submit to a "sexual addiction clinic" although he had broken no laws.

The Tiger Woods case serves as an illustration of the relationship between media image and the interests of capitalism. Woods' image was managed primarily by the International Management Group and had global interests in products ranging from Nike, Gatorade, AT&T, and various male toiletry products with companies like Gillette. Moreover, the impact of Woods' self-imposed hiatus from golf on the multi-million dollar golfing industry is incalculable and golf.com estimated that television ratings for golfing events without Tiger Woods were down 50 percent. Finally, as a result of the negative coverage of Woods' image and personal life he lost millions of dollars in endorsements.

In an article published in the February 2010 issue of *Vanity Fair* magazine Woods' persona public and private was noted as having the trappings of success because of his marriage to "a beautiful blond wife, Elin Nordegren, who was a former Swedish model ... props for the further crafting of image and garnering of those hundreds of millions of dollars in endorsements" (Bissinger, 2010). It was ironic the article associated Woods' success with his "blond" wife although he had athletically accomplished what he had set out to do; yet, the relationship with his wife appears to have temporarily contested and defied interracial taboos. However, once the infidelity of Woods was exposed he is caricatured as a threat to the Eurocentric capitalistic patriarchal paradigm. The mask of Woods' image was shattered by the news coverage revealing his troubles and flaws as a human being and it allowed the world to speculate and gaze upon him. Additionally, he is symbolically cast back among the black masses with comments interspersed within the *Vanity Fair* article that highlights preferences for various sexual acts and related contexts and notes crude racially charged sexual comments Tiger Woods made at the age of 22.

The first paragraph suggests that Tiger had never been seen in the midst of a human moment: "This was the first time we had ever seen him do something human, except perhaps for when, at the Buick Open last year, he was caught on video shaking his leg, apparently farting, and then grinning like a frat boy" (Bissinger, 2009, p. 83). This statement, like much of the article, suggests that Woods had everyone fooled into believing he was above error or making mistakes—bionic like. The only error or misstep we had seen him make was him losing his manners in public like the exotic savage *other* he really is. The emotion he displayed after winning his first tournament following the loss of his father or even the string of curse words he routinely spats when things go wrong on the course seem to have been forgotten. Are these not human moments?

In the very next paragraph of the article, Woods is compared to infamous O.J. Simpson insinuating not only scandal but also criminal activity. For example, the article states, "Tiger's little car ride was as pregnant with imminent implosion as the one taken by another sports celebrity on the San Diego Freeway, followed by a convoy of Los Angeles police cars, in 1994" (Bissinger, 2010, p. 83). Would it not be more appropriate to compare Woods to David Letterman who faced a more similar scandal (i.e. string of mistresses) months prior? The comparison to O.J. is a stretch. What are the similarities between the two? Okay, there are two black male athletes, two SUVs, and two white wives; otherwise, there is really no comparison. One case involved murder and a documented history of domestic abuse and the other involved tabloid reports and extramarital affairs, one involved criminal behavior and the other poor judgment, both are immoral, but the two scenarios are not the same. Comparing him to O.J. is an attempt to cast Woods as a criminally violent savage.

Mythical assertions permeate the article. For instance, the article implies that it is a given or a fact that professional basketball players are promiscuous. It states:

> When soccer player David Beckham was rumored to have been in sexual trouble, it may have been disappointing to his fans, but it was hardly surprising … The same with Alex Rodriguez. The same with Kobe Bryant. (Is there a player in pro basketball who doesn't screw around?) The same also with Bill Clinton and John Edwards and David Duchovny and Colorado minister Ted Haggard.
>
> (Bissinger, 2010, p. 86)

One may prefer to read the previous statements dominantly and agree that the article is merely mentioning other instances in which famed men have cheated or used poor judgment where women are concerned. However, the only black male mentioned is not only singled out, but he is also depicted as having no control over his sexual urges, reminiscent of the old stereotype and the common-sense notion that black men are sexual savages incapable of controlling their sexual desires. A similar assertion is made later in the article about Woods. For example:

> With the number of alleged paramours reaching 14 as of mid-December (a figure bound to multiply), it is safe to say that behind the non-accessible accessibility and seemingly perfect marriage

to a beautiful woman was a sex addict who could not get enough
… Even Hugh Hefner publicly disapproved of Woods' behavior,
decrying not that he had sex with other women but that he tried
to lie and cheat his way through his liaisons without manning
up to the fact that the marriage wasn't working.

(Bissinger, 2010, p. 145)

Again, this is suggesting that black men, especially those who are thought
to rely on their physical abilities and are aggressive (in the realm of sports),
cannot control their bestial urges and they cannot be trusted, particularly
when white women are concerned. Furthermore, this illustrates the level of
resentment and hostility levied at Woods because he stepped outside of
the zone or accepted parameters for those like him—a wealthy black male
athlete who married a white woman.

In many ways this article reproduces the same negative codes that have
historically characterized the treatment of blacks by news and entertainment media. Regardless of their achievements and successes in life they
remain marginalized and treated as the *other*. Woods may not identify
himself as a black man, and in all fairness, as result of his cultural heritage
as well as his slightly privileged upbringing, his experiences may not entirely
coincide with those often experienced by those more immersed within the
greater black community. However, racial politics of society ultimately
identify him as such. All of the fame and wealth he has amassed will not
change that as evidenced by the attention given to this incident.

Conclusion

As wealthy and accomplished as many African-American professional
athletes are, media representations continue to project a certain amount of
ambivalence. Though they are celebrated and admired for their discipline
and physical abilities, they are only accepted marginally as a means
of entertainment as they are often perceived as morally deficient. Media
portrayals have contributed to this mythical understanding of African-
American male athletes as criminal, animalistic, lacking intellectually, etc.
(Powell, 2008). Regardless of their economically elite societal status,
it remains "culturally taboo" for them to engage in interracial romantic
relationships, especially with white women, because when they do, the
scrutiny of them and their lives tends to increase.

Collins (2005) observes that one of the problems at the crux of
the matter of race is the fear of the "potential threat" caused by
African-American men's bodies as it is both admired and feared at the
same time. She maintains that a "new racism" exists today that places value

on physical strength, sexuality and violence as it relates to black men. She further maintains that this new racism, in some instances, generates a binary dual set of feelings in that "the physical strength, aggressiveness, and sexuality thought to reside in Black men's bodies generate admiration" by some and fear in others (p. 153). At times, African-American male athletes' bodies are admired and perceived as entertaining and at other times those same bodies are also sources of animosity as they appear in various forms of media. Thus, Collins (2005) suggests that the mere presence of the black male body can evoke fear regardless of his actions or intentions.

According to Collins (2005), although it is not applied as often to professional African-American male athletes as it is to the working class and less affluent counterparts, "all Black men are under suspicion of criminal activity or breaking the rules of some sort" (p. 158). And we see this assumption playing out in many sports-related news stories featuring or about African-American male athletes. With the recent Tiger Woods scandal, there were indeed attempts to turn what amounts to moral indiscretion into a criminal act. With the amount and level of coverage given to the issue, one would be surprised to learn that there was no criminal act involved. Woods received a traffic citation and that's about it. Shortly after news broke about Woods' extramarital affairs another story broke involving a physician who had treated him having ties to performance-enhancing drugs. The sharks were out for blood. Briefly following this breaking news were unsuccessful attempts to link Woods to steroids, but there was nothing there.

The perfect storm occurs when race, sex and wealth are intertwined. If Tiger Woods had checked into a drug rehab or some type of other facility, it likely would not have garnered so much attention. But once again, there's a mediated representation of a sex-crazed black male. This falls back on the familiar common-sense way that black men are depicted. As far back as the première of *Birth of a Nation*, black men have been portrayed as violent, sex crazed, and fixated on white women. It would not have been a big deal if Tiger Woods merely committed adultery, but the fact that he is a black man married to a white female and allegedly having multiple extramarital affairs with mostly white women outrages white patriarchy. The majority of the women who came forward claiming to have been involved with Woods appeared to be white. One has to wonder what the story would be or if there would even be a story or outcry if his wife and the women were of color.

Had this happened to someone like Tiger Woods a century ago, charges of rape would have likely been leveled because of the subject matter and alleged victims involved: sex and white women. First, because in parts of the U.S. interracial marriage was illegal. Second, married or not, it was socially unacceptable for black men and white women to interact under most circumstances. Likewise, if this had happened a century ago and Tiger Woods' wife was black, nothing likely would have come of it, because black women were not held in the same esteem, admired or respected as their white female counterparts.

Much has been made about Tiger Woods' well-crafted public image and the amount of energy and effort he put forth to cast himself as the ideal, nonthreatening gentleman. His livelihood was dependent on his well-crafted public image. Thus, it can be argued that America's power structure allows successful African-American athletes to become wealthy while at the same time maintain status quo hegemony (Campbell, 1995). So far, Tiger Woods has been hit where he can most feel it, in his wallet. The white supremacist capitalist patriarchal system of hegemonic control dictates the level of success allowed as well as the appropriate punishment when members of the subordinate group step out of line or cross long standing racial boundaries.

Once Tiger Woods stepped outside of the "accepted role" and outside of white patriarchy's boundaries he was reeled back in to submit to ridicule and public judgment. Mainstream media expressed animosity toward Woods because he did not come out, confess his sins and begin begging for white patriarchy's forgiveness. Many commentators and pundits pleaded with Woods to get ahead of the scandal and tell the public what happened and ask the public for forgiveness; however, in the days and weeks following the scandal, Tiger never said more than he did in the statements he released in the immediate aftermath via his own personal Web site. Tiger was asked to take control of the situation, but when he did not do so in the way that the media demanded, the scrutiny intensified. Maybe not talking was his way of saying everything.

References

Bigler, M. & Jeffries, J. L. (2008). "An amazing specimen": NFL draft experts' evaluations of black quarterbacks. *Journal of African American Studies*, 120–141.

Bissinger, B. (February 2010). Tiger in the Rough. *Vanity Fair*, 80–86, 144–145.

Campbell, C. P. (1995). *Race, myth and the news*. Thousand Oaks: Sage.

Campbell, R., Martin, C. R., & Fabos, B. (2009). *Media & culture: An introduction to mass communication*. Boston: Bedford/St. Martin's.

Collins, P. H. (2005). *Black sexual politics: African Americans, gender and the new racism*. New York: Routledge.

Coventry, B. T. (2004). On the sidelines: Sex and racial segregation in television sports broadcasting. *Sociology of Sport Journal*, 21, 322–341.

Davis, L. R. (1990). The articulation of difference: White preoccupation with the question of racially linked genetic differences among athletes. *Sociology of Sport Journal*, 7, 179–187.

Dines, G. (1998). King Kong and the White Woman: *Hustler* magazine and the demonization of Black masculinity. *Violence Against Women*, 4(3 June), 291–307.

Eastman, T. & Billings, A. C. (2001). Biased voices of sports: Racial and gender stereotyping in college basketball announcing. *Howard Journal of Communications, 12*, 183–201.

Eitzen, D. S. (2001). *Sport in contemporary society: An anthology* (6th ed.). New York: Worth Publishers.

Eitzen, D. S. & Sage, G. H. (2003). *Sociology of American sport* (7th ed.). Boston: McGraw Hill.

Entman, R. M. & Rojecki, A. (2000). *The black image in the white mind: Media and race in America.* Chicago: The University of Chicago Press.

Foss, S. K. (2004) *Rhetorical criticism.* Long Grove, IL: Waveland Press, Inc.

Frederick, B. R. (2007). *"This ain't NASCAR": Framing the Pacers-Pistons brawl* (Doctoral dissertation). Available from ProQuest Dissertations and Theses database. (UMI No. 3256436).

Hacker, A. (1992). *Two nations: Black and white, separate, hostile, and unequal.* New York: Scribner.

Hall, S. (2003). The whites of their eyes: Racist ideologies and the media. In G. Dines & J. M. Humez (Eds.), *Gender, race, and class in media: A text reader* (pp. 89–93). Thousand Oaks, CA: Sage.

Hoberman, John (1997). *Darwin's athletes: How sport has damaged black America and preserved the myth of race.* New York: Houghton Mifflin.

Kahn, L. M. (1991). Discrimination in professional sports: A survey of the literature. *Industrial and Labor Relations Review, 44*, 395–418.

Katz, J. (March 1992). Rock, rap and movies bring you the news. *Rolling Stone*, 33–40, 78.

King, C. R. & Springwood, C. F. (2001). *Beyond the cheers: Race as spectacle in college sport.* New York: SUNY Press.

Lapchick, R. E. (1991). *Five minutes to midnight: Race and sports in the 1990s.* New York: Madison Books.

Lapchick, R. E. (2000). Crime and athletes: New racial stereotypes. *Society, 37*, 14–20.

Moffitt, K. R. (2001). *The images of Black male athletes in British and American newspapers, 1990–1999: A comparative content analysis* (Doctoral dissertation). Available from Bell and Howell Information and Learning Company. (UMI No. 3030636).

Powell, S. (2008). *Souled out? How Blacks are winning and losing in sports.* Champaign, IL: Human Kinetics.

Rada, J. A. & Wulfemeyer, K. T. (2005). Color coded: Racial descriptors in television coverage of intercollegiate sports. *Journal of Broadcasting & Electronic Media*, 65–85.

Sailes, G. A. (1996). An investigation of campus stereotypes: The myth of black athletic superiority and the dumb jock stereotype. In R. E. Lapchick (Ed.), *Sport in society: Equal opportunity or business as usual* (pp. 193–202). Thousand Oaks: Sage.

Severin, W. J. & Tankard, J. W. (2001). *Communication theories: Origins, methods, and uses in the mass media* (5th ed.). New York: Addison Wesley Longman, Inc.

Sexton, J. (2008). *Amalgamation schemes: Antiblackness and the critique of multiracialism.* Minneapolis: University of Minnnesota Press.

Vanity Fair. (2010) Mission statement. Retrieved June 4, 2010 from: http://www.condenastmediakit.com/vf/.

West, C. (1993). *Race Matters.* Boston: Beacon.

Wilson, C.C., II & Gutierrez, F. (1985). Minorities and Media : Diversity and the end of mass communication. Beverly Hills, CA: Sage.

Woodward, J. R. (2004). Professional football scouts: An investigation of racial stacking. *Sociology of Sport Journal, 21*, 356–376.

Discussion Questions

1. Do you think that the mass media and news images and stories you read and see about people of color impact your perception of those that are of different cultural and ethnic backgrounds from yourself?

2. From a historical perspective, what role has ideology played in notions of race as it has been depicted and portrayed in mass media?

3. Do you agree with the assertion made in the "Old News vs. New News: The Infotainment Phenomena" section of the chapter that conventional or traditional journalism is no longer the rule, but is rather the exception in today's media environment and that the meanings and messages produced by infotainment outlets, like magazines, are similar to each other in that they both reproduce myths and stereotypes of people of color? Why or why not?

4. How has race been historically contained and controlled with respect to how news is reported?

5. How does the idea of race reproduced in the news serve the interest of capitalism and white supremacy?

6. Entman and Rojecki (2000) indicate that the media function as a gauge of cultural integration and as a potential accelerator either to cohesion or to further fuel cultural separation and political conflict. What do you think of this statement? Do you agree or disagree with it and is it relevant with regard to news coverage of athletes of color and sports?

Assignments

1. Using the Internet, look up articles, commentary and editorials addressing or discussing Kobe Bryant and Ben Rothlisburger's sexual assault allegations and compare and contrast the coverage. Are their stories treated more or less the same?

2. Examine a cross section of several issues of sports magazines (i.e. *Sports Illustrated* or *ESPN the Magazine*) as well as several editions of the sports section of your local newspaper and describe the stories that are about athletes of color. What is the tone of the coverage? Are the stories overwhelmingly positive, negative or is the coverage fair and balanced? Support your response with current examples.

3. Search for photographs and news footage (both print and video) of athletes of color both male and female and categorize and describe what you find. Indicate whether or not you notice any myths or stereotypes and whether they are positive or negative.

For Further Study

Books

Dates, J. & Barlow, W. (1993). *Split Image: African Americans in the Mass Media*. Washington, D.C.: Howard University Press.

Hunt, D. M. (2005). *Channeling Blackness: Studies on Television and Race in America.* New York: Oxford University Press.

Films/Videos

Griffith, D. W. (1915). *Birth of a Nation.*

Hall, Stuart (1997). *Race, the Floating Signifier.*
In this video Hall argues against the biological interpretation of racial difference. He asks viewers to pay close attention to the cultural processes by which the visible differences of appearance come to stand for natural or biological properties of human beings. Drawing upon the work of writers such as Frantz Fanon, he shows how race is a "discursive construct" and, because its meaning is never fixed, can be described as a "floating signifier."

hooks, bell (1997). *On Cultural Criticism.*
This is a two-part video in which hooks explores the theoretical foundations and positions that inform her work as well as explains why she uses the phrase "white supremacist capitalist patriarchy" to describe the interlocking systems of domination that define our reality.

Hurt, Byron (2006). *Hip-Hop: Beyond Beats & Rhymes.*
In this piece, Hurt examines the representations of manhood in hip-hop culture and engages issues of race, gender violence and corporate exploitation of youth culture.

Hurt, Byron (2006). *I Am a Man: Black Masculinity in America.*
In this documentary, Hurt explores what it means to be a black man in America as he confronts issues of race, and racism as well as the relationship between race and masculinity in America.

Riggs, Marlon (1987). *Ethnic Notions.*
In this documentary, scholars shed light on the origins and consequences of anti-Black stereotypes in popular culture from the antebellum period to the Civil Rights era.

CHAPTER 5

From the Water Cooler to the World Wide Web

Race and Audience Commentary on News Stories On-line

KIM M. LEDUFF AND ROBIN CECALA

Media history makes it clear that with the introduction of every new form of media technology there is a mixture of hope and fear that permeates society. Fisher and Wright (2001) explain that the utopian and dystopian views of the Internet are no different than the outlook surrounding earlier media technologies like the telephone, radio or television. They note, "Over time most communication technology has been perceived as both harmful and harmless in their social effects" (p. 5). In its earliest days of mainstream use, many viewed the Internet as a utopian technology that would allow people to expand beyond their real world boundaries and communicate across geographic and cultural borders. As Fisher and Wright write, "The Internet has been said to be as powerful if not more powerful than older technologies" (p. 5). Theoretically, no longer would people be limited by where they lived or by race or gender. This new environment would allow people to communicate in an anonymous fashion potentially with a global audience. But anonymity had a flip side.

One of the major dystopian views of this new media technology was also anonymity. There was the possibility that people could express ideas or opinions without accountability. Unlike face-to-face communication in the real world, in virtual reality people are not linked to a body or an identity. The Internet also allows people to deceive. Individuals can lie about who they are, where they are and what they believe. They can express offensive and potentially harmful and hurtful information without consequence. It sounds dangerous in theory, but Levinson (2009) points out that "some misuses and abuses of Web life predate new media and were already part of the older new media constellation from which new new media arose" (p. 169).

History also shows us that no matter how much we theorize about the societal impact of a new media technology at its inception, sometimes the technology has the potential to impact society and institutions in ways that cannot be imagined early on. As the world continues to use the Internet's multimedia capacity, interactive capabilities and adapts to the changes it initiates in society, we still don't know the definitive outcome. Over the last 10 to 12 years it has been interesting to observe how traditional media organizations have come to terms with the Internet. Audiences have also adapted to new technology. It changed where audiences get information, how they get it and more importantly how they respond to messages provided by mainstream media organizations. And the interactive nature of on-line communication has led to a relatively new and interesting dynamic between traditional news organizations and audiences and amongst audience members. On the utopian side, no longer is the debate about the day's news limited to the dinner table or the water cooler. The dialogue now takes place with complete strangers (or perhaps even close friends or relatives) protected by the anonymous nature of on-line forums provided by mainstream media organizations.

This is an examination of two studies that looked specifically at how audiences responded to news coverage of two very different issues with racialized components. The first study was conducted between August 20, 2007 and August 22, 2007. Twelve people were shot in New Orleans, Louisiana. Seven of them died; three were white, three were black, and one was Hispanic. Of those who survived, three were black and two were Hispanic. All of these incidents were initially reported in three stories on nola.com (The New Orleans *Times Picayune*'s Web site). The audience responses to these stories were critically analyzed. The second study consisted of an examination of news coverage in South Mississippi after an Immigration and Customs Enforcement (ICE) bust that took place in Laurel, Mississippi, in 2008. Over 300 illegal immigrants of Hispanic origin were taken in when they showed up for work at Howard Industries. Once again, audience responses to a week's worth of news coverage on HattiesburgAmerican.com were examined.

What Comments Can Tell Us About Readers

One might ask, why look at comments? If we go back to the earliest days of the newspaper, letters to the editor functioned as an important part of the paper. The comment might be looked at as a modern form of a letter to the editor that requires less effort on the reader's behalf. Because the comment can be published in an instant it is also not usually subject to the same level of thought before publication. Derrida (1994) calls this lack of thoughtful deliberation *accelerated rhythm* and suggests it is one of the pitfalls of the quick interactive nature of the Internet. It also appears that the media organization does a lot less gatekeeping. Editors typically only monitor the comments for profane language (in some but not all cases). Racism, sexism and offensive comments don't appear to get removed very often. Communication researchers have looked both at letters to the editor and more modern forms of audience participation in new media. Nader and Gold (1988) noted that in a 1934 edition of *The New York Times*, the letter to the editor section was described as a space for a "debating society that never adjourns, in which everything knowable is discovered" (p. 54). It might be found that a similar description could apply to on-line commentary. Wahl-Jorgensen (2004) looked at letters to the editor and noted that readership surveys suggest that audiences are more interested in what other members of the audience have to say about the news than what the typical journalist has to say (p. 92). But perhaps Levinson (2009) summarizes it best:

> The comment is clearly the most frequent form of sustained written discourse in the new media world. At their best comments serve not only as a voice of the people but as conveyors of truth and correction to a blog post epitomizing the democratic alternative to expert-driven information that is one of the hallmarks of new media (and has been developed to a fine art on Wikipedia) … At their worst comments can be vehicles for trolls to grab attention and can mar or derail an online conversation.
>
> (p. 22)

In their discussion of the utopian and dystopian view of the Internet, Fisher and Wright (2001) quote Timothy Luke (1998), who argues that because of the Internet "power shifts focus, speed overcomes space, orders become disordered, time moves standards, community loses centers and values change denomination as the setting of industrialized human agency are completely shaken'" (quoted in Fisher and Wright, 2001, p. 7). So exactly what is different about on-line communication that leads to the type of communication that might be observed in this case study? According to McKenna and Bargh (2005), there are essentially four main differences between communication over the Internet and in real life: First, it is possible to be anonymous on the Internet; second, physical distance does not matter on the Internet; third, physical appearance and visual cues are not present on the Internet; and, finally, time becomes immaterial (p. 197). In the earliest days of popular use of the Internet, this caused critics to be both skeptical as well as hopeful about what the Internet could offer in society. Today, as the Internet offers more advanced possibilities for interactivity and anonymous interaction, new concerns arise both for media professionals as well as audiences.

Lee (2005) argues that "the very possibility for people from different cultural settings to aggregate in an on-line group appears to condition the way hostility is discharged. There is a higher chance for the users of the Internet to make contact with others who have different political perspective, cultural taste, and national background than in other communication conduits" (p. 53). And it appears that this opportunity often becomes a reality in various on-line settings. Lee (2005) studied an on-line discussion formed to discuss the Branch Davidian Compound in April of 1993. The researcher noted that "many issues were raised and while one member of the group often held intense exchange with the others, most tried not to get hostile and emotional in the discussion" (p. 52).

McKenna and Bargh (2005) suggest that it is the process of *deindividuation* that allows users to feel safe posting extreme opinions. They note, "Deindividuation itself does not produce negative behavior. Rather it decreases the influence of internal standards or guides to behavior and increases the power of external cues" (p. 198). In other words, if the content of other posts appears to be hostile, they will mimic that behavior even if their personal standards in the real world would not normally allow such behavior.

Wall (2005) looked at blogs that are essentially like Web sites that can be posted by anyone. What she found was that "the voice of the typical blogger is personalized, opinionated, and often one-sided" (p. 161). But in addition to their own voices, most bloggers invited audiences to contribute and essentially engage in discussion. Wall notes, "On blogs audiences are often invited to contribute information, comments, and sometimes direct financial support. In effect, audiences sometimes co-create content and also serve as patrons" (p. 161). Essentially these sites function as "a sort of virtual town hall but one that can be and often is anonymous. These audience posts often consist of opinions" (p. 163). Like the previous study, Wall looked at issue-driven communication. In this case she looked at blogs regarding the War in Iraq. She found that most of the posts by audiences were indeed related to their opinions of the war.

Xiao and Polumbaum (2004) looked specifically at on-line audience posts in response to coverage of a serial killer in China. They found that certain themes arose in the audience discussions and they were often quite different from the themes that arose in news coverage of the crime. According to the researchers, "The major social reasons for the crime discussed by readers were growing disparities between rich and poor, discrimination against powerless social groups, and official corruption" (p. 5).

Based on this literature there is no conclusive evidence to suggest how closely audience responses will be tied to a particular topic when audiences are invited to respond to an article or blog or post to a newsgroup. The literature also suggests that in the on-line environment users feel free to be more honest and hostile in their commentary because they are anonymous.

Based on a quick scan of the responses to coverage of the two news stories examined in this chapter, it appeared that there were a number of features that audience responses had in common. Perhaps the most shocking feature of the posts was that the content was often rude and derogatory. Secondly, while anonymity is often considered a positive feature when using the Internet, there were often identifying characteristics offered in screen names that made those who posted a little less anonymous than they thought. Screen names often included identifying information and often times there was information such as location, race and level of education offered within the text of the posts. Based on surface observations this analysis was approached with five primary research questions:

RQ1: Which themes were most common in the audience comments posted?

RQ2: What percentage of posts were initial posts and what percentage were direct responses to previous posts from other screen names?

RQ3: Did certain users (based on screen name) dominate the dialogue in the responses?

RQ4: How often did individuals return to the site to post comments under the same screen name?

RQ5: How often did screen names appear to offer clues to real world name, race, gender, age or political affiliation?

Murder in New Orleans

The audience posts that were analyzed in this study were in response to three stories posted on nola.com. The first story, posted on August 20, 2007, was headlined, "Estranged husband kills wife, her boss" and was a double murder/suicide (Muskus & Hayes, 2007). The murderer/suicide victim and both murder victims were white. The second story posted on nola.com on August 21, 2007, was titled, "Five shootings leave three dead, two hurt" (McCarthy & Monteverde, 2007). In a span of less than 24 hours five separate shooting incidents took place across New Orleans. All the victims were black males. The third story on nola.com was posted on August 22, 2007, titled: "One killed four wounded in three separate shootings." In one shooting incident three Hispanic males were shot. (It was later reported that one died). The other two separate incidents involved black males, one murdered, the other injured.

We selected these three consecutive stories as a case study because the victims involved over the course of the three-day period were different racially. One goal of the study was to determine if there was a link between the story content and the content of the audience posts. The *level of analysis* for the purposes of this study was the posted comment; that is, we specifically examined the comments that were posted to attempt to answer our research questions.

There were a total of 135 comments posted by 95 different screen names. For the purposes of analysis, 18 themes were defined (see Table 5.1).

TABLE 5.1 Themes reflected in audience posts on nola.com.

Themes	
1.	Negative racial theme
2.	Anti-New Orleans theme
3.	Anti-city government theme
4.	Pro-New Orleans theme
5.	Positive racial theme
6.	Crime legacy to blame theme
7.	Law enforcement to blame theme
8.	Sympathy theme
9.	Anti-federal government
10.	Anti-state government
11.	Family structure lacking theme
12.	Religion needed theme
13.	Education system to blame theme
14.	Criticism of nola.com article theme
15.	Pro-city government theme
16.	Lack of mental healthcare theme
17.	Pro-national government theme
18.	Pro-state government theme

Over the course of the three-day period there were a total of 135 comments posted by 95 different usernames. Most names (71) posted only once, 17 posted twice, and five posted three times. Only two users posted more than that: one posted six times and another seven times. It is assumed that each screen name represents a different user. So based on these results, it appears that most people only post once.

There were 18 themes reflected in the audience posts over the course of the three-day period. It is important to reiterate that a single post could reflect multiple themes. The most common themes in the posts were the negative racial theme (in 32 posts), the anti-New Orleans theme (in 30 posts) and the anti-city government theme (in 26 posts). One extreme example of the negative racial theme was posted in response to the last story:

> Posted August 22, 2007 by *duke 1776*
> As I have commented before, this is a problem politicians cannot solve. When are the other races going to finally call out the blacks on what is largely their problem: inner city violence. I do not understand the black culture. At least Jews and Arabs hate the other race but value and cherish their own. As far as I can tell amongst the peoples of the world, only the Africans are this self-destructive. We must hold the black community accountable for what they are doing to this city.

This comment was an example of just one of the many racially charged posts that suggested that one group was to blame for the situation in New Orleans. Most of the racially charged posts looked at the murder rate in New Orleans as a black issue even though the coverage on the first day involved a white murderer and victims. Perhaps that incident, by nature of the circumstances, was looked at as an exception, while the news on the other two days constituted the rule. The commentary by *duke 1776* is perhaps one of the most outrageous examples of the type of negative racial themes reflected in audience posts. It makes sweeping generalizations about black culture as well as other ethnic groups that is stereotypical and damaging.

The second most common theme in the posts was the anti-New Orleans theme. Many users posted messages expressing their disgust with the city and their good fortune to have moved away either pre- or post-Katrina. This comment expresses the anti-New Orleans theme:

> Posted August 22, 2007 by *alleyezon3*
> After reading all this (expletive) I am so glad I moved away 4 years ago. I lived in New Orleans 27 years. You get tired of the same old excuses from politicians, the same old crime, the same

old dirty city. When is it going to change? People aren't cowards for leaving New Orleans and wanting a better life for their family. If anyone is a coward it's the same ignorant people that went back and are complaining that they "ain't getting nothing for free." New Orleans will be looked upon in a negative light for many years to come ...

The third most common theme overall was anti-city government. Most of these comments suggested that New Orleans Mayor Ray Nagin was to blame for the negative conditions in New Orleans:

Posted August 22, 2007 by *nolajohn1*

There is a great American city with a mayor whose family lives in another state. What kind of message does that send? It's safe enough for all you slobs who live and work here, but not safe enough for the mayor's family? Perhaps it's time to start a recall petition, and allow the Mayor to go to Dallas full-time with his family. This will permit serious minded folk to go about cleaning up the mess that the mayor, Riley and Jordan have allowed to fester.

Remember after Katrina there was a zero crime rate in New Orleans, but Nagin, Riley and Jordan have turned it into a free-fire zone.

The post offers negative criticism of Mayor Nagin, Police Chief Warren Riley and District Attorney Eddie Jordan, all three African American. It is similar to many posts during the three-day period that suggested that city officials were to blame. This type of criticism is not usually offered in such blatant terms in the local newspaper, but an anonymous audience member was able to offer open criticism in this on-line forum.

The second story, posted on August 20, 2007, was about a murder/suicide. The victims were both white. While the story received the fewest number of posts, overall, the theme most frequently reflected in the content of the posts was quite different from the primary theme in the latter days. It was only in posts after the story in which the victims were white that the sympathy theme was present. While some posts suggested that the person making the comment knew the family, most did not indicate close ties to the family but still offered a message of sympathy:

Posted August 20, 2007 by *Salita*

My family's thoughts and prayers are with both of the Price and Miquet's relatives. God is with you during this time of inconsolable pain and confusion.

There were no sympathetic messages in any of the posts on August 21 or 22. This could suggest one of a few things. It could simply be a reflection of a hegemonic attitude passed on for generations in this country that suggests that more importance is placed on crimes that victimize whites. Secondly, the coverage by nola.com may also be to blame for the type of audience responses. When nola.com reported the murder/suicide, pictures and a detailed analysis were included in the story. In the stories about the shootings of the black and Hispanic men, multiple incidents were combined and less detail was offered. While the shootings of the black and Hispanic men were treated as random crimes not worthy of extensive detail, the white murder/suicide was treated as an isolated incident affecting a suburban New Orleans community.

On August 21, 2007, the story was about five shootings, all involving black males, three of whom were killed. This story generated the most posts (a total of 78). The most common themes included in these posts were the anti-New Orleans theme, the anti-city government theme and the negative racial theme. The victims in the story on the second day of coverage were all black males. This is reflective of the type of crime that was most common in news coverage pre-Hurricane Katrina as well (LeDuff, 2009). It is not surprising that audience comments suggest disgust with city officials who appear to have done nothing to improve conditions and in turn fostered disenchantment with the city.

On August 22, 2007, the story posted on nola.com was about four shootings in New Orleans. One involved a black male who was murdered, and in a separate incident three Hispanic males were shot (one later died). The story generated 30 posts with the most common theme being the negative racial theme. The anti-city government theme and the legacy of crime theme tied for second most common comments on this day. The Hispanic victim crime stories posted reflected crime committed against a new population in New Orleans. Pre-Katrina, the Hispanic population was very small. Post-Katrina, that population grew because of the availability of construction jobs in rebuilding the city. It does not appear, however, that the race of the majority of victims in the story that day had any impact on the themes reflected in audience posts. While the anti-city government theme was most common, the second most common themes were the negative racial theme and the belief that the legacy of crime in the city was the primary issue. An excerpt from one post on August 22 incorporated a number of themes, but prominently displays the legacy of crime theme which was present in so many comments on the third day:

> Posted August 22, 2007 by *cosj*
> … all this kidding aside, because something is evil, but not new to a city (crime) it is still a poison pill that we must eradicate … we

need a sense of urgency, a feeling or a sentiment to motivate people to rid this city of its violence. If not, more and more people will leave.

Perhaps the real goal is to increase the gangsta culture, decrease the literacy level so that we can continue to self destruct …

One negative aspect of doing research of this nature is that there is no way to determine for certain whether or not the same individual posts under different screen names. There is also no guarantee that posts under the same screen name are posted by a single individual. This study was done under the assumption that each screen name represents a different person. Of all the posts, only 43 were direct responses to previous posts. On the first day there were 27 comments posted and five were direct responses to previous posts. On day two of the 78 total posts, 27 were direct responses to previous posts. The most dialogue actually occurred on day three. There were only two users who were excessive in their commentary. McKenna and Bargh (2005) found that "when taking part in a social gathering on the Internet a person cannot physically see the other people present, but he or she nonetheless becomes familiar with these people through their nicknames, e-mail addresses, or character names" (p. 199). There was a degree of familiarity evident here; unfortunately, it was usually conveyed through a negative tone. One such exchange was noted on day two among three users:

Posted August 21, 2007 by *Marykay1956*
First of all New Orleans needs to remove all Federal, State and local government and start over with all new people in government because everyone of them are corrupt starting from the US Attorneys office down to the Jefferson Parish Sheriff Department … The Mayor of New Orleans is a big JOKE, but you all voted for him after Katrina. We have most of your criminals that should have been put in prison in Louisiana a long time ago …

Response posted August 21, 2007 from *chola*
Marykay, I think you should focus on cosmetics, because your geographic advice of how to correct NOLA's problems is way off. First off it's the AG not the DA that is corrupt and Jefferson is not the police authority for New Orleans.

I guess from your post that you are a Texan, and there is no corruption in your state and the only criminals in Texas are from Louisiana. My next question to you is, are all Texans as dumb as Bush or just a few?

Response posted August 21, 2007 by *Marykay1956*
YES WE HAVE A SAY SO WHEN YOUR OWN PEOPLE
HAVE INVADED OUR CITY AND THEY ARE KILLING EACH
OTHER HERE. … I HAVE NO SYMPATHY FOR YOU. WE ARE
DEALING WITH ALL YOUR CRIMINALS HERE AND OUR
LAW ENFORCEMENT IS DOING WHAT THEY ARE SUPPOSED
TO DO. YOU ARE THE STUPID ONE.

Response posted August 21, 2007 by *borncountry*
Chola—you are an idiot. Are you reading your replies before
you hit post? And when you call others "dum," the least you could
do is spell it the right way.

Response posted August 21, 2007 by *chola*
Marykay, I must have hit a nerve huh, point is "don't throw
stones when you live in a glass house." Gotta go c-ya
Oh, borncountry, you must live on the border too …

Chola and *Marykay1956* were the most vocal of those who posted comments with *chola* posting seven times and *Marykay1956* posting six times. Most of their posts were defensive and usually insulting. Overall, positive exchanges were rare. Most screen names, however, only posted single comments. Very few of the screen names were posted on more than one day over the course of the three-day period. If this study were done over a longer period of time it might be more likely that the same screen names might recur.

While there is no way of knowing for certain who is behind a screen name, an attempt was made to determine if any of the screen names offered clues about who might be behind them. The 95 screen names were categorized to determine if they offered clues to political affiliation, race/ethnicity/culture, gender and geographic connection. There was only one screen name (*geedub2010*) that suggested political affiliation (as in "geedub" is a supporter of former Republican President George W. Bush). Only seven screen names suggested racial, ethnic or cultural group (e.g., *Russian*, *cajundelyte*). Gender was suggested in 18 screen names. Of those, eight incorporated what would typically be considered female names (e.g., *Janicej2*) and ten incorporated what would be considered male names or the word man (e.g., *DirtyPaul*, *movingman*). Geographic affiliation was evident in 19 screen names as well (e.g., *opelousas69*). And of those with geographic cues, 15 indicated New Orleans (*NO* or *NOLA*) in the screen name (e.g., *eastNO*, *ilovenola582*). Geographical connection and gender cues were most common in the screen names. Often, the content in the post reaffirmed the likelihood that the screen name characterized real world qualities about those who posted.

> Posted August 22, 2007 by *Leftno4good*
>
> It's so scary! It's a shame. This city is in need of some serious help … I mean what is it going to take to get New Orleans functioning properly? I would not want my dog to live in New Orleans!

The screen name might be translated to "left New Orleans for good" and based on the content in the post the person does not want to live in the city. Many of the screen names were reflective of the themes embedded in the posted commentary.

The results of this study show that the dialogue and debate that takes place in the comments section is not always reflective of the issues at hand according to the news organization that hosts that debate. Perhaps these posts might serve as a virtual thermometer measuring the hot issues on the minds of audiences, even if they are not the issues mainstream news outlets suggest are salient. The anonymity of the Internet allows audiences to not only address issues that are important, but to post strong opinions, debate, argue and sometimes insult one another in a way that would not be socially acceptable in other environments. This in turn has the potential to polarize audiences along racial lines, political lines and by other means—especially when some comments or screen names incorporate identifying information that makes their race, gender and social or political beliefs clear. But at the same time this study reaffirmed what Xiao and Polumbaum (2004) found: "Remarkably, voices seldom heard in conventional news items were projected and communicated in these discussions" (p.10).

The only difference in the posts in relation to the victims is that reactions to the white victims contained sympathy whereas the reaction to the other victims did not. As suggested earlier, there are a number of factors that could have been to blame for this reaction from audiences. But the fact remains that the treatment of inner city crime stories (which in the case of New Orleans usually involves African Americans) by traditional journalistic outlets causes audiences to become desensitized. That was clear in the content of these posts, especially those that expressed the negative racial theme.

Immigration Issues in South Mississippi

This study applied a similar methodology to examine audience reactions to stories directly related to an ethnic issue: immigration. Coverage of immigration is common in both national and local news coverage in America. Unfortunately, it appears that in American society today, the word *immigrant* is often equated with Hispanic people who may or in some cases may not be in this country illegally. Perhaps this is due to repeated and often stereotypical coverage of Hispanic immigrants in news in the U.S. at both the national and local level. This study looked specifically at news coverage at the local level in South Mississippi. Audience reactions to local news coverage of an Immigration and Customs Enforcement (ICE) bust that took place in Laurel, Mississippi, in 2008—the largest in ICE's history—were examined.

The impetus for this study actually began almost a year before ICE officials rounded up over 300 illegal immigrants of Hispanic origin on a regular workday at Howard Industries. In a September, 2007 issue of *The Hattiesburg American*, a headline read: "110% growth in Hispanic population in Jones County over six years." Right next to it: "Some link growth with higher crime rate." These headlines, side by side, served as a glaring example of the unfair treatment of Hispanic immigrants we observed in local media in South Mississippi. Post-Hurricane Katrina, there appeared to be few stories about the contributions of Hispanic people to the rebuilding of the area. The local media also treated Hispanic immigrants as second-class citizens, often not offering them the same protections or courtesies that would be offered American citizens. A prime example of the insensitivity was a story that aired on Hattiesburg's only local news channel, NBC-affiliate WDAM-TV, in the summer of 2007. In the story the reporter interviewed a Hispanic family that was in the country illegally. They noted that for their protection (because they were in the country illegally) the station was blurring their images. That was done in close-ups, but in a wide shot of the family sitting in their living room, their faces were clearly visible, making it possible for law enforcement officials to identify the family members.

In the story about population growth referenced above, when asked about the increase in the Hispanic population, a county administrator was quoted as saying, "Anyone who spends time driving around Laurel or Jones County can tell there are certainly a lot more here than five years ago … on some streets (Hispanics) is all you see." Both examples illustrate how local media dehumanize and generalize about a group that they often identify simply as "illegals."

On August 25, 2008 an incident occurred that illustrated more of the same treatment of Hispanic immigrants by media in South Mississippi. Even more insightful were the comments left by readers of the coverage on *The Hattiesburg American*'s Web site. It appeared that attitudes conveyed in the media coverage were also reflected in the reader posts. The Howard

Industries raid took place on August 25, 2008. The *Hattiesburg American*'s Web site, hattiesburgamerican.com, was monitored over the course of one week (seven days) and a census was done of all stories and posts generated that week. There were a total of 41 articles related to the raid posted on the Web site and a total of 246 posts were generated by readers. For the purposes of content analysis, 12 themes were defined (see Table 5.2). Before beginning the analysis of the posts, it is essential to look at the stories themselves. The titles of the stories (illustrated in Table 5.3) indicate how *The Hattiesburg American* framed the story of the ICE raid. As noted earlier, based on local media's treatment of the Hispanic population in this region of the country, it is no surprise that the responses were overwhelmingly negative. Some of the headlines to these stories alone prompted such negative discussion: "Attendance drops today in Laurel schools," "Applicants line up to take advantage of Southern job openings," "Pregnant young mothers eligible for alternative," "8 detainees charged with aggravated identity theft."

While there were multiple authoritative voices incorporated in the coverage from ICE, local government, local communities and Howard Industries, there were almost no voices from those members of the Hispanic community directly affected by the raid, especially as the sources of quotes or information. The most vocal representative of the Hispanic Community was a pastor of a local church who appeared to be of Hispanic origin.

TABLE 5.2 Themes reflected in posts on *The Hattiesburg American*'s Web site.

List of themes reflected in posts	
1.	pro-immigration
2.	anti-immigration
3.	racist
4.	pro-government
5.	anti-government
6.	pro-religion/church
7.	anti-religion/church
8.	taxes
9.	taking our jobs
10.	pro-business
11.	anti-business
12.	realists
13.	other

Table 5.3 Story headlines in *The Hattiesburg American* on the ICE raid.

Date	Story Headline
8/25	1. Activity light outside Howard headquarters
8/25	2. Immigrants rights group knew ICE raid coming
8/25	3. 350 detained by ICE
8/25	4. Pregnant young mothers eligible for alternative
8/25	5. Howard raid was result of union tip
8/25	6. Howard headquarters locked up
8/25	7. Laurel church aides undocumented workers' families
8/25	8. Howard Industries responds
8/25	9. Pastor: 8 members detained by ICE
8/26	10. New state law may not result in any charges against Howard Industries
8/26	11. 8 detainees charged with aggravated identity theft
8/26	12. State could become involved with children of detained parents
8/26	13. Attendance drops today at Laurel schools
8/26	14. ICE: 595 detained at Monday raid at Howard Industries
8/26	15. Employee verification system faulty some say
8/26	16. Residents lined up for jobs at Howard Industries
8/26	17. Officials say schools not involved in immigration raid
8/26	18. Two detainees charged with aggravated identity theft
8/26	19. Mack mum on raid
8/26	20. Husband told: "take care of the baby"
8/26	21. Federal raid nets 350 detainees from plant
8/27	22. Coincidence? Laurel school see attendance drop
8/27	23. Applicants line up to take advantage of southern job openings
8/27	24. Wicker stresses immigration enforcement
8/27	25. Feds hold 595 in Howard raid
8/27	26. Howard's contracts at stake
8/27	27. Residents have mixed feelings over Laurel raid
8/27	28. Detainees say employer sealed off escape routes
8/27	29. Federal raid affects Hispanic businesses
8/27	30. Eight detainees denied bond
8/28	31. Howard Industries releases customer statement
8/28	32. Immigrants, union saw tension rise
8/28	33. Feds claim 8 detainees stole ID's
8/29	34. ICE disputes that mace used in raid
8/29	35. Howard reassures customers
8/29	36. Detainees, families protest at Howard Industries
8/29	37. Lamar Schools: No parents detained in Laurel raid
8/30	38. Protestors seek paychecks
8/31	39. Raid points out need for serious reform
8/31	40. Raids shake up community
8/31	41. Howard cast big shadow in county, state

There were a total of 12 possible themes identified and, once again, multiple themes could be present in each individual post. Overall, the most common theme was the anti-immigrant theme, which was present in 116 posts. That was followed by the racist theme (those posts that incorporated blatant racist comments against any racial group) in 96 of the comments posted. Finally, the third most common theme was the anti-business theme, with 89 posts reflecting it. The fact that the most common was closely related to the story topic was very interesting because the result was not in line with the results of the New Orleans study or the results of the study done by Xiao and Polumbaum (2004). Both found that the themes incorporated in the content of posts to crime stories deviated far from the crime stories themselves. In other words, the audience talked about issues and events that were important to them rather than discussing the topic addressed in the article they commented in response to. Here, however, immigration was the primary topic discussed albeit in a negative manner. Perhaps audiences have such strong feelings and opinions about the issue that they feel the need to discuss it in detail. It may also be the result of audiences not being desensitized to the topic. Crime is a common occurrence on local TV news whereas stories about ICE raids are fairly new, particularly in southern Mississippi.

An example of an anti-immigrant comment was posted by screen name *dippitydeb*:

> Don't do like Texas over help or cater to the Hispanic population … In Texas the Hispanic population drains the welfare system and the kids never learn English and just cause problems in school. There are a few of them that break the mold, but the majority holds dragging things down as the norm. Don't turn Lamar County into little Mexico like parts of Houston and Pasadena, TX.

This post was also reflective of the kind of racism that was apparent in many of the posts. Huge generalizations were made about Hispanic people and most were offensive.

But comments were also made that suggested that people were unhappy with the way business was being conducted on behalf of large companies like Howard Industries and others who hire illegal immigrants and claim that they don't know of their status. An example of the anti-business theme was clear in a post by *JQPubliccitizen*:

> Upper management may claim that they were unaware that they had so many illegals working for them but that excuse is a crock.

Either everybody from the HR department on up had to be aware of what was going on or the managers of the company had to be dumber than the proverbial box of rocks and I seriously doubt that Howard Industries would have experienced the steady growth it has in recent years if it were the latter case.

There was a great deal of dialog that took place among those posting to the stories. Many times they were even insulting and condescending toward one another. In one exchange *JQpubliccitizen* responded to *missgal34* with:

Reading comprehension is a skill you should practice. I don't accept your reasoning …

This result was in line with the results of previous studies that suggest that people have no problem being rude to one another in these exchanges because of the anonymity of the Internet.

In this study, 134 (over half) of the comments came from users who posted more than once during the course of the week. This result might be deceiving because there was one user who was excessive. The screen name *Buzzm1* posted 32 times total in response to 15 of the stories. The next two screen names that posted most often were *Clevis* (who posted nine times total to three different stories) and *Dee123* (who posted eight times to two different stories). While most screen names had no real world indicators (129), it appears that the most common indicator incorporated in screen names was gender (in 63 names), followed by name (in 51 names), and, finally, geography (in 27 names). Once again, the assumption is that the screen names used incorporated labels representative of real world indicators. It is understandable that this might not be the case in some instances. An example of a screen name that gave real world indications was *mrsdcarey* (likely Mrs. D. Carey).

There was one respondent who posted excessively and that was *Buzzm1*. But it was interesting to note that quite often he posted the exact same response, perhaps in an effort to make a point. It was:

THERE WILL BE NO AMNESTY!!!
  OUR ACCEPTABLE IMMIGRATION REFORM
  #1 Secure the border!!!
  #2 Mandate E-verify for ALL Employees!!!
  #3 Mandate E-verify for NAY benefit!!!
  #4 Stop the Underground Economy!!!
  #5 End birthright Citizenship for illegals!!!

#6 End Chain Migration!!!
#7 Make English our Official Language!!!
#8 Cut off Federal Funds to Sanctuary Cities!!!
NOTHING MORE!!! NOTHING LESS!!!"

This response was reflective of many of the negative themes identified in this study. Unfortunately, there did not appear to be much challenge to this individual. It appears that the media's unfair treatment of Hispanic citizens and the propensity to equate illegal alien with Hispanic may have contributed to responses like these on behalf of most individuals who took the time to post comments. Unfortunately, not everyone is as anonymous as they may think. Quite often those who posted chose screen names that gave possible clues to their real world identities. Possible gender clues were given in almost one fourth of the screen names and many used what appeared to be given names.

Based on the results of this study, immigration is a hot button issue in south Mississippi, but the dialogue examined here is very one-sided and biased. The anonymity of the Internet allows audiences to not only address issues that are important, but to post strong opinions, debate, argue and sometimes insult one another in a way that would not be socially acceptable in other environments. Within the discussions, conversations developed between the posters. At times, these conversations are composed debates, but sometimes what begins as a simple expression of opinion becomes an all out attack by one poster on another. For example, in response to an August 26 article, *saltillogal1* questioned ICE's tactic of separating Hispanic-looking workers from the other workers in the plant while they examined their legal status. *Saltillogal1* said that this practice constituted discrimination and that it would have been less controversial if ICE had required everyone to prove legal status, not just those who "looked" Hispanic. The language and style of this post indicated that this was merely an expression of this one person's opinion.

The comment started an interesting dialogue. *Oakgrovehobbitt* agreed with *saltillogal1*, calling any tactic that targets people based on appearance a "slippery slope." A sarcastic dialogue then developed between *Oakgrovehobbitt* and another poster. *Clevis* wanted to know what other method *Oakgrovehobbitt* would suggest. Based on other posts by *Clevis*, it became clear that this comment was meant to be sarcastic. *Oakgrovehobbitt* did not rise to the taunt and simply suggested checking everyone. *Clevis* then wrote, "Well THAT would be efficient! Let's not hurt anyone's feelings. We can't do that!" Again, the emphasis of the capital letters and punctuation indicate the sarcastic intent of the comment.

This exchange was not unique. There were many sarcastic rants exchanged between posters that began with a simple impassive statement of opinion. Often, the initial post did not convey anything in its tone that would imply the poster was trying to provoke others. However, often these innocuous comments resulted in emotionally charged replies. As with the discussion between *saltillogal1* and *Clevis*, the rant is often one-sided. Discussions like these have the potential to polarize audiences along racial lines, political lines and by other means.

There were many posts that came across as overtly racist. Many of these postings call for the illegal immigrants to "go back" where they came from. For example:

> *Haudi62*: "Get this crap out of here. Send them the hell back where they came from."

> *Wesmb*: "…if they can't speak English, they are illegal!"

> *Lccat*: "Our FAMILIES are at the mercy of ILLEGALS and their Anchor Babies being murdered, raped, infected with disease or robbed. We can see the results of the ILLEGAL invasion in our courts every day!"

There is little room to interpret the language and style expressed in these comments as anything other than racist.

But these posts did not always go unchecked. Within the same group of posts was a comment from a self-professed Hispanic (legal) immigrant, *Edcaf*. The poster explained that he (she) has been a legal worker for seven years. *Edcaf*'s post also highlights several inaccuracies in the previous posts about the process of becoming a legal U.S. resident. The post further suggests that possibly the reason companies such as Howard Industries hire so many Hispanic workers may be the fact that they are hardworking; otherwise, they would not have kept their jobs. But in response to this attempt to defend illegal workers, another poster, *Standonfirst*, responded with the following:

> Jose, take your self pity and shove it where the sun don't shine. You are in no position to complain, much less attempt to castigate us on our uninformed opinion. Americans have no need to know the process because we were born here. Americans couldn't care less about your struggles to get here … because we were born here. Our opinions, whether informed or uninformed, gathered or given trumps yours every day of the week and twice on Sunday because we were born here!!!! … Your opinion is like the stuff for which

toilets were made—pure waste, it is not wanted and should be flushed immediately. Thank you for coming, hope you enjoy your stay but keep your trap shut on this one and when your Visa is up, go home.

Addressing *Edcaf* as "Jose," as well as telling him that his opinion does not matter and that nobody cares about his feelings indicates the overwhelmingly racist tone of *Standonfirst*'s post. This kind of exchange often occurred. Posters who tried to present facts and take the role as the voice of reason were often met with sarcasm, racist tirades or accusations that they themselves were "illegals" or employees of Howard Industries. Arguably, this kind of response tends to discourage those who want to have a positive discussion, especially since frequently the racist comments ended the discussion (i.e. there were no further posts). Ultimately, this problem limits the possibilities of this kind of forum since so often the opinionated posters squash the voices of reason.

In some instances, posters were critical of Americans too. The amount of discussion surrounding whether illegal immigrants were taking jobs from Americans or just taking jobs that Americans do not want was not surprising. For example, *mcouch, Azabache, DRANK, Bonhoeffer, derlehrer, GiveusLiberty* and *mrsdcarey* point out that if Americans did not want the Howard Industry jobs, then there would not have been so many people lined up outside the plant looking for work after news of the ICE raid broke.

However, many more posters expressed the belief that Americans ultimately do not want these jobs and are too lazy to do the jobs that illegal immigrants do. *Thuddy* wrote that the Hispanic workers were not taking jobs from Americans, but were doing jobs that Americans could do if they were not so lazy. This opinion was also supported by *MsHa10*, who wrote:

…Americans are lazy and always want something for nothing. Americans don't want to work! They want the "American Dream" handed to them on a silver platter.

Does Content Drive Commentary?

Though broad generalizations cannot be made based on the results of these two studies, there are a number of important lessons that can be learned from these analyses. First, it appears that when audiences are desensitized to a topic they are more likely to veer from the main topic of the story being covered. In New Orleans, crime coverage is nothing new, especially when it happens in the African-American community. Perhaps audiences feel that these incidents are isolated and won't affect them. Perhaps they hear similar stories so often, they are more concerned about how these stories tarnish the image of their community than what led to the actual crimes.

Immigration on the other hand is a hot button issue, especially in working class communities where people feel that those who are not U.S. citizens are offering competition for jobs in a bad economy. It is also an issue that gets attention not only in local media but is reinforced in the national media. As a result, audiences appear to have a great deal to discuss, especially when they feel that they may be affected.

There are also some important commonalities in these two studies. All in all, it appears that those who post feel that these spaces are an ideal forum to be rude to other posters and offensive to certain groups, possibly because they feel protected by a screen name. Many of the comments posted would not likely be spoken in real world company as diverse as the audience who reads these stories on-line.

The results of these studies indicate that user-generated content posted on Web sites run by mainstream news organizations brings a whole new dimension to the mass communication process. Lee (2005) notes, "Several unique structural and formal features of the Internet are believed to condition the way the Internet brings about changes in contemporary social interactions and cultural practices ... the blurring of geographical, written/spoken, public/private, and virtual real boundaries" (p. 61). First of all, these posts serve as commentary and therefore incorporate opinions—often un-edited opinions that are much stronger than those expressed in editorial sections. While the candor expressed in these posts may attract audiences initially, the offensiveness expressed in some user-generated content also has the power to repel audiences. According to Carol Christopher in a July 2007 article in the *Seybold Report*, media executives are grappling with how to deal with user generated content and the competition it offers traditional journalism. Perhaps the technology offers the audience a chance to tell the media what they should not only think about—but what to cover if they want to keep audiences coming back for news and information.

References

Derrida, J. (1994) *Specters of Marx*. Translated by Paggy Kamuf. New York: Routledge.

Fisher, D. R. & Wright, L. M. (2001). On utopias and dystopias: Toward an understanding of the discourse surrounding the Internet. Retrieved March 2009 from: http://.jcmc.indiana.edu/vol16/issue2/fisher.html.

LeDuff, K. (2009). *Tales of two cities: How race and crime intersect on local TV news*. Saarbrücken, Germany: Lambert Academic Publishing.

Lee, H. (2005). Implosion, virtuality, and interaction in an internet discussion group. *Information, Communication and Society, 8* (1), 47–63.

Levinson, P. (2009). *New new media.* Boston: Allyn & Bacon.

McCarthy, B. & Monteverde, D. (August 21, 2007) Five shootings leave three dead, two hurt. *The Times Picayune.* Retrieved August 30, 2007 from: http://blog.nola.com/updates/2007/08.

McKenna, K. & Bargh, J. (2005). Plan 9 from cyberspace: The implications of the Internet for personality and social psychology. In E. Bucy (Ed.), *Living in the information age* (pp. 193–203). Australia: Wadsworth.

Muskus, J. & Hayes, K. H. (August 20, 2007). Estranged husband kills wife, her boss. *The Times Picayune.* Retrieved August 30, 2007 from: http://blog.nola.com/updates/2007/08.

Nader, R. & Gold, S. (1988). Letters to the editor: How about a little down-home glasnost. *Columbia Journalism Review, 27*(3), 52–57.

One killed, four wounded in three separate shootings. (2007, August 22). *The Times Picayune.* Retrieved August 30, 2007 from: http://blog.nola.com/updates/2007/08.

Wahl-Jorgensen, Karin. (2004). A legitimate beef or raw meat? Civility, multiculturalism, and letters to the editor. *The Communication Review, 7,* 89–105.

Wall, Melissa. (2005). Blogs of war: weblogs as news. *Journalism, 6*(2), 153–172.

Xiao, L. & Polumbaum, J. (2004). Ideologies of crime coverage in Chinese online media: A case study of Chinese commercial portals' news content and interactivity. Paper presented at the Association for Education in Journalism and Mass Communication in Toronto, Canada, August 2004.

Discussion Questions

1. Have you ever posted a comment on a news Web site in response to a news story? Why or why not? Is it really all that different from posting a comment on a friend's YouTube video or Facebook status? How so?

2. If you encountered a racially charged message like the ones noted in this study, would you feel compelled to respond? Why or why not? Is there anything you fear about getting involved in such an on-line discussion?

3. On most sites that allow room for commentary, users can create an anonymous screen name to use in on-line discussion. Would you feel protected by that feature? Why or why not?

Assignments

1. Go to your hometown newspaper's Web site. Do they have a space for viewers to leave comments? Go to a local TV station's Web site. Is there room for commentary? If so compare and contrast the posts left on the site. How would you describe them?

2. Does your school newspaper have a Web site? Is there space for commentary? If so, look at responses to a few stories. What do the comments look like? Invite the on-line newspaper's editor to class for a discussion. What is the gatekeeping process when it comes to comments? Do they remove posts that are potentially offensive?

What are the criteria? Is it different from how the "letters to the editor section" is screened?

3. Can you think of other issues that might generate a great deal of discussion on-line? Do you think the discussion will be related to the issue or would it generate discussion about other issues?

Useful Tools on the Web

Virtual Communities Spark Coverage Ideas As Primary Season Ends
by Mallary Jean Tenore
http://www.poynter.org/column.asp?id=101&aid=144545

Immigration Status: When Relevant in Crime Stories?
by Mizanur Rahman
http://www.poynter.org/column.asp?id=58&aid=140153

Opening the Door to Better Immigration Stories
by Mary Sanchez
http://www.poynter.org/column.asp?id=58&aid=72344

CHAPTER 6

Ethnic News Media and Marginalization

African-American Newspaper Coverage of the AIDS Crisis

ROCKELL A. BROWN

The National Commission on Civil Disorders which was appointed by President Lyndon Johnson in 1968 and later became known as the Kerner Commission (1968) found that the residents of the "racial ghetto" were significantly less healthy than other Americans and that they suffered from higher mortality rates, higher incidence of major syndromes, as well as lower availability and utilization of medical services. As a nation, we have made tremendous strides in terms of health care for all, yet 30 years after Kerner racial disparities continued to exist on a broad scale (Boger, 1995), and in matters pertaining to health, the playing field continues to remain unequal for African Americans. African Americans experienced a variety of ailments and structural difficulties ranging from high blood pressure, sickle-cell anemia, homelessness, persistent poverty, drugs and crime at higher instances than other groups (Cohen, 1999). On the whole, African Americans continued to suffer at disproportionately higher rates and instances from an array of chronic and terminal illnesses and diseases than whites, even when socioeconomic factors are considered (Sylvester, 1998). For example, the infant mortality rate dropped significantly over the years; however, black infants are twice as likely to die within the first year as white infants. In fact, Boger (1995) maintained that while life expectancies overall have increased (including African Americans and whites), the average life expectancy for African Americans remained years shorter than that of whites.

This health care crisis is no more noticeable than in the effects of AIDS on African Americans. According to Chitwood (2002), "AIDS emerged at a time when it was believed by many that the threat of infectious syndromes in the United States had, for the most part, been eliminated" (p. 253). Unfortunately, like many other health issues and concerns, HIV and AIDS has become another, among an array, of chronic and terminal illnesses and syndromes in which African Americans suffer at disproportionately higher rates than other groups in the United States. Although it has no face and does not distinguish between poor and rich, gay and straight, old or young, or black and white, HIV and AIDS is spreading in epidemic proportions among people in Africa as well as others throughout the African Diaspora.

As the AIDS epidemic entered into its second decade, statistics began to more clearly reveal that the syndrome was disproportionately striking certain communities. By June 1992, the Centers for Disease Control and Prevention reported that African Americans accounted for 12 percent of the United States' population, but 30 percent of the AIDS cases (Shubert, 1992). Additionally, according to Shubert, at that time (the early 1990s), women with AIDS were overwhelmingly African American at a rate of 53 percent with Hispanic women accounting for 21 percent of AIDS cases; over 78 percent of pediatric AIDS cases were either African American or Hispanic. Shubert indicated that, early on, attention was diverted from risks that were most prevalent as a result of specific behaviors such as unprotected sex and sharing of needles because of widespread attempts to identify groups of individuals as being at-risk due to their sexual orientation, race or nationality.

The HIV and AIDS epidemic has been upon us for more than 25 years now, and even though media coverage of the issue got off to a relatively slow start, its spread did not. While the first reported case of AIDS was in 1981, it did not begin to receive continued or relatively consistent coverage until around 1985. This is not to say that individuals in mass media did not want to cover the syndrome or that they found it irrelevant or non-newsworthy, but simply, it was not an easy story to tell. Although lack of coverage was a general problem, it became particularly so for the African-American population.

As early as 1982, the Centers for Disease Control and Prevention (CDC) warned that African Americans may be at an increased risk for HIV and AIDS. Yet mainstream media paid little attention to its impact on marginalized groups (Hammonds, 1986; Krishnan, Durrah, & Winkler, 1997).

Theoretically, if coverage of health issues and concerns that disproportion-ately affect marginalized groups continues to be lacking or inadequate, then so will the public's knowledge regarding the syndrome and its subsequent ability to stem the epidemic. Since mainstream coverage of the impact it is having on the African-American community was lacking, the analysis of press coverage of the AIDS epidemic by African-American newspapers is important to determine how and what those outlets have selected or filtered for communities and audiences that are most at risk. This becomes an even greater concern when one considers that underrepresented groups such as African Americans are most at risk for HIV and AIDS and thus among those most in need of information regarding the syndrome. It thus becomes important to examine the content of media channels or outlets in which information regarding the syndrome is disseminated in an effort to better understand how the syndrome has been covered, reported on, framed and characterized for a media-reliant minority community that is at a much higher risk of con-tracting the syndrome.

While there is a plethora of research and literature concerning the mass media and its coverage and portrayal of health issues and of AIDS, much of the research has focused on the history of AIDS on the mainstream media agenda. The goal of this chapter is to examine how media outlets which serve marginalized or underrepresented groups have covered HIV and AIDS as well as to examine Cathy Cohen's (1999) suggestion that "secondary marginalization"—the mistreatment of African Americans *by* African Americans—may be a factor with regard to HIV and AIDS and the African-American community. Specifically, African-American newspaper coverage of HIV and AIDS from 1991 through 2001 is examined to better understand how HIV and AIDS information was disseminated, characterized and framed during that crucial second decade of the epidemic with special attention given to coverage of people with AIDS (PWA). It is important to have an under-standing of how the mass media frames complex issues, especially those pertaining to health because the characterization or presentation of the information may influence and or affect individuals' choices regarding health (Andsager & Powers, 1999) as well as public policy. This is especially relevant when the population in question is at a higher health risk. Historically, the Black Press is held with high esteem within many African-American communities and at times has served as gatekeepers and/or agenda setters within those communities. With HIV and AIDS infection growing at epidemic rates among blacks, it is important to recognize and understand how these outlets handled the issue during the second decade of the epidemic.

Ethnic Media and the Black Press

The exclusion or lack of coverage of people of color and their issues by mainstream media coupled with a need to advocate and inform gave birth to the ethnic or alternative press in the 1800s. The first Latino newspaper, *El Misisipí*, was founded in 1808; the first Black newspaper, *Freedom's Journal*, was founded in 1827; the first Native American newspaper, *Cherokee Phoenix*, was founded in 1828; and the first Asian Pacific American newspaper, *The Golden Hills*, was founded in 1854—all emerged as a result of crises being experienced by members of their communities that were not concurrently being experienced by whites (Wilson, Gutierrez, & Chao, 2003). For instance, *El Misisipí* mainly targeted Spanish-speaking readers that immigrated to the United States to escape war and political turmoil during the Napoleonic Wars in Europe. Likewise, the primary objective of the *Freedom's Journal* was to abolish slavery as well as to fight for the rights and better treatment of free Blacks. The *Cherokee Phoenix* was in large part established because of the desire of the Cherokee Nation leaders to unify Cherokees and others in support of the fight to keep their homeland. In addition, *The Golden Hills* English-language editorials often argued for fairer treatment of the Chinese as well as highlighted the contributions Chinese were making to society (Wilson, Gutierrez, & Chao, 2003).

The ethnic press of the 1800s focused on the social, cultural, and political dynamics affecting the communities of people of color. Furthermore, Wilson, Gutierrez, and Chao (2003) maintain that despite being founded for different groups at different times and in different places, there are other striking similarities among various ethnic presses. First, they all offered news about their communities that was not covered by the white press and provided alternative perspectives and views. Second, as mentioned above, they all emerged during times when their people were experiencing harsh treatment at the hands of whites through legal discrimination, social subjugation and violent oppression. Finally, these ethnic papers felt an obligation and need to respond to the negative manner in which their communities were depicted and perceived in mainstream white press. The tone of today's ethnic media is not as ignitable as in the past; nevertheless, "they continue to provide news, entertainment, and information alternatives to the general audience mass media" (Wilson, Gutierrez, & Chao, 2003, p. 286).

The newspapers targeted toward African Americans were collectively referred to as the "Negro Press" or "Black Press" (later called the Afro or African-American Press). The Black Press is often viewed as the corrective force for white biases in print media, and has traditionally covered African Americans and their issues and concerns very differently than that of the mainstream press (Dates & Barlow, 1993). Many Black Press publications exist primarily to report the news of the African-American community, to promote social awareness and activities within the culture and the community as a whole, as well as to advocate the advancement of issues that concern African Americans. By initiating and developing the Black Press, African Americans attempted to counter and exert control over the portrayal of African Americans and the issues pertaining to them and their livelihood (Wolseley, 1990). This historical tension with the mainstream press has allowed the Black Press to cultivate a close relationship with its African-American audience. African Americans often are more trusting of African-American news sources and tend to be more receptive of information coming from those sources.

The tone of the Black Press has varied over time, but it has always viewed the African-American community in a vastly different light and perspective from that of its mainstream counterpart (Dates & Barlow, 1993). Today's Black Press is less radical, and apart from the issue of race, some publications are even socially and politically conservative (Wolseley, 1990) and comfortable with mainstream party politics (Tinney & Rector, 1989). Nevertheless, the papers continue to be perceived as more credible and believable than their mainstream counterparts by many African Americans (Wolseley, 1990).

Cohen (1999) maintains much of the Black Press is influenced or guided by some type of political ideology in which publishers, editors and reporters are grounded. She indicates that differences exist between the old and new Black Press as many of the older, established and more popular African-American publications are more conservative and traditional in their approach to covering the African-American community and a topic like AIDS challenges their paradigm. According to Cohen, this paradigm includes the tendency and preponderance to portray and depict members of the African-American community and their leaders in a positive light. In contrast, the new Black Press is more concerned with empowerment of the community members it serves and with making its leadership more accountable (Cohen, 1999). Others endorse the model of the new Black Press which involves being an advocate as well as watch dog for the African-American community and this means covering the good, bad and, at times, embarrassing news impacting the community (Dates & Barlow, 1993).

Furthermore, according to Cohen, much of the popular African-American press is patterned after other indigenous institutions and organizations found in African-American communities, which are "dominated by the black church as well as black public officials who reinforce moral and conservative ideologies of acceptable behavior" (p. 248). It is as if there is a filtering system in place in which the morals and value systems of the clergy and elite members of the community are passed along to the leadership of the publications and thus prevent necessary information from being disseminated as needed, especially in regard to its impact on drug users and members of the gay community.

The Black Press Defined

There are certain qualifications that must be met in order for a publication to be considered a unit of the Black Press (Wolseley, 1990). Through investigation which included the reactions from leading black journalists during the late 1960s it was concluded that there are three qualifications that publications must meet: 1) Blacks must own and manage the publication as well as be the dominant racial group affiliated with it; 2) The publication must be intended for black consumers, thus it must deal with the interests and concerns of blacks; and 3) The publication must, as the report concluded, "serve, speak, and fight for the black minority" (Wolseley, 1990).

According to Wolseley (1990), the initial purpose of the Black Press during its inception in the early nineteenth century was to campaign for freedom of the slaves. Following the Civil War, its focus shifted to fighting for fair treatment and equal rights for black citizens in the areas of their daily lives such as access to public eating facilities, attendance at white colleges and universities, use of public beaches, and the like (Wolseley, 1990). However, after financing black publications became more difficult because subsidies grew increasingly difficult to obtain, publishers had to turn to advertisers for support (Wolseley, 1990). Therefore, many of the publications increasingly grew into business operations, thus decreasing their roles as crusaders. The Black Press of the late twentieth century and today exists primarily "to report the news of the black population and the particular local community, to give space to their own and others' opinions on many racially oriented matters, to promote the activities or the societies in which they exist, to present advertisers with a billboard or a spoken message, and to be the advocate for the black population" (p. 6).

Wolseley (1990) suggests that the Black Press is still a vital necessity for the African-American community because "all of the old battles have not yet been won and because there are so many new ones" (p. 9). African Americans have a need to know what's going on in their world as well as how various matters around the world affect them and their livelihood. Many black publications, especially newspapers, cover the "black society" in depth, which as of late, are still not covered by mainstream press and probably never will be (Wolseley, 1990). Additionally, the Black Press is needed because for many years African Americans have grown to mistrust a mainstream press that cannot be trusted to speak truthfully about African Americans. During the first half of the twentieth century, mainstream media and affiliated organizations were accused of favoring whites against blacks; thus, news was usually tailored to fit the publications' prejudices or at least those of their owners (Wolseley, 1990). For example, he further noted that both northern and southern newspapers "followed the practice of race identification of blacks only and of ignoring entirely anything but unfavorable black news" (p. 10).

Information contained in African-American newspapers provides their audiences with news of the African-American community as well as of national and international matters and events directly affecting African-American citizens (Wolseley, 1990). Although, usually, the emphasis and primary focus is on local or regional news and events, they also provide entertainment and editorial guidance (Wolseley, 1990). African-American newspapers often report news not covered by other publications, they interpret the news differently, and usually from an uncommon standpoint. Furthermore, African-American newspapers offer opinions about subjects and matters not typically dealt with by mainstream press discussing the same topics (Wolseley, 1990). Simply stated, African Americans still look to the Black Press for their version of the story and for an interpretation of the news and events that affect their central interest; thus, in meeting the necessary criteria to be considered a black publication, the African-American press helps to establish African-American identity as well as serve the African-American community (Wolseley, 1990).

AIDS and African Americans

As early as 1982 the Centers for Disease Control and Prevention warned that African Americans might be at increased risk for HIV and AIDS, and data from the following two years confirmed the trend (Krishnan, Durrah, & Winkler, 1997). However, it was not until 1987, five years after the initial warning, that the Centers for Disease Control officially acknowledged the looming epidemic with their first nationally sponsored conference, "AIDS in the Minority Community" (Jenkins, 1992; Krishnan, Durrah, & Winkler, 1997). Yet, over a decade later, those trends have continued as HIV and AIDS continues to affect African Americans disproportionately.

Over the past two decades AIDS has managed to secure a heavy grip on African Americans. Burkett (1995) chronicled the impact of the epidemic within the African-American community from 1987 through 1993. According to Burkett (1995), by 1987 almost one fourth of the nation's AIDS patients were black, although they only made up 12 percent of the U.S. population, and more than half of the nation's children with AIDS were black. Additionally, by 1987 it was observed that two out of every 100 women who gave birth in New York public hospitals were HIV infected and 84 percent of them were women of color, and during this same time the survival period from diagnosis to death was one to three years for whites whereas it was only 18 to 36 weeks for blacks (Burkett, 1995).

Burkett (1995) maintains that by 1989 black HIV positive newborns outnumbered white newborns eight to one, and in many American hospitals less than 1 percent of patients admitted were infected with HIV; however, in urban hospitals the virus was found in the blood of 30 percent of the black male patients alone. By 1990, even though women of color accounted for only 19 percent of the female population, they represented almost three quarters of reported AIDS cases among women (Burkett, 1995). According to Burkett (1995), by 1991, ten years into the epidemic, the nation had lost up to 100,000 lives to AIDS, and by then AIDS was the leading cause of death in New York and New Jersey among black women between the ages of 15 and 44. By 1992, it was observed that African-American women were becoming ill at a rate 14 times higher than white women and also in that year both Republicans and Democrats alike featured women with HIV at their conventions; neither was black even though the disease was already known to be taking a more devastating toll on African Americans than any other group (Burkett, 1995). Thus, Burkett (1995) maintained that by 1993 minorities accounted for more than half of the nation's reported AIDS cases and the AIDS rate for black men and women were five and 15 times higher than for white men and women respectively.

Duh (1991) suggests that the prevalence of AIDS in African Americans is higher for the same reasons that the prevalence of other diseases is higher and that is because their overall health status is lower, making them more prone to various diseases. He contends,

> The dual poor health and low socioeconomic status of blacks have been present for generations. In the late 1970s and early 1980s, blacks were poorer and less healthy. In the late 1980s, they were as poor or even poorer than they were before. In the late 1970s and early 1980s, when AIDS was emerging as a disease, it makes sense that AIDS would affect people who were less healthy already.
>
> (p. 21)

Thus, African Americans are at greater risks of contracting AIDS because they are more likely to be predisposed to conditions of poverty, drug addiction, and fatalistic perspectives of life, especially in the inner cities (Okigbo, Okigbo, Hall, & Ziegler, 2002).

African Americans fell behind in controlling the AIDS epidemic because of their slow reaction to the syndrome, which was partly due to the fact that the disease was viewed initially as one primarily affecting white gay men (Duh, 1991). African Americans were in denial regarding the presence and prevalence of the syndrome in blacks as well as the need to control it. As a result of the early stages of denial, African-American communities were lacking in the formation and establishment of grass roots, community-based organizations and programs geared toward fighting and controlling the epidemic (Duh, 1991). As AIDS began to grow rapidly among African Americans (as well as Hispanics), much of the media missed an opportunity to make a difference because they rarely told that story, because of fear of charges of racism (Mongerson, 1997). According to Mongerson (1997), "The result was lower awareness of the disease and how to combat it in the black community where people were the most vulnerable and the information was the most needed" (p. 133).

AIDS and News Coverage

Researchers have found that during the early years (1981–1985), the media did a relatively good job of informing the public and bringing the AIDS epidemic to the consciousness of the public (Cohen, 1999). Unfortunately, during that same time period, while individuals were aware of the syndrome, many did not have accurate information regarding transmission of the syndrome, personal risk factors/behaviors, or preventive strategies (Cohen, 1999; Dearing & Rogers, 1996). Furthermore, although the media did bring AIDS to the consciousness of the public, coverage and reporting of the syndrome was lacking during the initial years, and it was not really portrayed as a national issue nor was it on the main agenda until the illness and then death of actor Rock Hudson in 1985 and the attention given to the young school boy, Ryan White in 1990 (Dearing & Rogers, 1996; Signorielli, 1993). Coverage of those events served as a catalyst in humanizing AIDS, because prior to that the syndrome had a stigma associated with gays, IV-drug users, Haitians, and hemophiliacs (Signorielli, 1993). Additionally, Pickle, Quinn, and Brown (2002) maintain that early media coverage of AIDS "sensationalized and distorted information by portraying the lives of people with AIDS as isolated and desperate" (p. 428). They also suggest that initial reports regarding AIDS created a perception that there were actually moral dimensions surrounding AIDS because it was first reported to be a syndrome primarily affecting homosexuals and intravenous drug users.

The news media are the primary sources of AIDS information for the general public (Edgar, Hammond, & Freimuth, 1989). Nevertheless, a historical examination of media coverage of AIDS reveals that the rapid spread of the syndrome and its high mortality rate initially did not lead to widespread media coverage. In fact, prior to 1985, one could have assumed that the public and U.S. policy makers believed that AIDS was indeed intriguing, but that it was not a prominent national issue, at least not until after the death of Rock Hudson (Edgar, Hammond, & Freimuth, 1989). Edgar, Hammond, and Freimuth (1989) maintain that media interest and coverage of AIDS intensified and became more stable and sustained after Hudson's death.

They further suggest that the lag in early media coverage of AIDS was not consistent with media coverage of other health epidemics—which is unfortunate because "the news media are powerful sources of new information for the public and thus are primarily responsible for the first steps in the behavior modification process: exposure and awareness" (p. 3). Edgar, Hammond, and Freimuth (1989) maintain that the number of persons at risks or the number of deaths are often the factors that most influence the press's perception of the news value of a public health issue, and, therefore, coverage of AIDS expanded and exploded onto the networks and front pages once it was determined that the entire population was at risk for contracting the syndrome.

Cook and Colby (1992) viewed and analyzed the nightly news of all three major networks —ABC, CBS, and NBC —in an attempt to investigate coverage of AIDS between January of 1981 and April of 1987. They concluded "that the media did not merely reflect outside events but, instead, profoundly recast the epidemic for both public and governmental audiences" (p. 111). The researchers indicate that five major clusters of themes characterized AIDS nightly news coverage from 1981 through 1985. First it was viewed simply as a "mysterious syndrome" that gay men were blamed for because of their lifestyle. The second theme can be characterized as "the threat to the innocent" (the threat of AIDS beyond the originally identified risks groups). The third theme is the "epidemic of fear." The fourth theme can be characterized as "the search for the breakthrough," which was primarily an attempt to provide reassurance to calm fears that resulted from increased reports regarding the spread of the syndrome. Finally, the fifth theme was "the legitimating of AIDS" which emerged as a result of news about the most famous AIDS patient, Rock Hudson (Cook & Colby, 1992).

AIDS presented a slight dilemma for journalism as an institution for three reasons, according to Cook and Colby (1992): Gay men comprised the group initially associated with the virus, and collectively they did not achieved newsworthiness before 1981. Thus, with the exception of a few events during the 1970s, homosexuality and homosexuals had never been a part of news topics or issues of continuous concern. Second, because the subject of AIDS concerns matters pertaining to blood, semen, sexuality and death, it was not deemed as being tasteful, since journalists typically think of the audience by considering norms of taste when packaging the news. And third, the media were faced with the task and challenge to raise and increase the public's awareness without creating public panic; although the media are aware that they play a major role in educating and alerting, they are also careful not to be inflammatory (Cook & Colby, 1992).

In summary, mass media coverage of AIDS has evolved over the years as it has transitioned through several phases. Previous research reveals that media coverage of AIDS has been different from media coverage of other illnesses and matters in public health. During the early years, AIDS proved to be a difficult topic for reporters to handle because of 1) the population it was believed to primarily affect (i.e. the "undesirables" such as homosexuals and intravenous drug users), and 2) the modes of trans- mission and what it usually involved (blood, semen, sex, etc.). Furthermore, AIDS was also a challenging topic for reporters because, while it was neces- sary to keep the public informed and abreast of the latest developments regarding AIDS, they also had to be careful not to invoke panic. Additionally, response to AIDS by other institutions was also slow until it was recognized that AIDS was as big a threat to the mainstream as it was to those who were believed to be most at risk. Once that realization occurred, media coverage increased and became more sustained. According to Kinsella (1989) the rule that journalists often followed when covering AIDS was the closer the threat of the syndrome seemed to move toward those setting the agenda, the bigger the story became and more coverage was then provided.

The manner in which individuals react to health and health topics such as AIDS is related to how it is depicted and portrayed in the media (Nardi, 1990). Criticism of the lack of media coverage of AIDS and PWAs surfaced early in the epidemic (Watts, 1992); however, once AIDS reached promi- nence on the media agenda during the mid-1980s, coverage of the issue improved. Much of the literature suggests that the United States news media were very instrumental in framing AIDS (especially, during the early years) as some sort of plague that came about as a result of deviant behav- ior (Kinsella, 1989; Lester, 1992; Sontag, 1988). Sontag (1988) suggested that AIDS became a global event relatively fast because it affected the West, and, therefore, it could not be regarded as just another natural disaster. She further indicates that it has historical meaning and significance because it has been validated by the impact it has had on both the United States and Europe. Consequently, while the *New York Times* and other newspapers such as the *Washington Post* and *Los Angeles Times* have covered AIDS relatively extensively, their coverage has not always been balanced. Cohen (1999) suggests that mainstream coverage (specifically, the *New York Times*) was generally marginalizing to minorities especially to African Americans and Hispanics because of disproportionate coverage of the effect AIDS has had on their communities as compared with the mainstream population.

African-American Media and AIDS

The bulk of research that has examined coverage of AIDS in the media has excluded marginalized and underrepresented groups such as African Americans. There are some scholars who have criticized and discussed the disparities that exist socially, economically and politically when it comes to AIDS and the lack of coverage given to the impact that it has had on African Americans (Cohen, 1999; Worth, 1990). Mainstream media have done a poor job of chronicling the AIDS epidemic in the African-American community, which makes it necessary for black media outlets to fill in the gaps. What makes this issue all the more urgent is that, clearly, AIDS in the African-American community is an epidemic.

The *Amsterdam News*, which was founded in New York City in 1909, was considered Black America's paper of record. Thus, in its most influential period, it was for Black America what the *New York Times* was (and is currently) to mainstream America. Kinsella (1989) maintains that the *Amsterdam News* was its own agenda-setter because it covered issues and topics that were often overlooked entirely by the mainstream press, and, like other black newspapers, the *Amsterdam*'s circulation began to decline during the 1970s and 1980s. Consequently, when it came to AIDS coverage, the paper did not give much attention to the epidemic until 1987, and by then AIDS had begun to take its toll on Harlem and in other heavily populated African-American communities (Kinsella, 1989).

Furthermore, it was evident that the Black Press (at least the *Amsterdam News*) maintained a similar disposition as its mainstream counterparts regarding AIDS. According to Kinsella (1989), the managing editor of the *Amsterdam News*, William Egyir, felt that covering the epidemic would not have any real impact, especially among those with high infection rates (i.e. junkies from the barrio and the ghetto). While the *Amsterdam News* did a better job of covering AIDS than its other minority counterparts such as the *Caribbean News*, *El Diario-LaPrensa*, and *Noticias del Mundo*, its coverage was still lacking, maintained Kinsella (1989), because it was weak and often defensive. He suggests that the writing was often misleading as the paper would fail to provide explanations or details that would have provided its readership with more clarification and information especially as it pertained to the modes of AIDS transmission. He cited the following as an example: in April of 1987, the paper reported that white homosexuals contracted AIDS from "action" between themselves and that the majority of blacks and Hispanics contracted it as IVDU; however, the problem was that the paper neglected to explain that the "action" was "presumably and quite possibly oral sex" and that "IVDU" was "intravenous drug use" (Kinsella, 1989, p. 245).

Cohen (1999) examined the New York *Amsterdam News'* coverage of AIDS beginning in 1983. She found that a pattern emerged for covering AIDS, which was intact by 1985. Her research indicated that the major players and themes involved with AIDS remained constant, although the frames used by reporters evolved over time. Cohen (1999) suggests that the staple of coverage by the *Amsterdam News* were articles that highlighted the words and actions of black leaders, as well as controversies surrounding possible interventions, involvement in government agencies and alternative treatments. One can deduct from Cohen's investigation that although there is room for improvement of coverage by the Black Press, it is likely to do a more comprehensive job of covering the epidemic as it relates to the African-American community than their mainstream counterparts.

Cohen indicates that the first articles on AIDS did not appear in any African-American newspaper until the end of 1983, two years after it was first mentioned in mainstream media. Coincidentally, it was also in 1983 that the CDC first began providing the racial breakdown of AIDS cases. It was coincidental because the African-American press did not emphasize or really cover AIDS based on reports from public health officials, especially those concerning persons marginalized within the community. Cohen suggests the African-American press fell back into its familiar routine by focusing on the actions taken by black elites and prominent African-American organizations concerning AIDS. She maintains,

> Thus, holding true to the tradition of the old black press, positive reporting emphasizing the awarding of grants, the holding of public hearings and community forums, and other generally symbolic events sponsored most often by black public officials were the mainstay of early reporting on AIDS in the News. Complementing these topics were other acceptable subjects, such as black and Latino children with AIDS, alternative drug therapies for AIDS, and conspiracy theories about the development of AIDS.

(p. 197)

Through her examination of the *Amsterdam News*, Cohen (1999) found that by 1986 about seven dominant themes were prevalent in AIDS coverage. Furthermore, she found that the reporting was guided by three fundamental practices of the Black Press usually found in the introductions of the stories. The introductions produce frames revolving around historical mistrust of the white/mainstream establishment, efforts to over-emphasize the positive or mainstream characteristics of the African-American community as well as attempts to make moral and value judgments about activities and behaviors considered an embarrassment to the African-American community.

Cohen (1999) concluded that the popular African-American media sources analyzed did not provide extensive or in-depth coverage of AIDS and when it was covered, predictable frames were prevalent. There was paucity in coverage regarding those most vulnerable to AIDS. She found that the most popular frames in these publications were the threat of AIDS to heterosexuals, symbolic acts of African-American leaders and conspiracy/genocidal theories. Furthermore, Cohen explains that the popular African-American press' lack of extensive AIDS coverage was most evident when its coverage is compared to that of *City Sun* and the other alternative presses in the African-American community. Although their coverage was imperfect as suggested by Cohen, it was more in depth and inclusive than their popular African-American counterparts as they were critical of both dominant and indigenous institutions and organizations regarding their response to AIDS.

Cohen maintains that the glaring difference in coverage between the popular African-American press and its alternative counterparts are that the latter attempted to transform the consciousness of its audience, largely African American, by presenting AIDS as a policy issue as well as a public health issue, whereas the former often reinforced the same frames and themes found in mainstream press. She states, "In choosing to distance and misrepresent the AIDS epidemic as it developed in black communities, the black press let stand, and in some cases reinforced processes of secondary marginalization and ideologies of otherness that designated certain segments of the community as not worthy of group resources, activism, or coverage" (p. 248).

Additionally, Pickle, Quinn, and Brown (2002) conducted one of the first investigations of multiple African-American newspapers' coverage of HIV/AIDS. They found that most of the articles analyzed displayed a "critical attitude" toward the government and the "AIDS establishment" regarding their commitment to saving the lives of minorities. Furthermore, their investigation revealed that the frames that were evident often reflected distrust and rational concerns that were rooted in the historical context of

American race relations, including the legacy of the Tuskegee study. Their findings are similar to Cohen's with regard to frames that relate to conspiracy and mistrust.

Likewise, I examined AIDS coverage in four African-American newspapers over a ten-year period, from 1991 through 2001 (Brown, 2003). Specifically, the newspapers that were examined include: the *Atlanta Inquirer*, *Michigan Chronicle*, the *Oakland Post*, and the *Washington Afro American*. Newspapers in Atlanta, Oakland, and Washington, D.C. were selected because each had a substantial African-American population; each had an established African-American newspaper which had been in existence for a number of years; they were located in different geographical regions within the U.S.; and each (with the exception of Washington, D.C.) was located in a state with high rates of HIV/AIDS infection in the African-American population. Furthermore, at the time, all three of these cities were within the top ten metropolitan areas with high rates of AIDS and HIV infection according to surveillance data obtained through the Centers for Disease Control and Prevention. Although Detroit was not within the top ten, it still merited attention because almost half of the reported AIDS cases within the state of Michigan occurred in Detroit.

The investigation sought to determine which issues and topics related to AIDS were covered most often as well as how they were framed to aid in understanding the meaning and prominence given to the issue by the papers. Additionally, I was also interested in the African-American newspapers' coverage of people with AIDS (PWA). I examined the frames because framing focuses and navigates attention to certain aspects of an issue, while ignoring or minimizing attention to other factors. Thus, information that is presented repeatedly in the media is what most individuals notice and recall about a particular issue (Bennett, 1995).

Overall, I found: 1) During the early portion of the second decade of AIDS, coverage was low, but it increased each year and eventually leveled off; also, during the 10-year period under examination, cumulatively, the majority of the articles appeared from 1998 through 2000, almost 20 years into the epidemic; and it was not until 1995 that all four of the papers covered AIDS with some consistency. 2) The topics covered or selected most frequently by the papers were those that compared AIDS to other illnesses and diseases or social problems or mentioned it among an array of social problems; statistical data pertaining to AIDS infection rates and trends; and preventive efforts. 3) Roughly half of the articles appearing in the papers examined specifically pertained to AIDS and the African-American community and the majority of those addressed prevalence rates and prevention; however, only few of them concerned PWAs and of those only a small number addressed matters such as discrimination. Of the 477 articles examined, 53 (about one out of nine) were about PWAs. Furthermore, coverage of AIDS victims was low during the early 1990s (beginning of the second decade), and then it gradually began to increase and then coverage peaked in 1995. After 1995, coverage again leveled off, and then it shot up again once more in 2000, but then coverage dropped off in 2001. 4) Prevention frames exceeded both political and economic frames.

My findings further support Cohen's notion that African-American newspapers have in many instances engaged in "secondary marginalization" with regard to AIDS. For clarity, let's first define what is meant by marginalization. Here it is meant to refer to those instances in which those who are underrepresented (i.e. minority in terms of political and social power relations) are treated as less significant and less valued members of society; ultimately, they are kept at the periphery of "American" society (Campbell, 1995). According to Cohen (1999),

> a group is marginal to the extent that its members have historically been and continue to be denied access to dominant decision-making processes and institutions; stigmatized by their identification; isolated or segregated; and generally excluded from control over the resources that shape the quality of their lives. Much of the material exclusion experienced by marginal groups is based on, or justified by, ideological processes that define these groups as "other."
>
> (p. 24)

Thus, it is fair to say that African Americans as well as members of other ethnic groups experience marginalization at the hands of various mainstream institutions, including the mass media. Therefore, "secondary marginalization," according to Cohen, occurs as a result of "advanced marginalization," which occurs when certain members of a marginalized group secure privilege and mobility as well as some degree of power or access to or within dominant institutions. Ultimately, those members who have achieved such status (black elites or bourgeoisie) end up engaging in their own form of marginalization, "secondary marginalization," which involves a reproduction of a rhetoric of blame and punishment that ends up being directed at those most vulnerable and stigmatized within their community. This is what I believe happened with AIDS, the African-American community and the popular African-American newspapers.

Ironically, the Black Press came into existence partly as a result and as a response to marginalization experienced by blacks in America. Although its purpose and role has evolved over time, it has still been expected to serve as an agenda-setter and advocate for the African-American community. Members of marginalized groups depend on their own indigenous institutions like African-American as well as other ethnic newspapers for accurate and reliable information (Cohen, 1999). However, with regard to AIDS, it reneged as findings from this analysis suggest that the African-American newspapers examined had no sustained or consistent agenda nor did it fulfill the role of advocate. Most noticeable is the paucity of coverage of people with AIDS which has led to secondary marginalization. This is likely because those that own, operate and/or run indigenous institutions like the historical Black Press tend to be privileged members of the marginalized community who maintain a conservative ideology when it comes to matters pertaining to morals and values as well as because of who it was believed to impact: injection drug users, gay men and lesbians, and poor women—those segments of the community that are often ignored, deemed unimportant and not worthy of resources, activism or media coverage (Cohen, 1999). Those in the later group are often treated as an embarrassment to the larger community.

As evidenced above, research examining the Black Press' handling of AIDS has been sporadic and limited as well as marginalizing. It is necessary to look to African-American media to gain a comprehensive understanding of how complex issues and subjects such as AIDS concern or impact African Americans. Thus, African-American media, especially newspapers, must recognize the power that they possess within the African-American community to be one of the dominant forces setting the agenda for social, political, as well as health issues like AIDS.

According to Dearing and Rogers (1996), during the early years, the media initially framed AIDS as a gay issue because many of those who first contracted the virus were affiliated with the gay community. However, once it was acknowledged that the virus could and was being transmitted by needle sharing, blood transfusions, as well as homosexual contact, the media frame of AIDS became one characterizing the virus as primarily affecting certain segments of the population, but not everyone else. Dearing and Rogers (1996) maintain that the way in which AIDS was framed greatly affected the news value of the epidemic during the early 1980s.

Conclusion

The relationship between mass media and African Americans has been strained since the early days of the American press during the seventeenth century (Wilson & Gutierrez, 1995). The clash between the news media and African Americans can historically be attributed to racism and overt discrimination by media organizations. As a social and cultural institution, mass media coverage of minorities and issues affecting minorities has and continues to reflect a bias, often attributed to racist and hegemonic ideologies (Center for Integration and Improvement of Journalism, 1994; Kerner Commission, 1968).

Examination of early news coverage reveals intentional neglect of persons of color as they were not included in the reporting of the news; thus, suggesting they were not relevant to society and further signaled the status afforded nonwhites by Anglos. Excluding or not covering persons of color or issues relevant to them served to reinforce white supremacist dominant ideology that impacted both nonwhites and whites, understanding of their social positions in society. According to Wilson, Gutierrez, and Chao (2003),

> Insofar as the gatekeepers of public information—and by extension, their constituent audience—were concerned, people of color were not an important consideration in the conduct of social affairs. In the colonial era this was made clear in such a sacrosanct document as the Declaration of Independence, wherein the phrase "all men are created equal" was understood to exclude women, Native Americans, and Blacks. The point was so obvious that there was no need to insert the word "White" between "all" and "men." … Ultimately, exclusion from coverage in news media signified exclusion from American society, because the function of news is to reflect social reality.
>
> (p. 117)

As previously stated, this early treatment of persons of color by the press has left a lasting impact as it has influenced the nature and extent of the coverage and treatment of persons of colors and issues relevant to them over time. This pattern of coverage is evident when examining the history of news coverage of AIDS. Early on, mainstream news coverage of AIDS did not feature any frames pertaining to African Americans even though early indications suggested that the African-American community was at increased risk. According to Wilson and Gutierrez (1995),

> The preponderance of such reporting has led some observers to say the news media have offered an image of non-Whites as "problem people," which means they are projected as people who either have problems or cause problems for society. The legacy of news exclusion thus leads to the general audience seeing people of color as a social burden—the "us versus them" syndrome carried to another dimension.
>
> (p. 158)

News coverage of African Americans and other people of color as well as the issues that concern them are often ignored by mainstream news organizations, and this type of treatment places African Americans and others of color on the outskirts of American society and culture (Campbell, 1995). Therefore, according to Campbell (1995), the underrepresentation of minorities in news coverage ultimately "contributes to a marginalization of the lives and interests of people of color" (p. 35). Much of the literature concerning news coverage of minorities suggests that minority communities and issues concerning them are usually ignored or stereotyped by mainstream news organizations (e.g. Campbell, 1995; Entman, 1992; Pease, 1989). Pease (1989) maintains that little progress was made by minorities by the late 1980s in having their concerns heard and addressed and their problems reported on by the mainstream press, and AIDS has been no exception. Unfortunately coverage in popular African-American newspapers has not been much better.

While early mainstream media coverage of AIDS was slow and lacking, the coverage provided by the African-American press was not much better as it has tended to underplay almost every aspect of the disease that has claimed the lives of African Americans (Kinsella, 1989). AIDS coverage by popular African-American newspapers is similar to coverage by popular African-American magazines (Brown, 2003; Cohen, 1999; Krishnan, Durrah, & Winkler, 1997) in that the majority of the information simply reinforces existing knowledge and information regarding the disease. According to Cohen (1999),

> Overall there has been very little reframing of AIDS to awaken the consciousness of black communities and mobilize their political strength in response to this epidemic. Instead, AIDS has most often been represented as an individual medical/moral problem caused, depending on your perspective, by bad people or salvageable individuals engaged in bad behaviors.
>
> (p. 288)

As is evidenced by the present analysis, the popular African-American newspapers have done a mediocre job in their coverage of AIDS, even as it specifically pertains to African Americans. The coverage needs to expand by focusing more on people with AIDS (PWAs) and their concerns as well as by focusing more on the policies and economics involved.

Furthermore, certain issues (such as drug use/abuse, homosexuality, discrimination, and transmission) that are central to the AIDS discussion need to be covered more comprehensively by the papers. Findings indicate that the African-American newspapers of today do provide basic or general coverage of AIDS. However, in several instances their coverage has been marginalizing. The papers along with other African-American media outlets (alternative media outlets, Black radio, magazines, and Web sites) need to partner with government and health agencies, members of the community, activists and most importantly those personally impacted to develop more effective health and AIDS information campaigns. It is vital for African-American media outlets like the African-American newspapers to become more assertive in health information dissemination because of the shared experiences, cultural norms and racial identification that typically exists between African-American media and the African American community, and because they are perceived to be more credible and believable than their mainstream counterparts (Wolseley, 1990).

African-American newspapers are usually located in key neighborhood locations within many African-American communities such as barbershops, hair salons, churches, and local black-owned businesses. Therefore, the information contained in them may lead to discussions within the greater community. The combination of media and interpersonal channels can be an effective way of reaching a population that is suffering disproportionately from the AIDS epidemic.

AIDS in the African-American community poses a major social problem as it threatens to jeopardize some of the social and political strides that have been made among African Americans. Throughout much of the 1980s the faces of AIDS that many Americans saw on billboards, television, newspapers, public health pamphlets as well as charitable requests were typically white, gay and male, even though AIDS was already carving a path throughout much of the African-American community (Burkett, 1995). If traditional mainstream approaches and paradigms continue to be used ineffectively to combat HIV and AIDS in African Americans, the effect may have a devastating impact on the African-American population as a whole. Furthermore, the practice of secondary marginalization can be costly and damaging—costly in terms of the lives lost and affected and damaging to growth and esteem of members within the community.

African-American newspapers as well as other African-American media outlets need to do a better job of covering AIDS, by seriously and aggressively covering issues of policy, economics, as well as the politics and discrimination surrounding the syndrome. As suggested by Krishnan, Durrah, and Winkler (1997), African-American media outlets need to serve multiple roles as reinforcers, agenda setters as well as gatekeepers as it pertains to dissemination of AIDS information in the African-American community. After all, as Wolseley (1990) indicated, the Black Press exists "…to be the advocate for the black population" (p. 6).

Finally, the concerns mentioned above regarding the Black Press and its propensity to reproduce that which is found in mainstream media may pose similar problems for other ethnic media as well. For example, many ethnic news and entertainment outlets follow or adhere to similar business models as their mainstream counterparts in that they are sustained largely through advertising revenue. Thus, this makes them susceptible to other hegemonic capitalistic processes as well—prioritizing profit over advocacy. Other ethnic media also need to be concerned about the issue of secondary marginalization and aware that their coverage of important issues can have the same marginalizing effect that has traditionally been the mainstream media's problem. In a fight to survive and sustain, much ethnic media have unintentionally become just another outlet for advertisers to use to target and reach consumers of color as much of their content has become increasingly commercial (Wilson, Gutierrez, & Chao, 2003) as the bark remains without the bite.

References

Andsager, J. K. & Powers, A. (1999). Social or economic concerns: How news and women's magazines framed breast cancer in the 1990s. *Journalism and Mass Communication Quarterly*, 76(3), 531–550.

Bennett, W. L. (1995). *News, the politics of illusion*. White Plains, NY: Longman Publishers.

Boger, J.C. (1996). Race and the American city: The Kerner commission report in retrospect. In J.C. Boger & J.W. Wegner (Eds.), Race, poverty and American cities (pp. 3–76). Chapell Hill, NC: The University of North Carolina Press.

Brown, R. (2003). Framing the second decade: A content analysis of African-American newspaper coverage of AIDS from 1991–2001 (Unpublished doctoral dissertation). Wayne State University, Detroit, MI.

Burkett, E. (1995). *The gravest show on earth: America in the age of AIDS*. Boston: Houghton Mifflin Company.

Campbell, C. (1995). *Race, myth and the news*. Thousand Oaks, CA: Sage.

Center for Integration and Improvement of Journalism (1994). News watch: A critical look at coverage of people of color. *A Report from the Center for Integration and Improvement of Journalism*. San Francisco State University, p. 44.

Chitwood, D. D. (2002). United States. In K. McElrath (Ed.), *HIV and AIDS: A global view* (pp. 253–271). Westport, CT: Greenwood Press.

Cohen, C. (1999). *The boundaries of blackness: AIDS and the break down of black politics*. Chicago: University of Chicago Press.

Cook, T. E. & Colby, D. C. (1992). The mass-mediated epidemic: The politics of AIDS on the nightly network news. In E. Fee and D. M. Fox (Eds.), *AIDS: The making of a chronic disease* (pp. 84–122). Berkley: University of California Press.

Dates, J. L. & Barlow, W. (1993). *Split image: African Americans in the mass media* (2nd ed.). Washington, D.C.: Howard University Press.

Dearing, J. W. & Rogers, E. M. (1996). *Agenda-Setting*. Thousand Oaks, CA: Sage Publications.

Duh, S. V. (1991). *Blacks and AIDS: Causes and origins*. Newbury Park, CA: Sage Publications.

Edgar, T., Hammond, S. L., & Freimuth, V. (1989). The role of the mass media and interpersonal communication in promoting AIDS related behavior change. *AIDS and Public Policy*, 4, 3–9.

Entman, R. M. (1992). Blacks in the news: Television, modern racism and cultural change. *Journalism Quarterly*, 69 (2), 341–361.

Hammonds, E. (1986). Race, sex, AIDS: The construction of "other." *Radical America*, 20(6), 28–36.

Jenkins, B. (1992). AIDS/HIV epidemic in the Black community. In R. L. Braithwaite & S. E. Taylor (Eds.), *Health issues in the Black community* (pp. 55–63). San Francisco: Jossey-Bass.

Kerner Commission (1968). *Report of the National Advisory Commission on Civil Disorders*. New York: Bantam.

Kinsella, J. (1989). *Covering the plague: AIDS and the American media*. New Brunswick: Rutgers University Press.

Krishnan, S. P., Durrah, T., & Winkler, K. (1997). Coverage of AIDS in popular African American magazines. *Health Communication, 9*(3), 273–288.

Lester, E. (1992). The AIDS story and moral panic: How the Euro-African press constructs AIDS. *The Howard Journal Communication, 2* (3&4), 230–241.

Mongerson, P. (1997). *The power press: Its impact on America and what you can do about it*. Golden, CO: Fulcrum Publishing.

Nardi, P. M. (1990). AIDS and obituaries: The perpetuation of stigma in the press. In D. A. Feldman (Ed.), *Culture and AIDS* (pp. 159–168). New York: Praeger Publishers.

Okigbo, C., Okigbo, C. A., Hall, W. B., & Ziegler, D. (2002). The HIV/AIDS epidemic in African American communities: Lessons from UNAIDS and Africa. *Journal of Black Studies, 32*(6), 615–653.

Pease, E. C. (1989). Kerner plus 20: Minority news coverage in the Columbus Dispatch. *Newspaper Research Journal, 10*(3), 17–38.

Pickle, K., Quinn, S. C., & Brown, J. (2002). HIV/AIDS coverage in Black newspapers, 1991–1996: Implications for health communication and health education. *Journal of Health Communication, 7*, 427–444.

Shubert, V. (1992). Introduction. In M. E. Hombs (Ed.), *AIDS crisis in America: A reference handbook* (pp. 1–25). Santa Barbara, CA: ABC-CLIO.

Signorielli, N. (1993). *Mass media images and impact on health: A sourcebook*. Greenwood Press: Westport, Connecticut.

Sontag, S. (1988). *Illness as metaphor and AIDS and its metaphors*. New York: Doubleday.

Sylvester, J. L. (1998). *Directing health messages toward African Americans: Attitudes toward health care and the mass media*. New York: Garland Publishing, Inc.

Tinney, J. S. & Rector, J. J. (1989). *Issues and trends in Afro-American Journalism*. Washington, D.C.: University Press of America.

Watts, E. A. (1992). *The agenda setting effect of reporting cure research on polio and AIDS in newspapers, news magazines, and network television news*. Unpublished doctoral dissertation, Ohio University, Athens.

Wilson, C. C. & Gutierrez, F. (1995). *Race, multiculturalism, and the media: From mass to class communication*. Thousand Oaks, CA: Sage.

Wilson, C. C., Gutierrez, F., & Chao, L. M. (2003). *Racism, sexism, and the media: The rise of class communication in multicultural America* (3rd ed.). Thousand Oaks, CA: Sage.

Worth, D. (1990). Minority women and AIDS: Culture, race, and gender. In D. A. Feldman (Ed.), *Culture and AIDS* (pp. 111–136). New York, NY: Praeger.

Wolseley, R. E. (1990). *The Black Press, USA*. Iowa State University, AMES.

Discussion Questions

1. Do you feel there is a need for ethnic newspapers and other ethnic media today? Why or why not?

2. What do you think about what Cohen refers to as secondary marginalization? Do you think that it is valid in explaining how AIDS was covered by black newspapers? Why or why not?

3. What are some issues or concerns today that ethnic presses might address differently than their mainstream counterparts (i.e. war in Afghanistan or Iraq, health care, immigration, etc.)?

4. Should ethnic news and entertainment outlets cover health issues that impact their respective communities differently than their mainstream counterparts? Does it matter? Why or why not? And, if so, how should they go about doing so?

5. Revisit the sections in the chapter that discuss the past and present role of the ethnic and Black Press ("Ethnic media and the Black Press" and "The Black Press defined") and indicate whether or not today's ethnic and black publications meet those criteria and objectives. Cite current examples that support your response.

6. What challenges might ethnic and alternative media face in their advocacy role as a result of increased media consolidation in the era of media conglomeration?

Assignments

1. Examine multiple copies or editions of selected ethnic newspapers in your community and identify the topics most frequently covered by the papers as well as the frames or themes most commonly found in the articles about those topics. Are there any noticeable patterns in the coverage?

2. Look through alternative and ethnic newspapers and describe the coverage given to health issues and topics. Indicate what diseases or health conditions are covered as well as the frames and themes most often associated with the health issue or topic. For example, let's say you notice coverage is given to breast cancer. What do the articles about breast cancer mention or address (i.e. victims or persons affected, treatment options, risk factors, research, etc.)?

3. Compare and contrast a mainstream newspaper and its ethnic newspaper counterparts' coverage of HIV and AIDS or other health topics such as diabetes, hypertension, cancer, etc. and describe the differences and similarities in the coverage. Do the ethnic papers cover the topics differently or reproduce similar frames as the mainstream publications?

4. After examining several editions or issues of an ethnic publication, write an essay critiquing its coverage of health issues and topics and consider sending it to the publication's editor. The critique can offer positive and/or negative feedback. Indicate what the paper is doing well as well as what areas need improvement. Be sure to offer suggestions for improving coverage of health related issues.

5. Compare and contrast the advertising content of your local mainstream newspaper with that of the ethnic presses in your community and indicate whether or not the ads are the same. What type of health related products and services are most often featured? How do the products and services advertised compare to the editorial content as it pertains to health? For example, are there advertisements for cigarettes and/or alcohol as well as articles and editorial content pertaining to various types of cancers, diabetes, heart disease, etc.?

For Further Study

Books

Shilts, R. (2000). *And the Band Played On.* New York: St. Martin's Press.

Films/Videos

Adelman, Larry (2008). *Unnatural Causes ... Is Inequality Making Us Sick?*
This is a seven-part documentary series exploring racial and socio-economic inequalities in health by examining some root causes.

Epstein, Elaine (2002). *State of Denial.*
This documentary examines the claims by some South African government officials that HIV does not lead to AIDS even as data indicated that South Africa had one of the highest incidences of HIV infection.

Nelson, Stanley (1998). *The Black Press: Soldiers without Swords.*
In this piece, archival footage and interviews trace the history of African-American newspapers and journalism from the antebellum period to the Civil Rights Movement.

Riggs, Marlon (1995). *Black is ... Black Ain't.*
In this, his final film, Marlon Riggs debates Black identity, white critiques, sexism, patriarchy, homophobia, colorism and cultural nationalism all while chronicling his personal journey with AIDS.

Spottiswoode, Roger (1993). *And the Band Played On.*
This movie is based on the book by Randy Shilts that brought the AIDS epidemic to public attention and chronicles the political neglect the disease faced at its onset.

Web sites

Pew Research Center for the People and the Press:
http://people-press.org/

Centers for Disease Control and Prevention:
http://cdc.gov

PART 2

Covering Race

Contemporary Case Studies

CHAPTER 7

Simple Incivility or Outright Racism? How Newspapers Covered Joe Wilson's Outburst during Obama's Congressional Health Care Address

KIM M. LEDUFF

Does the election of President Barack Obama indicate that America has transcended its sordid racist past? One need only briefly survey news coverage in America since Obama's election to the presidency to confirm that racism is alive and well. The feel-good images of the Obama family the night of the election and the masses that gathered in D.C. for the inauguration were quickly overshadowed as Obama began his day-to-day work as President of the United States. And no matter how racially neutral the president attempted to keep his dealings—race has somehow crept in as a factor on numerous occasions.

The interesting thing about this new wave of racism as covered by the news media is that it is often couched in partisanship. In other words, the definitions of political affiliation seem to have taken on new meaning, especially in media coverage of political debate. The term Democrat has come to be associated with extreme liberalism, and since Obama's election, a synonym for acceptance of non-white and non-traditional values in America. Republican, on the other hand, has come to mean extreme conservatism and acceptance of whiteness as representative of what it means to be the norm or the standard in American society. On occasion, some news organizations frame it as a battle of good against evil (and who is good and who is evil appears to be determined by the network or publication one chooses).

This study consists of an examination of newspaper coverage of one particular incident that illustrates this new era of racism disguised as "politics as usual." One of the first issues Obama chose to tackle as he assumed the presidency was health care. News coverage of turbulent town hall meetings where people of opposing political parties yelled at one another and at politicians attempting to present the president's plan were America's first indication that Obama's plan was not going to go over easily. And it was clear from the visuals incorporated in the newspaper and TV coverage that the feud was not just Democrat versus Republican, but, often, Black versus White. On September 9, 2009, President Obama addressed Congress in regards to his plan for health care reform. During the speech he addressed the fact that illegal immigrants would not be covered under his plan when he was interrupted with a boisterous, "You lie!" from Republican Representative Joe Wilson of South Carolina. That incident brought into question whether or not the action was indicative of a clear lack of respect for the president or if it might have more to do with his being African American.

Needless to say news commentators jumped on the bandwagon immediately after the speech, pondering the motives behind Wilson's actions. Wilson apologized quickly and Obama accepted—but the mass media didn't drop the controversy so easily. It was a column published in the *New York Times* on September 13, 2009 that really turned up the tension. In her column, titled "Boy, oh, boy," Maureen Dowd wrote, "Surrounded by middle-aged white guys—a sepia snapshot of the days when such polls ran Washington like their own men's club—Joe Wilson yelled 'You lie!' at a president who didn't. But, fair or not, what I heard was an unspoken word in the air: You lie, boy!" (Dowd, 2009).

A week or so later, former United States President Jimmy Carter spoke out as well. It was reported by a number of news outlets that in an interview with NBC News Carter explained that in his opinion Wilson's outburst indeed had to do with a lack of respect for Obama simply because of his race. "I think it's based on racism," Carter said. "There is an inherent feeling among many in this country that an African-American should not be president" (Bluestein, 2009, n.p.). Carter went on to suggest that this type of behavior was characteristic of much of the behavior seen on behalf of extreme conservatives in this country since Obama's election.

This chapter is a critical analysis of newspaper coverage following Obama's speech and Wilson's outburst. In an effort to determine how newspapers covered the events, three publications were examined: *The Chicago Tribune* (because Chicago is President Obama's hometown); *The State* of Columbia, South Carolina (the largest newspaper in Representative Wilson's home state), and finally, the *Atlanta Journal Constitution* (from Jimmy Carter's home state). The goal was to determine if there was a difference in how the events were covered and what type of follow-up stories and features were published after the speech, the outburst, and Carter's claims of racism.

A History of Racism

In order to analyze the media coverage of the fallout after Obama's speech, it is first necessary to understand a little about the history of race relations in the United States and the remnants of that history today. Many would like to believe that America changed for the better for African Americans after the Civil Rights Movement. While it did in some ways, in others, things remained the same and in some respects got even worse. While outright racism may no longer be acceptable in American society or commonly represented in American media, it does not mean that it no longer exists. It also does not mean that individuals in this society are unconscious of the stereotypes and assumptions about minority groups that are the direct result of the poor treatment of black people historically. Unfortunately, many of those ideas and beliefs are still applied whether consciously or unconsciously in American media. Because media are cultural industries, American audiences often take these messages in passively and apply them unconsciously or subconsciously in the real world.

Today, racism manifests itself in a variety of ways in society. Campbell (1995) looked specifically at a variety of forms of contemporary racism, including one he described as *traditional racism*, which "regards white Americans as superior and privileged. It considers people of color to exist outside of mainstream society; it marginalizes minority group members if not ignoring them all together" (p. 37). McConhay (1986), Sears (1988), Chiricos and Eschholz (2002), and Entman (1990) identify *modern racism* as yet another form. Entman (1990) defines modern racism by explaining that it "eschews overt expressions of racial superiority or inferiority and is characterized instead by a diffuse 'anti-black effect—a general hostility toward blacks'" (p. 332). Finally, Jhally and Lewis (1992) describe *enlightened racism* as "the attitude of liberal whites who point to the social and economic success of a few African Americans as representative of the state of all African Americans in the US. They argue that racism is not a factor in social and economic oppression of Blacks in America" (quoted in

Campbell, 1995, p. 110). A more prevalent form of racism that permeates society today is what is known as "everyday racism." According to Essed (1991), "One major feature of everyday racism is that it involves racist practices that infiltrate everyday life and become part of what is seen as normal by the dominant group ... everyday racism does not exist as single events but as a complex of cumulative practices" (p. 288). This is very similar to what Gilliam and Iyengar (2000) define as *new racism*, which is closely tied to conservative beliefs in modern society. "New racism is thought to be symbolic, subtle, covert, hidden, and underground. Although the meaning and measurement of the new racism has varied widely from study to study and has been the basis of much controversy, there is a general agreement that racial attitudes have become increasingly tied to support for traditional American values"(p. 566). New racism appears to be in line with the forementioned new definition of Republican that is often alluded to in media coverage.

White Privilege and the News

The theoretical basis for this analysis is founded in Critical Race Theory (CRT). Christopher Metzler (2009) notes that "CRT was born out of the reality that the formal legalistic approach to civil rights in America began but did not end the conversation about how Blacks experience racism and how Whites have the privilege of opting out of the conversation unless it provides succor to their own self-interest" (p. 399). According to Delgado and Stefancic (2001), the CRT movement "considers many of the same issues that conventional civil rights and ethnic studies discourses take up, but places them in a broader perspective that includes economics, history, context, group- and self- interest, and even feelings and the unconscious" (p. 3). The theory's roots extend as far back as the mid-1970s when a group of legal scholars and activists realized that the waves of change following the Civil Rights era of the 1960s were starting to die down. In some instances, America's justice system even appeared to revert back to its pre-civil rights state. Derrick Bell, who is African American, and Alan Freeman, who is white, were pioneers of Critical Race Theory. "Both were deeply distressed over the slow pace of racial reform in the United States and decided that new approaches were needed to expose and deal with the less obvious though just as deeply entrenched types of racism that characterized modern time" (Delgado & Stefancic, 2001, p. xiii).

One specific area of Critical Race Theory also allows researchers to examine race by acknowledging the inherent privilege of "whiteness" and analyzing race from a perspective that recognizes that privilege.

Martha Mahoney (1995) argues that "this country is both highly segregated and based on the concept of whiteness as 'normal.' It is therefore hard for white folks to see whiteness both when we interact with people who are not socially defined as white and when we interact with other white people, when race doesn't seem to be involved" (p. 306). Theodore Allen (1994) in *The Invention of the White Race* says that racism was invented to establish social control over others whether it be racial or socioeconomic others. Others have also examined white privilege in the context of politics in the United States. Christopher Metzler (2009) looked specifically at how white privilege shapes many white Americans' views on racism in this country:

> The "typical" White person in a postracial America situates racism in the past; embraces formal equality; believes that America has done so much for Blacks and yet Blacks never seem to think that it is enough; walks on eggshells around blacks for fear of saying something offensive; believes in interracial dating so long as it is not their son or daughter who is marrying Black; does not see themselves as racialized, but basks in White privilege; believes that Blacks use race as an excuse for failure, that blacks who are successful are the exceptions; believes that pretending that race does not matter makes it true; and still harbors and makes decisions based on the powerful marker of race that is embedded in American racial reality.
>
> (p. 402)

Social critic and activist Tim Wise also acknowledges the inherent benefits of whiteness, but argues that denial of racism emanates squarely from "the collision between the rhetoric of equality and the crushing evidence of inequality and injustice" (p. 64). In other words, when whites view the success of someone like Obama, they assume that all minorities have an equal shot at being successful and doing well in this country. They do not recognize that often times black failure is not due to lack of ability, but vast inequalities that still exist for many in this country because of a combination of racial discrimination and socioeconomic status. Just as the Civil Rights Movement signified a monumental step forward for America, so did the election of Barack Obama. But unfortunately the election of a black president did not serve as an indication that America "has arrived" when it comes to eradication of racism. Instead, the news coverage following Obama's election appears to incorporate the racialized side of many of the major issues that have recently risen to prominence.

The Exception—Not the Rule

As the first African-American president, Obama's election suggested a shift of sorts in the American mentality. But within the first year of his presidency it soon became evident that perhaps we as a society had not changed as much as some might have thought. In an essay titled, "Uh-Obama: Racism, white voters and the myth of color blindness," Wise wrote about the impact that Obama's election might have on America. The article was written prior to his election, and Wise noted that "many a voice has suggested that Obama's success signifies something akin to the end of racism in the U.S., if not entirely, then surely as a potent political or social force. But, of course, the success of individual persons of color, while it certainly suggests that overt bigotry has diminished substantially, hardly speaks to the larger social reality faced by millions of others" (Wise, 2008, March 6). Cultural critic bell hooks (1994) argues that we must "critique and question the politics of representation that systematically devalues blackness" (p. 181). The mass media is unfortunately one of those systems. She continues: "To intervene and transform those politics of representation informed by colonialism, imperialism, and white supremacy, we have to be willing to challenge mainstream culture's efforts to erase racism by suggesting it does not exist" (p. 181). While Obama's election is a historic milestone, it has the demonstrated potential to give Americans a false sense that all is well and fair amongst the races in this country. In her column following the speech, Dowd also addressed the fact that Obama's experience is not the experience of many minorities in America: "Barry Obama of the post-'60s Hawaiian 'hood did not live through the major racial struggles in American history. Maybe he had a problem relating to his white basketball coach or catching a cab in New York, but he never got beaten up for being black" (Dowd, 2009).

The goal of this chapter is to look at newspaper coverage after Wilson's outburst during Obama's speech to determine if, a) media coverage indicates that indeed we are not living in a post-racial society, b) newspapers cover events from differing perspectives depending upon the region of the country and in turn shape how readers think about issues and events, and c) Obama's election may have done something quite opposite of what most people thought it would do. But it has opened the floodgates for dialogue in the media and in society about race relations in America; d) Media coverage attempts to mask racial issues behind politics, especially since Obama's election.

This study consists of a qualitative analysis of newspaper stories that were published in the month following Obama's speech. The primary research questions are:

RQ1: How much coverage was found in each publication in the month following Obama's speech and Wilson's outburst?

RQ2: What similarities and/or differences were found in the coverage featured in the newspapers?

RQ3: When Jimmy Carter spoke out, were there any notable differences in the coverage?

RQ4: How frequently was race incorporated as part of the story?

RQ5: Did it ever appear that political party was used as a euphemism for race in order to make the story more palatable for readers?

Regional Coverage of a National Issue

For the purposes of this study, newspaper coverage of Obama's health care speech, Wilson's outburst and Carter's claims between September 10, 2009 and September 30, 2009 were critically analyzed. Three newspapers were chosen for this analysis: *The Chicago Tribune, The State*, and the *Atlanta Journal Constitution*. Each newspaper's archives were searched using three terms: "Obama health care plan," "Joe Wilson" and "Jimmy Carter," between September 10, 2009 (the day after the speech) and September 30, 2009. The results from each search were then sorted. Opinion pieces were removed as well as stories that were not relevant to the speech.

Semiotic analysis is perhaps the best method of determining the possible meanings and interpretation of the content of these articles by audiences. Arthur Asa Berger (1995) credits Ferdinand de Saussure for the basis of semiotic analysis, which suggests that signs consist of the signifier and the signified. The language and references used in the articles (the signifiers) will be analyzed to determine how they might have been decoded by readers (the signified).

Shaping Audience Interpretations

Perhaps it is a sign of the times and the distressed state of the newspaper industry, but the first interesting note came during the search for coverage following the speech. All three publications depended very heavily upon wire coverage for stories. Initially there were few stories that actually were done by reporters working for the chosen publications. *How much coverage was found in each publication in the month following Obama's speech and Wilson's outburst? The Chicago Tribune* featured 13 articles, between September 10 and September 30, that addressed the events that took place on September 9, and the fallout that ensued. There were 12 stories from the *Tribune news service* and one from the *Associated Press*

(*AP*) wire. This result alone might suggest that perhaps the stories might not be as slanted in favor of Obama as one might have imagined they would be if covered by Chicago writers. *The State* of South Carolina featured 15 articles related to the speech and the outburst between September 10 and September 30. Eight of the stories were from McClatchy newspapers and written by one writer, James Rosen. There were four stories written for *The State* by their own staff writers. The newspaper also published three additional related stories: one from the *New York Times*, one from the *Beaufort Gazette* and one from the Associated Press. The *Atlanta Journal Constitution* published a total of 10 stories related to the incident. There were five stories from AP and five original pieces between September 10 and September 30.

Though *The State* had the most coverage, there was a similar amount of coverage in all three newspapers. It is also important to note that in all three publications the earliest reports following the speech were front-page news. The *Atlanta Journal Constitution* had a little less coverage than the other two newspapers and depended heavily on AP for content. Perhaps this suggests that because the other two newspapers had such close ties to the characters involved in this controversy, they dedicated more space to the story and follow up. But, numbers only tell so much. The content of the articles was indeed more telling and will be examined in an effort to answer the remaining research questions. Each newspaper appeared to cover the story in a way that indicated support for the politician involved who was geographically tied to the newspaper's home state. *The State* was especially supportive of Joe Wilson.

The second research question was: *What similarities and/or differences were found in the coverage featured in the newspapers?* It didn't take very long to determine that there were some differences in the way Wilson's outburst was framed when looking at *The Chicago Tribune* and *The State*. Perhaps the most telling data for this analysis came in the first paragraphs of the first stories published in each newspaper that addressed Wilson's outburst during the speech. Below are the leads from each story:

The State, September 10, 2009 by James Rosen
Washington—U.S. Rep. Joe Wilson, a Republican from South Carolina, stole the spotlight Wednesday evening by yelling out, "You Lie" during President Barack Obama's address to Congress on health care reform.

The Chicago Tribune, September 10, 2009 by Nicholas & Simon
Washington—When President Barack Obama Addressed Congress Wednesday night he got an unusual greeting: "You Lie!"

Atlanta Journal Constitution, September 10, 2009 by Erica Werner

In his speech to Congress Wednesday, President Barack Obama said that the changes to health care that he's proposing "would not apply to those who are here illegally." That prompted Wilson, a South Carolina Republican to shout "You lie!" from his seat in the House chamber. Wilson later apologized for his outburst, but he didn't back down from his claim.

These leads alone suggest that the framing of the story was different for readers in South Carolina. It is important to note here that the writer of the story published in *The State*, James Rosen, is a correspondent for *McClatchy Newspapers* and writes specifically for South Carolina newspapers. Perhaps in an effort to hold the attention of readers from Wilson's home state, Rosen approached the story with a lead that almost makes Wilson seem like a celebrity (and hero) by crediting him with "stealing the spotlight" (9/10/09). It is important to remember that Wilson's outburst was an expression of a lack of respect not only for the president, but Congress as well. It would seem that a politician's constituency might be somewhat embarrassed by the ill mannered actions of its representative, but the language used (the signifier) had the potential to be interpreted by audiences to mean that Wilson is a hero of sorts for challenging formality and tradition. While *The State* covered the incident and the events that followed more extensively than the other publications observed in this study, the content of the coverage clearly signified a conservative slant and support for Representative Wilson. Perhaps this is not surprising coming from a newspaper written to attract a very conservative readership. The danger, however, is that it is presented to audiences as unbiased and factual news.

The argument could also be made that *The Chicago Tribune* chose to lead the story with Obama because he is from Illinois. But the author, Richard Simon, is actually a writer for *The LA Times*. California also supported Obama, so the journalist is used to writing for a more liberal audience. But judging from past news coverage and in comparison to the lead from the AP that was published in the *Atlanta Journal Constitution*, the approach taken in both of these leads is more in line with what one would have expected in a follow-up story on a presidential speech. Had there been no outburst, the story would likely have begun with the most important points in Obama's speech. Yes, Wilson's outburst was newsworthy and did make for an attention grabbing lead, but this serves as a good example of how a journalist's word choice and story arrangement can impact audience interpretations of a story. The fact that he is described as "stealing the spotlight" suggests that Wilson's agenda somehow became more important than Obama's.

In the coverage that followed in *The State* Wilson indeed stole the show when it came to the stories published. One element of the coverage that was particularly interesting had to do with Wilson's run-ins with a Democratic representative from South Carolina, James Clyburn. In a story titled, "Wilson's outburst thrusts him on national stage," Wilson boasts about the support he received for his actions: "'I've been very pleased at the number of people who have told me that what I said is what they felt,' Wilson told McClatchy newspapers" (Rosen, 9/11/09). While the article notes that he apologized and Obama accepted, it also notes that "Clyburn, the highest ranking African American in Congress, threatened Wilson with a House sanction unless he issued an apology to his fellow lawmakers" (Rosen, 9/11/09). On September 12, in an article titled, "2 words = nearly $2 million," Clyburn's "threat" is mentioned again: "Clyburn and House Speaker Nancy Pelosi threatened to pass a 'resolution of disapproval' unless Wilson apologizes on the House floor. Clyburn asked three times and Wilson refused" (Rosen, 9/12/09). In this story there is no mention of Clyburn's race. But once again, from a semiotic perspective, the signifier and signified are very important here. Most readers in the state who are familiar with state politics would likely know that Clyburn is black. His name alone signifies his race and his liberal stance on issues just as Wilson's name signifies his conservative stance. The choice of the word "threatening" to describe his request for an apology from Wilson also signifies to audiences that the black, liberal politician is dangerous to the conservative, white politician who has been celebrated in the local news for his actions against the president. In fact, Wilson's actions the night of the speech and in other instances noted in the newspaper coverage are much more hostile than Clyburn's demand for an apology, but the language used to describe those events is much milder and is likely interpreted by audiences to mean that the conservative representative has to act out to protect his conservative views and the rights of his conservative constituents. It is important to note that at this point no allegations of racism on Wilson's behalf have been made in the coverage in *The State*. Clyburn's race and position are only mentioned as background in one story. But in two later articles it is interesting how racism suddenly becomes a consideration in light of the comments made by Jimmy Carter that garnered national attention.

In a later *State* article published on September 13, titled, "Wilson's shout keeps on echoing," Clyburn is mentioned again, but there is no mention of his race or any allegations of racist behavior on Wilson's part. There is, however, a short vignette about Clyburn's outrage over Wilson's actions in

South Carolina. It reads: "Clyburn was startled last month when Wilson hosted a raucous town hall meeting with 1,000 people, most of them angry conservatives at Keenan High School. The school in Clyburn's district is three blocks from his home and Clyburn's children attend it" (Rosen, 9/13/09). The story does not state it explicitly, but once again there are a number of interpretations that are likely made by readers based on this statement. The audience can easily decode what this incident is really about. And the truth is that this is a prime example of using political party to signify underlying racial issues. The impetus for Clyburn's outrage is signified in the language used in the story. It isn't the fact that Wilson crossed territorial lines that angers him. The interpretation likely made by local audiences goes something like this: Clyburn (who is African American) and his children (who are African American) live in a neighborhood (that is mostly inhabited by African Americans) and near his kids' school (which, from one look at its Web site, is clearly attended by mostly African Americans). And why is Clyburn outraged when a meeting is heavily attended by "conservatives" at his children's school? Because in this article "conservative" is code for wealthy and white Wilson supporters, who oppose a minority president and who would not likely set foot in his neighborhood or in the school under ordinary circumstances. Wilson and his supporters clearly chose the location to make it loud and clear to Democrats (translation: less wealthy, liberals and blacks, who don't always fall in line with the Republican version of "standard American values" and who they believe might unfairly benefit from Obama's plan) that they will not support it! While the interpretation might not be politically correct and the newspaper would not dare use this language, the underlying interpretation was indeed partially confirmed in an article published September 19, 2009.

"Wilson Debate Reopens Deep S.C. Wounds" was the title of the September 19 story in *The State*, and in this article the same conflict with Clyburn was addressed with additional information. The article read: "Clyburn also said he was furious about Wilson's decision to hold a town hall meeting at Keenan High school whose student body is virtually all black. Wilson told McClatchy, 'The decision to move the town hall meeting to Keenan high school was a last minute change in order to accommodate an anticipated larger crowd.' Clyburn ticked off three nearby schools in Wilson's district that could have been used" (Rosen, 9/19/09, n.p.). In the article Clyburn also cites other acts on Wilson's behalf that might have been considered racist, including membership to groups that support white supremacy, fighting to keep the confederate flag on the capitol dome and making vile comments about Strom Thurmond's bi-racial daughter Essie Mae Washington-Williams. What happened between September 13 and September 19 that suddenly made it okay to discuss the racist element of Wilson's behavior? Jimmy Carter's statement initiated the debate. The fact that Carter is white made it okay to suddenly have the conversation in the media. Had it been a black politician who said that Wilson's actions were racist, the discussion that ensued would more than likely have been attributed to a minority being overly sensitive. *The State,* as well as other newspapers, now had the okay to address the racial element of what had only been addressed previously in code: Democrat or liberal signifying black, and Republican and conservative signifying white.

The third question addressed in this study was: *When Jimmy Carter spoke out, were there any notable differences in the coverage?* The answer is a resounding yes.

In all three papers no overt mention of racism was made until Carter spoke out on September 16. Perhaps the publications were leery of mentioning racism because Obama never attributed it to that. But as soon as Carter opened the floodgates, the claims poured in. In the *Atlanta Journal Constitution*, the first article that addressed the issue was from AP, titled, "Wilson's son disputes Carter's claim of racism." In the story the son, Alan Wilson, defends his father saying: "There is not a racist bone in my dad's body … He doesn't even laugh at distasteful jokes. I won't comment on former President Carter. But I know my dad and it's just not in him" (Bluestein, 9/16/09). The fact that there was an article published defending Wilson in the conservative state before Carter's comments were even explored was an important note. The next day Ernie Suggs of the *Constitution* wrote in an article titled "Carter: Attacks unprecedented, former President stands by remarks about Wilson," he addresses Carter's comments to NBC and also incorporates comments from two sources. One, Robert Watson, is an African-American professor at Hampton University (a historically black institution). The other is the Republican National Committee Chairman, Michael Steele, who also happens to be African American. They have completely opposing views on Carter's comments. Watson argues that Carter is correct, while Steele suggests that calling it racism is a distraction on behalf of Democrats (Suggs, 9/17/09). The article does not identify the race of the two experts—perhaps the author crafted this in an effort to signify to audiences that the conflict is indeed about politics rather than race if two African Americans don't even agree on the motive. Not that all blacks must agree, but media coverage often suggests that they all should. This signifies to readers that blacks can't even agree on Wilson's motives, therefore they should not jump to conclusions so easily or take Carter's claims as gospel truth.

The Chicago Tribune also began to address race after Carter spoke out. It wasn't until an article published on the 16th in *The Chicago Tribune* that the race card gets thrown in. The article ends with the mention that Jimmy Carter called Wilson's outburst "an act of racism." But what was interesting about the coverage from *The Chicago Tribune* was that it was more about Obama's efforts to shift the discussion away from race no matter how hard the media attempted to bring it back there. More than any other publication, the story titles incorporated Obama's name (as opposed to Wilson's). And after Carter's announcement, *Tribune* writer Mark Silva published an article titled "In media blitz Obama says vitriol isn't racism based," in which he wrote, "In a calm manner, Obama also addressed the fervor of the current debate, suggesting much of the 'vitriol' aimed at him in protests stems from a natural fear of 'big changes' in government and not as much as former President Jimmy Carter has suggested, because opponents cannot accept that an African American is President" (9/21/09). The story recounted appearances Obama made on TV in the days following the incident with Wilson and discussed his attempts to downplay the possibility that Wilson's actions were race based. He cites an interview on CNN: "Obama disagreed with Carter, saying that the invective instead reflected the kind of turmoil that is common 'when presidents are trying to bring about big changes. Are there people out there who don't like me because of my race? I'm sure there are, … that's not the overriding issues here'" (Silva, 9/21/09, n.p.). The story then referred to another interview on ABC: "Obama was asked by ABC's George Stephanopoulos if it frustrates him when his own supporters 'see racism when you don't think it exists.' Obama responded 'I think that race is such a volatile issue in this society, always has been, that it becomes hard for people to separate out race being a sort of part of the backdrop of American society, versus race being a predominant factor in any given debate'" (Silva, 9/19/09). The coverage in *The Chicago Tribune* portrayed Obama as recognizing that race is an issue for some, but it is not "his" issue at the time. It is important to think about what this signified to readers in a state that supported Obama and his mission of change. The language used here suggests to audiences that the president does not acknowledge or support the notion that racism was Wilson's motivation. The message supports an idealistic and utopian view of post-racial America that many Obama supporters hoped his election signified. This evidence surrounding the incident squarely opposed that notion (as confirmed in the *State's* coverage), but the coverage in the *Tribune* downplayed the racial element and could have easily been interpreted by audiences to mean that those who suggested racism (like Carter "an old president") were simply locked in antiquated thinking (unlike Obama, "the new president"). This has the potential to be even more dangerous than the blatant racism of the past because it ignores a dangerous condition in America.

Research question 4 was: *How frequently was race incorporated as part of the story?* It appears that in all three publications race or racism did not become an integral part of the story until Carter spoke out. The reader would have to have a deeper knowledge of politics to pick out the nuances suggesting racism in the newspaper coverage prior to Carter's statement. Politicians of different races and political affiliations were often pitted against one another in quotes, but there was no mention of racism specifically. For example, in one of the first articles published in *The State*, Clyburn was referred to as "a close political ally of Obama." But as noted earlier, a well informed reader would understand that this signified an underlying set of meanings. The context suggests a bond deeper than political affiliation: Perhaps they have a similar agenda because they are both black as well. *The Chicago Tribune* only published three stories that addressed racism, not surprising if in fact the publication is upholding the president's wish to play down the race issue. The *Atlanta Journal Constitution* only published three articles related to race, mostly in response to Carter's claims. *The State* published eight stories that addressed racism—perhaps to defend the outspoken representative from their state. But often there was an attempt to make it appear more about politics than race.

And finally, *Did it ever appear that political party was used as a euphemism for race in order to make the story more palatable for readers?* There were a few stories that attempted to portray the events as "politics as usual." A story in *The Chicago Tribune* addressed the fact that Congressman John Shimkus of Illinois walked out on Obama's speech and there was no uproar surrounding his actions (9/11/09). Others compared Wilson's actions to other incidents that had happened amongst politicians in the past. In an article written by Carolyn Click, titled, "And this was before CNN!" in *The State*, she examined the Brooks-Sumner affair when South Carolina Republican Preston Brooks beat U.S. Senator Charles Sumner with a cane on the floor of the U.S. capitol in 1856. According to Click, "Sumner (became) a martyr in the North and Brooks a hero in the South. Historian Walter Edgar wrote in his book 'South Carolina: a History.' One newspaper wrote that fragments of the stick are begged as sacred relics. Brooks received canes, silver loving cups and other tokens from Southern admirers" (Click, 9/13/09).

The State also re-published an article from the *New York Times* in which Gen. Colin Powell was quoted:

"You can find pictures where Bush was called all kinds of names, with all sorts of banners being held up and burned in effigy.

I've seen it in every Presidency," Gen. Colin Powell, who was secretary of state under Bush, said in an interview. Powell said he believed Obama was arguably facing even more apparent hostility, but he blamed the current partisan Internet and cable news culture for amplifying the more extreme voices, not necessarily racial bias. "The issue is not race, it's civility," Powell said.

(Zelney & Rutenberger, 2009, Sept. 18)

The Chicago Tribune also published a story reminding readers this wasn't the first case of incivility: "There have been many examples of the breakdown in civility on Capitol Hill over the years, including Vice President Dick Cheney directing an obscenity at a senator on the Senate floor in 2004" (9/11/2009). The article also cited the Brooks-Sumner incident. What did these stories signify to audiences? It depends on what city the reader lived in and the context of the story. For those in Chicago, perhaps it signified that it isn't always about race. For readers in South Carolina, perhaps it signified that Wilson isn't alone in his actions and, therefore, maybe he isn't such a bad guy (or a racist) for shouting at the president. When a story is observed in the context of other coverage it can indeed signify something very different for readers in different parts of the country depending on what they are exposed to on a regular basis.

Is the Obama Era Truly a Post-Racial Era?

Critical Race Theory was born out of frustration with the Civil Rights Movement. The outcome was not as promising as many hoped it would be for minorities in the U.S. At the beginning of this study the goal was to find out if media coverage since Obama's election suggests that we are living in a post-racial America. Based on the results of this study, Obama's election does not appear to have had the unifying force that many hoped it would amongst the races in America. Whether or not that is the message across the U.S., however, cannot be addressed in a blanket statement based on the results of this study. While in some places the dividing lines appear to have become more pronounced, in others they are often glossed over.

While sweeping generalizations cannot be made based on the results of one study, the results indicate that there are some important considerations American audiences should take when depending on local media (in this case newspaper) for information. The Obama-Wilson incident clearly shows that even though we elected Obama, America is by no means a post-racial society. As Wise (2008, March 6) notes, "The fact that old fashioned bigotry has diminished substantially hardly speaks to the larger social reality" (p. 16). Secondly, Wise notes that Obama's downplaying of events has much to do with his success amongst white voters: "His success actually *confirms* the salience of white power. If, in order to be elected, a man of color has to pander to white folks, in ways that no white politician would ever have to do to people who were black or brown, then white privilege and white power remain operative realities." Wise suggests that the only reason Obama was elected was "because he managed to convince enough whites that he was *different*, and not *really* black, in the way too many whites continue to think of black people, that according to every opinion survey, is not too positively" (p. 16).

It also appears that where you live in this country may have some impact on how news stories are framed. In this case, readers of *The State* saw more about Wilson than anyone or anything else involved in the incident. There were attempts to rationalize his actions, remind citizens of South Carolina's history, and portray an African-American politician (James Clyburn) as overly sensitive and threatening. In much the same vein, the *Atlanta Journal Constitution* published an article allowing Joe Wilson's son to come to his defense in light of Carter's claims of racism, before even exploring Carter's claims in depth. On the flip side, *The Chicago Tribune* focused primarily on Obama and downplayed the racial element just as the president did. So, yes, it appears that the publication one reads and the connection to the characters involved in a news story indeed shapes how the story gets relayed to readers. Another important note is that the two Southern papers covered the story in a more similar fashion than the midwestern paper. This suggests that the region of the country in which a newspaper is published may also shape the content contained and the angle from which stories are told.

So what exactly does Obama's election mean for race relations in this country? It may have done something quite opposite to what most people expected. As Metzler (2009) notes, "Obama's postracial idealism told Whites the one thing they most wanted to hear: America had essentially contained the evil of racism to the point at which it was no longer a serious barrier to black advancement" (p. 403). But clearly Wilson's actions paint a different picture. Wise (2008) notes the danger of looking at a minimal number of black success stories (like Obama) and equating them with opportunity for all in America. He says that

> to use individual success stories, like that of Oprah, or any-one else—Bill Cosby, Condoleeza Rice, Robert Johnson, or whomever—as proof that racism and white privilege don't exist, or at least aren't significant problems, is nonsensical. After all, (Madame C.J.) Walker became a millionaire in 1911, even in the

midst of what everyone would admit was a racist, white suprema-cist, and viciously fascist society as regards black people. But so what? Did that mean that folks shouldn't have been fighting for anend to racism simply because a few individuals had been able to "make it"?

(p. 70)

One only need look back at the events surrounding Hurricane Katrina in New Orleans only a few short years ago to see in living color the vast inequity that exists in this country. We haven't resolved the issues of racism and classism in the 50 years since the Civil Rights Movement. Obama's election most certainly does not prove that we have moved beyond what was seen in New Orleans post-Katrina and similar situations in major American cities across the country. As Metzler observed, "No one contests the symbolism of President Obama's election. What is contested is the role of race and racism in his election, his reluctance to engage in race in any meaningful way, and whether his election as the first Black President of the United States will be relegated to a mere symbolic footnote in the racial historical discourse" (2009, p. 399).

Do the media hide racial issues behind the mask of politics since Obama's election? It is difficult to say if the problem is the media or the politicians themselves. Any critical race theorist would likely credit white privilege as the force that gave Wilson the courage to yell at the country's highest political official and not think twice about the possible racial implications that would follow. But the media often do a complicated dance when covering these sorts of issues. For example, *The State* and *The Chicago Tribune* identified incidents of incivility in the past downplay-ing the Obama-Wilson incident, but for differing reasons. Dowd, however, made a head-on claim: "No Democrat ever shouted 'liar' at W. when he was hawking a fake case for war in Iraq." Dowd (2009, n.p.), like Carter, surmised, "Some people just can't believe a black man is president and will never accept it."

In *The New Republic*, John McWhorter (2009) wrote, "We are talking about a racism more complicated than the bigotries of old, a racism intertwined with other brands of animus ... it's a kind of racism whose perpetrators usually do not consciously recognize it in themselves, and would heartily resist owning up to it if presented with the charge" (p. 79). Republican Party members likely recognize that it is Obama's ability to downplay his own race and racial issues that makes him appealing to white Democrats. In an effort to sway opinions (as Maureen Dowd pointed out in her article) there appears to be "frantic efforts to paint our first black president as the Other, a foreigner, socialist, fascist, Marxist, racist,

Commie, Nazi; a cad who would snuff old people; a snake who would indoctrinate kids—had much to do with race" (Dowd, 2009). This isn't politics as usual.

This incident was not the last that Obama faced regarding race. While on the one hand there appears to be some bias or slant in the way stories of this nature are covered regionally, there is a positive side to this. Obama's election has opened the door for conversations about race in places where the subject was considered taboo. Hopefully, that dialogue can continue and conversations about race can lead to a true shift in American mentality rather than the symbolic one initiated by Obama's election. Obama is no doubt in an awkward position that many African Americans find themselves in when placed in a position of power. How does one address issues of race without coming across as pushing a personal agenda? It is a challenge, but perhaps the president can take steps toward unifying people across racial and political lines for the betterment of all people. And, in turn, maybe the media can go back to more objective coverage rather than diluting it in an effort to remain politically correct or attract a certain politically inclined readership.

References

Allen, Theodore. (1994). *The invention of the white race*. London: Verso.

Associated Press (2009, September 10). Text of the speech. *Atlanta Journal Constitution*. Retrieved December 15, 2009 from: http://www.ajc.com/news.

Associated Press (2009, September 26). No lie, Wilson is now a GOP star. *The Chicago Tribune*. Retrieved December 15, 2009 from: http://www.chicagotribune.com/news.

Berger, Arthur Asa. (1995). *Cultural criticism: A primer of key concepts*. Thousand Oaks: Sage Publications.

Bluestein, G. (2009, September, 16). Wilson's son disputes Carter's claim of racism. *Atlanta Journal Constitution*. Retrieved December 15, 2009 from: http://www.ajc.com/news.

Campbell, Christopher. (1995). *Race, myth and the news*. Thousand Oaks, CA: Sage.

Carter again cites racism as factor in Obama's treatment (2009, September 17). *CNN*. Retrieved December 15, 2009 from: http://www.cnn.com/2009/POLITICS/09/15/carter.obama/index.html.

Chiricos, Ted & Eschholz, Sarah. (2002). The racial and ethnic typification of crime and the criminal typification of race and ethnicity in local television news. *Journal of Research in Crime and Delinquency, 39*(4), 400–420.

Click, C. (2009, September 13). And this was before CNN! *The State*. Retrieved December 15, 2009 from: http://nl.newsbank.com/nl-search/we/Archives.

Delgado, R. & Stefancic, J. (1997). *Critical white studies: looking behind the mirror*. Philadelphia: Temple University Press.

Delgado, R. & Stefancic, J. (2001). *Critical race theory: an introduction*. New York: New York University Press.

Donahue, W. (2009, September, 13). Constituents turn out to jeer, cheer. *The State*. Retrieved December 15, 2009 from: http://nl.newsbank.com/nl-search/we/Archives.

Dowd, Maureen. (2009, September, 13). Boy, oh, boy. *The New York Times*. Retrieved December 15, 2009 from: http://www.nytimes.com/2009/09/13/opinion/13dowd.html.

Entman, Robert M. (1990). Modern racism and the image of blacks in local television news. *Critical Studies in Mass Communication*, 332–345.

Essed, P. (1991). *Understanding everyday racism*. Newbury Park, CA: Sage.

Gilliam Jr., Franklin D. & Iyengar, Shanto. (2000). Prime suspects: the influence of local television news on the viewing public. *American Journal of Political Science*, *44* (3, July), 560–574.

hooks, b. (1994). *Outlaw culture*. New York: Routledge.

Jhally, S. & Lewis J. (1992). *Enlightened racism: The Cosby Show, audiences, and the myth of the American Dream*. Boulder: Westview.

Keefe, B. (2009, September 16). You lie outburst Georgia's rep. Johnson says remark reflects racial undercurrents. *Atlanta Journal Constitution*. Retrieved December 15, 2009 from: http://www. ajc.com/news.

Keefe, B. (2009, September 17). GOP opens fire on czar power Obama aide points out use of advisers started with Nixon. *Atlanta Journal Constitution*. Retrieved December 15, 2009 from: http://www.ajc.com/news.

Keefe, B. (2009, September 19). Wilson's outburst unusual. *Atlanta Journal Constitution*. Retrieved December 15, 2009 from: http://www.ajc.com/news.

Levey, N. (2009, September 11). Obama's healthcare speech helps unify Democrats. *The Chicago Tribune*. Retrieved December 15, 2009 from: http://www.chicagotribune.com/news.

Levey, N. (2009 September 14). President Barack Obama dismisses "you lie" outburst by Joe Wilson. *The Chicago Tribune*. Retrieved December 15, 2009 from: http://www.chicagotribune. com/news.

Mahoney, Martha. (1995). Racial construction and women as differentiated actors. In R. Delgado & J. Stefancic (Eds.), *Critical White Studies: Looking behind the mirror* (pp. 305–309). Philadelphia, Temple University Press.

McConahay, J. B. (1986). Modern racism, ambivalence, and the modern racism scale. In S. L. Gaertner & J. F. Dovidio (Eds.), *Prejudice, discrimination, and racism* (pp. 91–125). Orlando, Academic Press.

McWhorter, J. (2009, October, 7). Color blind. *New Republic*, 7–8.

Metzler, C. J. (2009). Barack Obama's Faustian bargain and the fight for America's racial soul. *Journal of Black Studies* , *40*(3), 395–410

Muskal, M. (2009, September, 10). Obama accepts rep. Joe Wilson's apology. *The Chicago Tribune*. Retrieved December 15, 2009 from: http://www.chicagotribune.com/news.

Nicholas, P. (2009, September 13). Yes we can pass overhaul crowd tells President. *The Chicago Tribune*. Retrieved December 15, 2009 from: http://www.chicagotribune.com/news.

Nicholas, P. & Simon, R. (2009, September, 10). Obama addresses congress on health care: the time for games has passed. *The Chicago Tribune*. Retrieved December 15, 2009 from: http:// www.chicagotribune.com/news.

Phillips, N. (2009, September 11). Would plan ensure illegal immigrants? *The State*. Retrieved December 15, 2009 from: http://nl.newsbank.com/nl-search/we/Archives.

Romney taunts Democrats with memories of Carter. (2009, September 19). *Atlanta Journal Constitution*. Retrieved December 15, 2009 from: http://www.ajc.com/news.

Rosen, J. (2009, September 10). Obama offers compromises. *The State*. Retrieved December 15, 2009 from: http://nl.newsbank.com/nl-search/we/Archives.

Rosen, J. (2009, September 11). Wilson's outburst thrusts him on national stage. *The State*. Retrieved December 15, 2009 from: http://nl.newsbank.com/nlsearch/we/Archives.

Rosen, J. (2009, September 12). 2 words = nearly $2million. *The State*. Retrieved December 15, 2009 from: http://nl.newsbank.com/nl-search/we/Archives.

Rosen, J. (2009, September 13). Wilson's shout keeps on echoing. *The State*. Retrieved December 15, 2009 from: http://nl.newsbank.com/nl-search/we/Archives.

Rosen, J. (2009, September 14). I am not going to apologize again. *The State*. Retrieved December 15, 2009 from: http://nl.newsbank.com/nl-search/we/Archives.

Rosen, J. (2009, September 15). Wilson shouts; tourists stay out. *The State*. Retrieved December 15, 2009 from: http://nl.newsbank.com/nl-search/we/Archives.

Rosen, J. (2009, September 16). U.S. house punishes Wilson. *The State*. Retrieved December 15, 2009 from: http://nl.newsbank.com/nl-search/we/Archives.

Rosen, J. (2009, September 19). Wilson debate reopens deep S.C. wounds. *The State*. Retrieved December 15, 2009 from: http://nl.newsbank.com/nl-search/we/Archives.

Sabulis, T. (2009, September 13). Wilson outburst unusual. *Atlanta Journal Constitution*. Retrieved December 15, 2009 from: http://www.ajc.com/news.

Sears, D. O. (1988). Symbolic racism. In P. A. Katz & D. A. Taylor (Eds.), *Eliminating racism* (pp. 53–84). New York: Plenum.

Sidoti, L. (2009, September 27). Wrestling with how to talk about race. *The State*. Retrieved from: http://nl.newsbank.com/nl-search/we/Archives.

Silva, M. (2009, September 11). Obama, administration officials pay tribute to 9/11 victims. *The Chicago Tribune*. Retrieved December 15, 2009 from http://www.chicagotribune.com/news.

Silva, M. (2009, September 11). Downstate lawmaker takes a walk during President Barack Obama's speech. *The Chicago Tribune*. Retrieved December 15, 2009 from: http://www.chicagotribune.com/news.

Silva, M. (2009, September 21). Obama says he's got to step up his game. *The Chicago Tribune*. Retrieved December 15, 2009 from: http://www.chicagotribune.com/news.

Simon, R. (2009, September 10). Apology after calling Obama a liar. *The Chicago Tribune*. Retrieved December 15, 2009 from: http://www.chicagotribune.com/news.

Simon, R. (2009 September 11). Outrage over rep. Joe Wilson's outburst isn't dying down. *The Chicago Tribune*. Retrieved December 15, 2009 from: http://www.chicagotribune.com/news.

Smith, G. (2009, September 11). The reaction to Joe Wilson. *The State*. Retrieved December 15, 2009 from: http://nl.newsbank.com/nl-search/we/Archives.

Suggs, L. (2009, September 17). Carter: attacks unprecedented former president stands by remarks about Wilson. *Atlanta Journal Constitution*. Retrieved December 15, 2009 from: http://www.ajc.com/news.

Wallsten, P. (2009, September 16). Health care overhaul; Obama shift on insurance for Immigrants surprises advocates. *The Chicago Tribune*. Retrieved December 15, 2009 from: http://www.chicagotribune.com/news.

Werner, E. (2009, September 10). Rep. Joe Wilson is wrong. *Atlanta Journal Constitution*. Retrieved December 15, 2009 from: http://www.ajc.com/news.

Werner, E. (2009, September, 10). Obama uses iffy math on deficit pledge. *Atlanta Journal Constitution*. Retrieved December 15, 2009 from: http://www.ajc.com/news.

White House: Criticism of Obama not based on race (2009, September 17). *The State*. Retrieved December 15, 2009 from: http://nl.newsbank.com/nl-search/we/Archives.

Wise, T. (2008). *White like me*. Brooklyn: Soft Skull Press.

Wise, T. (2008, March 6). Uh-Obama: white voters and the myth of color blindedness. Retrieved November 8, 2009 from: http://www.lipmagazine.org/~timwise/Obama.html.

Zelney, J. & Rutenberger, J. (2009, September 18). Obama tries to sidestep debate on race. *The State*. Retrieved December 15, 2009 from: http://nl.newsbank.com/nl-search/we/Archives.

Discussion Questions

1. When you watch television news or read newspapers, do you notice that some sources appear to have more of a conservative slant and others a more liberal slant? What networks, publications, etc., appear to be biased? In what political direction were they biased?

2. Do you think that the coverage of the health care debate was accurate and fair? Does it appear that the media favored Obama's agenda or the Republican agenda?

3. The results of this study suggest that a city's connection to the characters involved in the story may indeed impact the amount of coverage and angle of the coverage to which the audience has access. In your opinion, how does your local newspaper cover the federal government? Have you observed differences in the coverage of the

Obama administration versus the coverage of the George W. Bush administration?

4. Based on the coverage of this event and what you learned in this study, would you say that racism was behind Wilson's outburst or was it an act of incivility? On what grounds do you base your opinion?

5. Do you think that Obama's race played a role in the opposition towards health care reformation by Republicans? Do you think things would have been different if he were white?

Assignments

1. Find the coverage of Obama's speech and Wilson's outburst in your local newspaper. Does there appear to be a slant in the coverage? Would you classify it as liberal, conservative, or neutral? Is it in line with how your state voted in the last presidential election?

2. Look at coverage of the health care debate in your local newspaper. Does there appear to be a slant in the coverage of the issues. Does the local newspaper's coverage appear to reflect an opinion on the debate?

3. During the Clinton Administration, First Lady Hillary Clinton attempted to take on health care reformation. Find coverage of that initiative. What similarities and differences do you identify in the coverage? Does Hillary's gender appear to play a role in the opposition based on the coverage you found?

4. Find an article on-line related to Obama's health care plan. Is there a place for audience commentary? What kinds of comments are readers making? Are they related to the issue or do other issues arise in the discussion? What are some of the other issues that audiences seem concerned about?

For Further Study

View a segment of the speech and Wilson's outburst:
http://www.youtube.com/watch?v=NR_Ol3VA37o.

"Outburst at Obama prompts discussion about covering cultural divides" by Angie Chuang:
http://www.poynter.org/column.asp?id=58&aid=171620.

"In S.C., one road divides two ways of thinking: Views on Obama, and race, hold firm" by Phillip Rucker:
http://www.washingtonpost.com/wp-dyn/content/article/2009/09/21/AR2009092103775.html.

"How race affects attitudes towards Obama, health care" by Ezra Klein:
http://voices.washingtonpost.com/ezraklein/2010/01/how_race_affects_attitudes_tow.html.

CHAPTER 8

The Real Price of Oppression

Fox News Coverage of the Virginia Tech Shooter

KIM M. LEDUFF

Violence in schools is nothing new in this country. The simple mention of the word Columbine brings back emotion for many Americans no matter how near or far they live from Littleton, Colorado. More recently, America was also chilled by the events that transpired on April 15, 2007, when 32 people were murdered on the campus of Virginia Polytechnic Institute and State University (Virginia Tech). At the time, it was (and still remains) the largest mass shooting in U.S. history. But perhaps what was most surprising to audiences was who was responsible for the murders. He did not fit the stereotype of the typical murderer involved in many of the high profile mass shootings covered in U.S. news—young, white, male who is socially awkward and often angry or frustrated at the time. The shooter was indeed a troubled young man, named Cho Seung-Hui. He was born in South Korea and moved to the U.S. with his family in 1992 at the age of eight years old.

This study looks at one particular Fox News special, *Crime Scene: The Virginia Tech Massacre*, as an example of how national news coverage might be used to empower audiences and improve society rather than simply reporting the facts. I don't claim that the Fox special is representative of all reports that were done in response to the Virginia Tech Shooting. This case study uses one singular example to make a point about a common pattern observed in national network coverage of tragedy. Local news and even national evening news programs are limited by the short length of their programs, usually 30 minutes. Reporters are limited by the time they have to put a story together and the short amount of time they are given in the newscast to tell the story. As a result, audiences are given headlines as opposed to in-depth reporting that not only reports the facts, but the social effects and the possible solutions.

Long-form news reports like the one-hour special on Fox News that will be examined here have an advantage. This type of explanatory journalism is usually produced over a few days or weeks. There is more time to tell the story and include important details such as background and future social implications that are left out of short reports. Unfortunately, sometimes these long-form reports fall short of their potential. This is especially problematic when a news event offers a "teachable moment" for society. In the case of Virginia Tech, the teachable moment might have been to examine what went wrong in the case of Cho Seung-Hui and how society could prevent something like this from happening again. Actually, the host Greta Van Susteren opens the special by saying that the goal of the show was to do just that, but a critical examination of the long-form report identifies where it (like other national news reports about the case) missed the mark.

Television messages and images have been examined and scrutinized by a number of media scholars. But sometimes what isn't there is equally telling. It is important to preface this research by making it clear that the researcher is in no way attempting to empathize with or excuse the actions of the perpetrator in the case of Virginia Tech. The events that transpired on the campus of Virginia Tech will remain an indelible scar in American history. But what I will attempt in this critical analysis is to construct "the back story." In other words, traditional news storytelling is flawed in that it doesn't allow much room for background. Television reports do a reasonable job of telling us breaking news and events and pointing out what's wrong with society, but seldom do these reports take the time to look at the historical, social and perhaps even psychological issues that often underlie the crime and disruption that frequently lead in the news.

Framing the News

It is important to approach this study by examining the norms of narrative storytelling in television news. All stories have frames. Entman (2007) defines framing as "the process of culling a few elements of perceived reality and assembling a narrative that highlights connections among them to promote a particular interpretation. Fully developed frames typically perform four functions: problem definition, causal analysis, moral judgment and remedy promotion" (p. 100). Television news stories in their most primitive form are scripts/narratives/tales. And like the author of any narrative there is a desire on behalf of the news story creator to set up irony, surprise and perhaps even a climax in the context of the story. The story may be told during one newscast or it may be told in a series of stories in multiple newscasts (follow-up stories).

Communications scholars (for example, Abelson, 1976, 1981; Gilliam & Iyengar, 2000) have borrowed from the field of cognitive psychology and examined the news script. According to Gilliam and Iyengar (2000), the script is defined as a "coherent sequence of events expected by the individual, involving him either as a participant or as an observer" (p. 561). Others have expanded the concept to embrace narrative or text-based scripts which appear in fiction, humor, advertising and television news reports (Black, Galambos, & Read, 1984; Graesser et al., 1980; Sulin & Dooling, 1974; all in Gilliam & Iyengar, 2000). Over time it is clear that news stories have come to adopt a certain format. These formats or formulas have become common practice for journalists. Gilliam and Iyengar (2000) point out that "in many cases script-based expectations are so well developed that when people encounter incomplete versions of the script they actually fill-in the missing information and make appropriate inferences about what must have happened" (p. 561).

So in the case of this long-form report, I will look at pieces of the script and dialogue in the Fox News special about the Virginia Tech shooting. The goal will be to determine if the script and traditional reporting conventions somehow limit the story. I will also critically examine places where the viewer is left to make inferences and draw conclusions that might counter the goals set out by the production team to understand how this happened and what we as a society can do to keep it from happening again.

The Asian Stereotype

As noted in the introduction, the ethnicity of the shooter was a surprise to American audiences. Perhaps they were surprised because their perception of Asian Americans is likely influenced by the stereotypes they encounter in American mass media. One of the biggest problems for the Asian American in American news media is that they are largely ignored. Lind (2010) describes this as "symbolic annihilation":

> The concept is rooted in two assumptions: that media content offers a form of symbolic representation of society rather than

any literal portrayal of society, and that to be represented in the media is in itself a form of power—social groups that are powerless can be relatively easily ignored, allowing the media to focus on the social groups that really matter. It's almost like implying that certain groups don't exist.

(p. 5)

There is limited coverage of Asian-American life and culture in the news media, and when there is coverage it can be quite stereotypical.

The literature indicates that historically there have been two often repeated stereotypes of Asians and Asian Americans that have prevailed in the media. According to Kawai (2005) "the model minority" is probably the most influential and prevalent stereotype for Asian Americans today. The stereotype dates back to the 1960s. The other stereotype, the yellow peril, is a Western stereotype and has a somewhat longer history and dates back to the medieval threat of Genghis Khan and the Mongolian invasion of Europe (Marchetti, 1993, in Kawai, 2005). In the U.S., however, it signified the apprehension about Asian migration and the fear that they would overtake the nation in the late nineteenth and early twentieth century (Fong, 2002; Kawai, 2005; Lee, 1999).

Kathy Rim (2007) identifies additional stereotypes of Asian Americans reinforced by American mass media. The "victim minority" is the image of Asians as victims of "discrimination, social problems and hate crimes" (p. 37). The "problem minority" is the image of Asians as "participants in crime and resistors of assimilation" (p. 37). This is a quite different approach. As Alverez, Juang, and Liang (2006) note, "Minimal attention has been devoted to the range of Asian American experiences with racism such as verbal insults, harassment, differential treatment and so forth" (p. 478). This is the case not only from a media studies perspective, but from the field of psychology as well.

Harrell (2000) identified six ways people of color might experience racism-related stress:

1. *Racism Related Stress*—major incidents of racism in areas such as housing, education, occupation, and so forth.
2. *Vicarious Racism and Stress*—observing a racist incident.
3. *Daily Racism and Micro Stress*—chronic racial slights and degradations such as being overlooked or ignored.
4. *Chronic Contextual Racism and Stress*—chronically inadequate living conditions resulting from the unequal distributions of and access to resources.

5. *Collective Racism and Stress*—an understanding of the impact of racism on one's racial group.

6. *Transgenerational Racism and Stress*—an understanding of historical traumas directed at one's group.

(p. 479)

Using Harrell's framework, this study will examine how the Fox News special conveyed the impact that these stressors might have had on Cho. It appears that all these forms of stress were part of Cho's daily existence, but did the documentary make that clear and suggest ways that American society could improve the situation for others who face similar challenges in this society? Or was this situation portrayed as a fluke and Cho as an exception to the rule?

This critical analysis will begin with a brief description of the entire news special including descriptions of important visuals, interviews and narration. According to Arthur Asa Burger (1995), this is known as the denotative reading. Once the facts are presented as they were in the story, I will then analyze how the racism-related stressors were evident in the piece and whether or not the report made it explicit for audiences how each form of stress might have contributed to the incident. This is the connotative reading, according to Berger. The goal, once again, is to examine how the media might fall short when it comes to helping audiences understand how we've gone wrong, how we can change for the better and limit the chance of tragedies such as this one from happening again.

Reading a Crime Scene: The Virginia Tech Massacre

The Fox News special begins with Van Susteren on the campus of Virginia Tech. She begins by explaining that it was the site of the largest mass murder in U.S. history with 32 victims. She explains:

> It was a horrifying massacre carried out over a span of hours by a disturbed English undergraduate who most people knew nothing about. He was a most quiet man in a quiet university town. How did it happen? Why? Was there any way to prevent it? Tonight our Fox News team will take you as far as we can into the darkest corner of Blacksburg, Virginia. The violent mind of Seung-hui Cho and the crime scene where he killed 32 people and himself.

She then goes on to talk about where Cho came from. His story is described as the classic American success story. His family moved from

South Korea to Centerville, Maryland, in 1992 when he was only eight years old. But, Van Susteren notes, "It appears there were red-flags." She then explains that his aunt describes him as an idiot and says that in an interview on Fox's *O'Reilly Factor*, a grade-school classmate said Cho made a hit list as a child, suggesting that his troubles began at an early age. According to the report, his family owned a dry cleaning business and his parents did their best to give their kids the best education possible.

The report then shifts to his college experience at Virginia Tech. His classmates and a professor talk about his demeanor in class. They say he didn't speak much, but that his writing was disturbing and very violent. A black female English professor, Lucinda Roy, describes him as "quite arrogant and deeply insecure." He wrote disturbing and very violent stories in his English classes. As a result, students approached professors with concern. Cho was referred to university counselors but refused services. But this wasn't the only time his mental health was questioned. Students notified campus police of disturbing phone calls made to a female student on campus. As a result, Van Susteren explained, "Cho's creepy behavior didn't change."

In an on-camera interview, Charlotte Peterson, a white female student at Virginia Tech, explained an encounter she had with Cho:

> He friended me on Facebook. He had sent a message … really random and weird. It wasn't until a few weeks later one of the girls in my class sent me a message warning me. Saying … Charlotte listen, this guy was stalking me. I had to get a police report against him a restraining order. So I just wanted to let you know. I saw you were friends with him and this is the guy in our class, so just be careful.

A white male campus police officer then explains that the investigation resulted in a report that Cho was depressed, but that his insight and judgment were normal. Outpatient treatment was ordered by a school counselor.

Van Susteren then notes that Cho had talked with classmates about the Columbine killers and then draws a parallel between this event and an event that took place on the campus of the University of Iowa in 1991. Gang Lew, a Chinese Ph.D. candidate, killed five people and himself on that campus. She then explains that a book about those events was found on the syllabi of a number of English courses at Virginia Tech and that perhaps Cho had encountered the story. Van Susteren describes Cho as "not a ticking time bomb, but a bomb with a fuse lit for all to see." She also notes that six days before the shooting he began shooting a video.

It is at this point that the images of Cho become important to the story. Over and over again a picture that looks like a mug shot (likely his ID photo) is shown. It is shown as an extreme close-up; only his eyes appear. There are also multiple images of guns shown with his photo. Van Susteren explains how Cho, the gunman, entered the first crime scene, a dorm. She explains that just after 7 a.m. the gunman entered a dorm and approached Emily Hilshir, a white female and "a 19-year-old freshman with a beautiful smile." The two got into a shooting match.

> Van Susteren: Some suggested they were romantically involved but this was most certainly false. She had a long-time boyfriend and no one recalls seeing Emily and Cho together. But who knows what was going on in Cho's mind.

The visual image of Cho at this point is the mug shot tinted red. Van Susteren says that in the next room is senior resident assistant Ryan Clark, a black male. She explains that the last thing Clark does on this earth is try to help Emily. Cho shoots both of them and the calls to 911 begin. Police arrive on the scene, think it is a domestic violence case and order everyone to stay put. Meanwhile, Cho, the real shooter, is preparing his next move. There was a two-hour intermission. Apparently at that time he went to his room to shoot a video that would surface later. NBC News received correspondence from Cho including photos, video and writing that may have been produced in that interval. His roommate Karan Grewel explains to Fox how lucky he feels to have not been there in the room at that point.

At this point the video made by Cho is shown. In it he says:

> You had a hundred billion chances and ways to have avoided today. … Crucify me! You loved inducing cancer in my head, terrorizing my heart and ripping my soul all this time.

Van Susteren then says:

> This is the last you'll hear of Cho's voice tonight. Fox News has made the decision to broadcast only limited amounts of [Cho's] video and only when necessary.

She then begins the next segment:

> The non-stop rantings of the madman who was teased for mumbling in grade school and who spoke so little in three years at

Virginia Tech that classmates assumed he wasn't fluent in English were express mailed to NBC.

In the next block she refers to Cho as a lunatic and explains that he killed, paused, re-grouped, re-armed and mailed out a package. But she explains there were glimmers of heroism in the midst of the chaos. An FBI agent explained that there was nothing spur of the moment about Cho's actions. After a two-hour break, he walked across campus, uninterrupted, to Norris Hall. He headed to a German class where he killed a 35-year-old white male professor, Jamie Bishop, who is described as "destined to be a success." Meanwhile, Virginia Tech police were after the wrong person.

She notes that "the evil of Cho was overshadowed by the courage of average citizens." She explains, "As the deranged killer walked to the second floor … he walked into a classroom and fired on 11 students and a professor" (who was an East Indian male). He then walked into a French class and killed four more. Van Susteren explains how students and faculty made efforts to block doors and thwart Cho's attempts. She also explains how one professor who was a Holocaust survivor used his own body to shield his students and was killed.

Most of the sound bites incorporated in this segment were from white male and female students who either witnessed the events or knew the victims. Van Susteren then explains that he killed himself and an image that he sent to the news station with a gun to his head is used for the visual.

The final block begins with Van Susteren explaining that "we need a frank discussion on campus and across the county about how this happened and how we can prevent it from happening again. Virginia Tech will be a name like Columbine or Kent State that conjures up a wound in American life." She goes on to talk about the Convocation held on campus, attended by President and Mrs. George W. Bush. She explains that funerals were held across the nation and abroad for the victims. She notes that Cho's sister issued a statement on behalf of his family. Van Susteren then questions where things might have gone wrong: "Was the bloodshed necessary? Should the university have been harder on him for stalking? Were there issues with counseling? Was security lax? Should police have been more aggressive?" The story then shifts to what the public thinks. According to a poll, 19 percent of registered voters think we need tighter gun control. But 71 percent still think that even with it a madman like Cho will find a gun.

She then says that students who knew the killer and how strange he was wondered if they were somehow responsible. But Ed Falco, Cho's play-writing teacher, explained:

We all saw that he was troubled and we all recognized the violence in his writing. Please hear me when I say this: It was our responsibility not yours. There is no need to add to the pain and guilt.

Van Susteren ends the piece by reiterating that society and individuals need to take precautions to keep something like this from happening again. She explains that Cho is the guilty one as we see a montage of the victims. She closes the piece by noting that Virginia Tech awarded degrees to all the victims posthumously.

As noted in the literature review, Harrell (2000) identifies multiple levels of stress that might impact members of minority groups in society. The Fox News special begins by suggesting that the goal of the piece is to see what may have gone wrong and what we can do to prevent it from happening again. By the end it removes all the blame from society and instead places it all back on the perpetrator as though all the issues that led to his actions developed in a vacuum.

Each form of stress identified by Harrell (2000) was evident in the piece, but whether or not the story made it clear for audiences that these stresses led to Cho's actions is not always evident. While this news special identifies the stressors, it failed to connect the dots and explain how the compounded stress led Cho to destruction of himself and others. Instead, he was depicted as an outsider who was an exception to the rule of the model minority. The media often depicts Asian people as docile and undetectable in society. In this case, Cho is depicted as making his presence known—but for all the wrong reasons. The report could have done a better job of helping audiences understand that by passively accepting stereotypes, they are not taking an active role in preventing something like this from happening again.

Racism Related Stress

According to Harrell (2000), one example of racism related stress often takes place at the institutional level. The education environment is one place where one might experience it, and in an environment at a mainstream higher educational institution there are stresses that minority students are likely to face. In the case of Cho, he did not fit the mold of the "model minority." In the news story his classmates' reports indicate that they didn't see him as brilliant and passive in the classroom. Because he was quiet, most assumed he couldn't speak English. One teacher even described him as "quite arrogant and deeply insecure." Perhaps he didn't appear to make an effort to quietly assimilate. As a result, Cho apparently felt ostracized by his peers. That was clear in the video message he created that was briefly shown in the Fox News special.

Previous research indicates that the "model minority" stereotype alone places great stress on young people of Asian descent. Wong and Halgin (2006) noted results of a survey that indicated Asian students "do not like having expectations pinned on then, believing that such labeling marginalizes them from mainstream society" (p. 40). It was clear based on how students and even teachers described Cho that he was seen as odd and in this narrative his oddity was indicated by the fact that he didn't fit the model minority stereotype.

"Vicarious Racism," "Daily Racism" and Stress

Vicarious racism has to do with observing a racist incident and *daily racism* has to do with the first hand experience of racism. Both also lead to stress on behalf of the individual experiencing the racism. For the purposes of this analysis, these two forms of racism were examined in combination because they are closely related. The video of Cho was an expression of a young man in serious pain.

> Cho: You had a hundred billion chances and ways to have avoided today. … Crucify me! You loved inducing cancer in my head, terrorizing my heart and ripping my soul all this time.

It was quite clear from the sound bites from classmates as well as the descriptions by Van Susteren that the pain he felt was no figment of his imagination. Classmates thought he couldn't speak English because he was quiet. His advances toward white female colleagues were consistently rejected because he was seen as weird. This is not to say that he did not have personal issues, but perhaps the way he was treated on campus compounded his mental health issues. He clearly felt alienated and ostracized.

Nowhere in the piece were audiences told about the campus climate for Asian students. It would have been helpful and useful to hear what other students of Asian descent experienced on campus. Was the environment welcoming? Or did they too have experiences similar to Cho? Is there the possibility that Cho saw his peers being treated in a similar fashion? Is this something common on college campuses across the country?

It is a typical news convention to tell a story with an ending that leaves audiences with a figurative "good taste in their mouths." And even in this tragic case the story ended with an attempt to wrap the story up in a neat little package for the viewer, rather than investigating the possibility that something larger was at stake. Van Susteren poses the notion that students who knew the killer and how strange he was wondered if they were some-how responsible. This is immediately followed by a sound bite from one of Cho's teachers, Ed Falco, who says:

> We all saw that he was troubled and we all recognized the violence in his writing. Please hear me when I say this: It was our responsibility not yours. There is no need to add to the pain and guilt.

Who is he referring to when he says "our"? Professors? University officials? Adults in society? It is unclear. Van Susteren then ends the piece by reiterating that society and individuals need to take precautions to keep something like this from happening again. But as far as what those precautions are? That is never addressed in the piece.

Chronic Contextual Racism and Stress

Perhaps the greatest factor missing from this story is that no one bothered to examine why Cho refused counseling services. According to Chou (2007), Asian-American youth have the highest incidents of teenage depression. Perhaps Cho's behavior had cultural roots rather than being simply an act of defiance. For some ethnic groups, the need for counseling services is considered a weakness. In no way did the story address that issue. Wong and Halgin (2006) suggest that mental health counselors need to realize the immense pressure that some young Asian people feel to live up to the model minority stereotype "as well as their shame and reluctance to reveal personal difficulties when they do not live up to this model minority image"(p. 48). The story alludes to the fact that counselors who saw Cho in essence missed something, but the report does not delve into how often that happens.

Chou (2007) notes that she interviewed Asian Americans "from several different ethnic groups, ages, geographic locations and recurring themes prevailed … All these Asian Americans shared a common thread of marginalization of identity that affects their lives" (pp. 6–7). She notes that they had similar coping patterns: "These similarities force a critical look at the alarming rates of mental illness within the Asian community. Some techniques used to deal with discrimination are overachievement assimilation, memory suppression, and hopeless with-drawal" (p. 7).

Collective Racism and Stress

The documentary attempts to draw parallels between Cho and another Asian student who wreaked havoc on a different university campus years ago. Gang Lew was a Chinese Ph.D. candidate at the University of Iowa in 1991. He killed five people on campus and then killed himself. But instead of focusing on the similar forms of stress and racism that the two men may have experienced, the connection is attributed to the possibility that Cho may have encountered a book about the incident at the University of Iowa during his college experience. Apparently, a book about the incident was on the syllabi of a number of English courses at Virginia Tech. We aren't told if Cho was in any of those classes, but the inference is made that he was. Chou (2007) explains that the model minority stereotype "detracts from the hardships Asian Americans are facing as they try to become socially integrated into US society ... Asian Americans still feel isolated and inadequate" (p. 2). This was something that could have been addressed if the audience had been allowed to hear from other Asian students. But even in this case, they remained invisible.

Transgenerational Racism and Stress

From the beginning of the documentary Cho is portrayed as a product of his family, but his family is never given a voice. The only thing we hear is that his aunt thought he was an idiot. Cho's family fit the stereotype of the model minority according to the report. Van Susteren describes their story as "the classic American success story." They moved to this country and opened a business (a cleaners, reinforcing a common stereotype for Asians in this country). Their goal was to work hard to provide a better life for their kids. According to Wong and Halgin (2006),

> Since the 1960's the popular press and media have portrayed Asian Americans as the "model minority"—successful minorities who have quietly moved to the pinnacle of success in various contexts through hard work and determination. Asian Americans are often depicted on television as restaurant or convenience store owners who arrived in the United States with no money and worked long hours to finally own a piece of the American dream or as eye glass-wearing awkward nerds who spend countless hours in the library reading math and science books.
>
> (p. 38)

Here the audience was allowed to fill in the blanks, because they've heard the story before—Cho's family did everything right, but he didn't live up to expectations. Wong and Halgin (2006) also note that they have found that "for Korean students in particular academic success is seen as a way to climb the social ladder and they often feel obligated to do so for their parents" (p. 41).

This was yet another instance of how what wasn't included in the coverage was as telling as what was. Cho's family was not given a voice in this piece. In the end, Van Susteren did note that his sister issued a statement on the family's behalf, but the content of the statement was not included in the story. There was no mention of his family's take on the tragedy or an opportunity to hear from them (or anyone of Asian descent) in the story. Once again, this group is depicted as silent.

Learning from the Media

Stearns (2008) looked at the media circus surrounding the Virginia Tech shooting in his article "Texas and Virginia: A bloodied window into changes in American public life":

> Media representatives descended like wolves, including TV anchorpersons for two of the three leading networks. Finding relatively little to report about directly, given the fact that the incident was over and the scene sealed off, commentary focused on often replayed shots of exterior scenes and peripheral police activity, spiced above all by constant efforts to elicit emotional reactions from students and others near the scene. If this weren't enough, and many commentators later argued that the actual substance was quite limited and quickly tiresome, the visual media but also the press, sought to stir things up by shock head-lines, provocative music, and efforts to imply that someone must be called to account for such a tragedy.
>
> (p. 303)

Television has the power to make people think about things, but often news organizations do not utilize that power to its full advantage. It would be naïve to suggest that in all cases media practitioners have the time or the wherewithal to produce deeply analytical and critical news stories that ponder the best way to improve society. That is simply not the nature of the daily news beast. But on occasion there are stories that demand a little extra time and a little extra effort in hopes of preventing history from repeating itself.

The documentary serves as a good model for what the long-form news story might emulate. Yes, these are two different forms of media with differing conventions, but as network news organizations look for ways to improve their product and hold on to audiences, perhaps they might be open minded and look at ways to improve existing conventions.

Mass media practitioners need to identify teachable moments that help viewers think twice about what they think and how they behave. There were multiple lessons to be learned in the case of Virginia Tech. There were lessons about racism and oppression as well as how we as a society sometimes drive people to dark places whether intentionally or not. Very often stereotypes that we encounter in media determine how we interact with others in the real world and we may not even be conscious of it. In Michael Moore's documentary *Bowling for Columbine* there is one poignant segment in which he talks to shock rocker Marilyn Manson about the fact that many blamed him and his music for the events that transpired at Columbine. Moore asked Manson what he would tell the shooters if he'd had a chance to talk to them. In response he simply said he wouldn't talk—he would listen. That seems to be exactly what Cho needed—the opportunity to express the isolation and pain that he felt. When NBC News got the video from Cho they made the choice to show it. The network was immediately challenged by the public who wanted to hear more about the victims in this tragedy rather than the person responsible. The audience response was admirable and understandable, and NBC's decision to pull Cho's video was logical. Cho's actions are indefensible, but the short clip of his video that was incorporated in this story made it clear that this young man was in serious pain and mental distress. Further investigation into what led him to this place might have been beneficial to audiences and truly led to the goal that Van Susteren set out to accomplish at the beginning of the special: "How did it happen? Why? Was there any way to prevent it?"

References

Abelson, R. P. (1976). Script processing in attitude formation and decisionmaking. In J. S. Carroll & J .W. Payne (Eds.), *Cognition and social behavior* (pp. 33–45). Hillsdale, NJ: Lawrence Erlbaum.

Abelson, R. P. (1981). The psychological status of the script concept. *American Psychologist*, *36*, 715–729.

Alvarez, Alvin, Juang, Linda, & Liang, Christopher. (2006). Asian Americans and racism: when bad things happen to "model minorities." *Cultural Diversity and Ethnic Minority Psychology*, *12*(3), 477–492.

Burger, Arthur Asa. (1995). *Cultural criticism: a primer of key concepts*. Thousand Oaks: Sage.

Chou, Rosalind. (2007). *Malady of the model minority: White racism's assault on the Asian American psyche*. Conference Paper, American Sociological Association Meeting, 1–20.

Entman, Robert. (2007). Framing bias: media in the distribution of power. *Journal of Communication* *57*, 163–173.

Fong, T. P. (2002). *The contemporary Asian American experience: Beyond the model minority* (2nd ed.). Upper Saddle River, NJ: Prentice Hall.

Gilliam Jr., Franklin, D. & Iyengar, Shanto (2000). Prime suspects: the influence of local television news on the viewing public. *American Journal of Political Science*, 44 (3, July), 560–574.

Harrell, S. P. (2000). A multidimensional conceptualization of racism-related stress: Implications for the well-being of people of color. *American Journal of Orthopsychiatry*, 70, 42–57.

Kawai, Yuko. (2005). Stereotyping Asian Americans: The dialectic of the model minority and the Yellow Peril. *The Howard Journal of Communication*, 16, 109–130.

Lee, R. (1999). *Orientals: Asian Americans in popular culture.* Philadelphia: Temple University Press.

Lind, Rebecca Ann. (2010). *Race/gender media. Considering diversity across audience content and producers.* Boston: Allyn & Bacon.

Rim, Kathy, (2007). Model, victim, or problem minority? Examining the socially constructed identities of Asian-origin ethnic groups in California media. *Asian American Policy Review*, 16 (June).

Stearns, Peter N. (2008). Texas and Virginia: A bloodied window into changes in American public life. *Journal of Social History*, Winter, 299–318.

Wong, Frieda & Halgin, Richard. (2006). The "model minority": Bane or blessing for Asian Americans. *Journals of Multicultural Counseling and Development*, 34, 38–49.

Discussion Questions

1. Asians have consistently been stereotyped as "the model minority" in American mass media. Can you think of stories about Asian Americans commonly covered by the local news in your state or community? Do the frames fall in line with this stereotype?

2. Mass media scholars suggest that when audiences see repeated images and frames in the media, they begin to associate certain groups of people with certain behaviors. When you heard about the Virginia Tech shooting, whom did you imagine was responsible? Why do you think you imagined the person you did?

3. There has been concern since the shootings at Columbine High School in Littleton, Colorado, that it is dangerous to cover school shootings for fear of copycat events. What are your thoughts on this matter? Are there ways to cover these events so that audiences can learn how to prevent these incidents from occurring again?

Assignments

1. Watch Michael Moore's *Bowling for Columbine*. This long-form documentary is an examination of what might have led to the events that took place at Columbine and examines why violence is a problem in the U.S. What do you think of the way Moore examined the issues? He is often criticized for being subjective and staging events in his documentaries. Did you see examples of this? What was the value of the in-depth investigation that took place in the long-form documentary as opposed to shorter news stories covering similar events?

2. Violent events have occurred at a number of schools and on college campuses over the years. As a class, assign groups to an event or pick one event and find any news articles related to it, either on-line or in the newspaper archives. You will likely find breaking news coverage of the violent events as they unfolded, but how often do you find follow-up coverage of what might have led to the violence? Why is this important and useful?

For Further Study

1. Roy, Lucinda. (2009). *No Right to Remain Silent: The Tragedy at Virginia Tech*. Harmony Press.
2. Kellner, Douglas. (2008). *Guys and Guns Amok: Domestic Terrorism and School Shootings from the Oklahoma City Bombing to the Virginia Tech Massacre*. Paradigm Publishers.
3. CBS. *60 Minutes*. "*The Mind of an Assassin*" (air date: April 22, 2007) (DVD).

CHAPTER 9

"Nappy-Headed Hos"

Media Framing, Blame Shifting and the Controversy Over Don Imus' Pejorative Language

HAZEL JAMES COLE AND CHERYL D. JENKINS

> I'm a woman, and I'm someone's child ... I achieve a lot. And unless they've given this name, a "ho," a new definition, then that is not what I am.
>
> (Kia Vaughn, Rutgers University basketball player)

Members of the 2007 Rutgers women's basketball team that should be best known for "a gritty season that brought them within a game of the championship" are instead, according to syndicated newspaper columnist Leonard Pitts (2007), "famous as the objects of a misbegotten attempt at banter between radio shock jock Don Imus and his radio broadcast producer Bernard McGuirk" (n.p.). In a column on the incident, Pitts recounts the dialogue between Imus and McGuirk as follows:

> "That's some rough girls from Rutgers ... Man, they got tattoos ..."
> "Some hard-core hos," observes McGuirk.
> "That's some nappy-headed hos there," says Imus.
>
> (n.p.)

Those words, commercially broadcast on the *Imus in the Morning* radio show on April 4, 2007, stunned not only the black community and women across this country, but mainstream audiences as well. The result was a firestorm of controversy focusing on race, gender and language in America. The women's basketball team comprised of eight African-American and two Caucasian players would become part of the national debate around Imus' offensive remarks. Further, the controversy would spark Civil Rights activists like the Reverend Al Sharpton, president of the National Action Network, to call for Imus' resignation.

Imus' remarks, considered derogatory, sexist and racist, were reviled by members of the media and the general public alike. As such, the media's coverage of this controversy, the cancellation of Imus' show by the MSNBC cable television network following his remarks, and his subsequent firing by CBS Corporation after a brief suspension by the network became an area of important critical inquiry, particularly in media studies.

The purpose of this chapter is to examine not only how the mass media covered the events that encompass the Imus controversy, including his remarks, his apology and his firing, but, more specifically, the media's shift from focusing coverage on Imus' controversial statements and subsequent repercussions to that of the tribulations of the hip hop culture and the use of misogynistic language in song lyrics by rap artists following the public apology by Imus.

Using the theoretical underpinnings of critical, cultural discourse analysis, this chapter incorporates *framing analysis*, examining specific media events concerning the controversy as texts to explain the motivations of the media to describe certain facts, themes and words to garner maximum interest among viewers and readers. The Imus controversy set the stage for a larger moral discussion of black language in the media and music industry with the focus shifting from racism and white America to black rappers and sexist, misogynistic language in rap music. Racial insensitivity is not uncommon in America or in the media; however, Imus' borrowing of the black race's cultural signifiers proved to be a nearly fatal, career-altering mistake for the white, 66-year-old radio personality known as the "I-Man."

Shifting the Blame

When examining the coverage related to this controversy, it is apparent that hip hop became the scapegoat for Imus' use of racist and sexist language. Moreover, Imus' obvious use of "blame shifting" in this controversy and the media's framing of this incident to validate that shift is both a palpable case of image restoration as well as an example of the ideological construction of reality. This shift in media focus has ideological and functional implications that were not explored in coverage of the controversy.

Indeed, media framing is the essential theoretical structure that guides our examination of the coverage of this media event. Because journalists determine the approach to coverage of news events and issues in the media, framing affects how readers and viewers comprehend those events and issues. Journalists routinely engage in the process of "framing news" or in organizing ideas for making sense of relevant events and suggesting what is at issue and, as such, examining this process provides critical context for the discussion of coverage of controversial topics like the Don Imus comments. The ideological aspect of this issue is also important to note because dominant ideologies often provide essential guiding frameworks in critical analyses and discourse. According to Benshoff and Griffin (2004), "Dominant ideological functions that exist in society and structured in a largely pervasive way, aid in how a culture thinks about itself and others, as well as who and what it upholds as worthy, meaningful, true, and valuable" (p. 9).

The Don Imus controversy is a classic example of the dominant ideological view that has functioned in American society since the country's founding. Critical scholars as well as postmodern feminists like hooks (1994), Gaines (1986), and Mies (1998) refer to "white patriarchal capitalism" as a dominant ideology functioning optimally in U.S. society that structures how we think about ourselves and others. This ideology is more commonly associated with the critique of American films and suggests that the values of the dominant culture are "hierarchally placed to maintain and perpetuate the values that uphold exploitative and oppressive systems" (hooks, 1994, p. 117). This ideology works to "naturalize the idea that wealthy white men deserve greater social privilege and to protect those privileges by naturalizing various beliefs that degrade other groups—thus making it seem obvious that those groups should not be afforded the same privileges" (Benshoff & Griffin, 2004, p. 9).

From a hegemonic standpoint, the American mass media is still a white-male-dominated corporate structure. The initial media response to the Imus controversy was minimal compared to the eventual more "sympathetic" regard for his words once he, the MSNBC network, its parent company and the show's sponsors were challenged by activists across the country. The seeming lack of fear of retribution for his comments as a shock jock (be they offensive or racially insensitive) speaks to the notion of a greater social privilege for certain segments of society. The traditional pattern that follows this "protection of social privilege" and the protection of power in a "white patriarchal capitalistic society" is protest from marginalized groups that suffer from the glass ceiling created in the corporate culture that exists in a "privileged society." African Americans "marched" in front of the offices of MSNBC, and political activist Sharpton led the charge for the firing of Imus. Sharpton's response is in line with hook's (1994) analysis of race representation:

> If black folks are to move forward in our struggle for liberation, we must confront the legacy of this unreconciled grief, for it has been the breeding ground for profound nihilistic despair. We must collectively return to a radical political vision of social change rooted in a love ethic and seek once again to convert masses of people, black and nonblack.
>
> (p. 246)

The charge of activism by Sharpton goes further than benefiting one marginalized group, as those who protested Imus' actions were from various minority groups in society.

What followed the protests and subsequent firing was a shift in the rhetoric about Imus' comments and just where those who protested should direct their anger. In an effort to minimize the damage to his now bruised reputation, Imus issued an apology through the media to those he offended by his comments. Public figures and celebrities commonly issue apologies following controversial matters that play out in public as part of the process of image rebuilding or restoration in defense of their claim of innocence and/or alleged ignorance. The process or function of crisis management uses aspects of public relations to "minimize harm to an organization or individual in emergency situations that could cause irreparable damage" (Williams & Olaniran, 1998, p. 387). Imus' apology was part of a traditional function of public relations that would emerge as a necessary means to showcase him in a light that is uncharacteristic of his behavior—one where he uses the media to communicate his apology for the error of his ways.

Communication scholar Benoit (1995) argues "apology/excuse/account behavior is a common feature of human behavior" since attacks on a person's image is a serious matter (p. ix). Benoit suggests that "our image or reputation is extremely vital to us" and whenever that image is threatened, "we feel compelled to offer explanations, defenses, justifications, rationalizations, apologies, or excuses for our behavior" (p. 2). Initially problematic for Imus after issuing his apology was the question of sincerity by some in the media. Associated Press writer Jocelyn Noveck (2007) noted in her article, "Imus critics say apologies are hollow," that apologizing has little merit if there are no consequences for actions. She writes, "It's a familiar dance that plays out ever more frequently in our popular culture. A public figure transgresses, and we wait to dissect the apology. Was it sincere enough? Contrite enough? Specific enough? Did he feel our pain?" (n.p.).

Further complicating the matter was Imus' use of the apology to shift the blame to certain segments of the African-American community, a behavior that served his goal of protecting his reputation. Blaney and Benoit (2001) list "denial" and "evading responsibility" as major categories in image repair strategies. The denial category has a subcategory of "shifting blame" which Blaney and Benoit state is an "attempt to lay responsibility for the transgression on another part" (p. 16). The categories are part of a larger model of image restoration that has two guiding assumptions. First, "communication is best conceptualized as a goal-directed activity" and second, "maintaining a positive reputation is one of the central goals of communication" (Benoit, 1995, p. 63).

The model of image restoration is a central function in Imus' attempt to regain credibility and restore his personal and professional reputation. The use of apology in this particular communicative event ultimately served as a strategy to 1) rebuild his image, and 2) pit Imus up against the corporate structure that provided the revenue and airwaves for his dissemination of sometimes divisive and controversial rhetoric. Specifically, for MSNBC, as a white-dominated corporation that represents the dominant ideology in society, managing crises well, even if it means firing a controversial white male, will result in longevity, credibility and, essentially, a healthy bottom line for the corporation. MSNBC had to determine how to emerge as a leader in managing race relations in the early twenty-first century. The company had a lot to lose if it made a misstep in its judgment regarding consequences for Imus, specifically the loss of sponsors and advertising revenue. MSNBC executives had to make a decision to show its stakeholders, employees, advertisers, sponsors, key publics and its competitors that making a firm, necessary decision was in the best interest of all. This was essentially a form of apologizing and serves the goal of illuminating crisis while also "maintaining a positive reputation."

Don Imus, on the other hand, tried apologizing by shifting blame in order to protect his reputation. Benoit (1995) posits that the *Theory of Image Restoration* "focuses on one particular goal in discourse: restoring or protecting one's reputation" (p. 71). Further, Benoit suggests that for one's reputation to be threatened, a "reprehensible act must have been committed" (p. 72). For Imus, his use of racist, sexist language met this criterion. For MSNBC, a lack of consequential action would have been reprehensible and unconscionable, a risk to its reputation it could not afford.

Both aspects of image restoration played out in the media and, thus, both Imus and his corporate sponsors were able to effectively carry out an important aspect of crisis management and image re-building, which is the use of the mass media to construct realities for their audiences. In the case of the Don Imus controversy the media serves as both channel and audience in the flow of message dissemination. Imus used media to communicate his rhetoric and apology and, in turn, media outlets and major media figures like Oprah Winfrey used their platforms to discuss the very thing that Imus blamed for his racist and sexist comments, the hip hop community. In this instance Winfrey and others begin to validate the shift in blame, specifically Imus' assertion that the hip hop community should bear the brunt of the blame for his scandal. There is an abrupt shift in coverage of this controversy following Imus' apology that makes the news event more of a "black cultural" issue and less of a "racist and sexist" one.

As such, the subsequent framing of the Imus controversy by the media and the dual role this powerful cultural industry takes on in this controversy subtly undergirds the notion that the media became a "target audience" that was manipulated into constructing a reality that Imus' racist language was a part of a bigger problem in the African-American community's sub-culture known as hip hop. Imus used media to defend his image and reputation by shifting the blame away from his racist, sexist remarks and cleverly redirects the controversy to a now mediated discourse on the "in group" language of the hip hop culture; the media in turn creates momentum not necessarily about Imus' comments, but follows the blame to the hip hop community. This framing of the media event suggests that the more relevant issue at hand has broader context than initially thought. This point is important to note because journalists' framing of issues—that which is deemed newsworthy—provides the critical background necessary to make sense of news events in general.

Framing and Issues of Race

In general, news framing is the process by which media gatekeepers define and construct issues or events. Literature on media framing suggests that news and information have no intrinsic value unless embedded in a meaningful context which organizes and lends it coherence (Griffin & Dunwoody, 1997; London, 1993). As such, framing provides a way to make sense of relevant events and shapes the way issues are viewed.

When journalists frame information, they organize the concepts that reside in texts and public discourse and provide the reference points in which viewers make sense of issues like crime, natural disasters and ideological debates. This allows both the originators and the recipients of the message to make sense of the information conveyed. Moreover, to frame is to "select some aspects of a perceived reality and make them more salient in such a way as to promote a particular problem definition, causal interpretation, moral evaluation and/or treatment recommendation" (Entman, 1993, p. 52). So, according to Entman and Rojecki (2000), to suggest that a news report "framed" a drive-by shooting as a gang war story means that the account included aspects of the event that summoned an audience's stored cognitive perceptions about gang members.

In addition, frames originate both within and outside of news organizations. Influences that may affect the way media frame issues and events can include journalists' personal values, ideological constraints imposed on the medium, and market forces (Kraeplin, 2008). Richardson and Lancendorfer (2004) state that media frames are important in two respects: 1) they reflect the larger public discourse, and 2) they can influence public opinion. Poindexter, Smith, and Heider (2003) note that "much of the power of framing comes from its ability to define the terms of a debate without the audience realizing it is taking place" (p. 527).

Moreover, framing is the process by which a communication source constructs and defines a social or political issue for its audience (Nelson, Oxley, & Clawson, 1997). Framing itself becomes a political phenomenon because "the extent to which certain dimensions are stressed, or framed, over others" contributes to the public's interpretation of specific events (Haider-Markel, Delehanty, & Beverlin, 2007, p. 588). Research has increasingly begun to examine the process through which the mass media highlight varying aspects of topics to build and maintain issue salience over time. Unfortunately, some of those constructs are overtly biased when it comes to covering news events that feature minorities and people of low economic status. Most industry leaders today acknowledge the media's shortcomings in covering minority communities, issues of race and racism, and ideological and political divides between racial and ethnic groups.

As such, the metaphoric frames that make up most media coverage, which, according to Watson (2007), are so because they are imprecise and allow for a degree of flexibility, are continuous representations influenced by ideological, social and cultural cues. Hall (1990) states that media are part of the dominant means of ideological production. What they produce is precisely representations of the social world, images, descriptions, explanations and frames for understanding how the world is and why it works as it is said and shown to work. The obvious aspects of cultural influence and differences affect interpretations of media frames in a way that media scholars have highlighted in varying degrees. In particular, the treatment of race and issues of racism when covered by the media reveal intrinsic attitudes of media professionals that are inherent in societal ideologies that may already be present.

Janice Peck (1994) suggests that the treatment of racism, as revealed in her study on a series about race on the syndicated *The Oprah*

Winfrey Show, draws on ideologies of race that members of society see and feel every day. Her study focused on how the show framed popular discourse on race:

> These are part of the material social conditions into which we are born, and within which we acquire racialized identities, develop an understanding of others based on racial positioning, and interpret social relationships through racial categories … We have to speak through the ideologies which are active in our society and which provide us a means of "making sense" of social relations and our place in them.
>
> (p. 92)

Other scholars have suggested that coverage of sensitive issues relating to class, poverty, crime and race in this country, such as the Imus controversy, the treatment of young defendants in Jena, Louisiana, and most notably the Hurricane Katrina disaster and its aftermath, reveal that a deep racial divide continues to exist in the United States, one that permeates all aspects of society, including the media (Haider-Markel et al., 2007; Kraeplin, 2008; Lavelle & Feagin, 2006; Morris, 2006). The perpetual image of poor African Americans wading through polluted flood waters and being described by media correspondents as "looters" and "refugees" implies the mainstream media's tendency to use overt racial bias when reporting about segments of the minority community.

In the instance of the Don Imus controversy, media coverage that placed blame on the hip hop community, which consists of large numbers of minority artists and fans, rocked journalistic convention that news could escape the influence of modern or aversive racism, an influential theory that proposes that while most white Americans today consciously adhere to egalitarian ideals and perceive themselves as non-prejudiced, they may have recognized negative feelings about blacks (or other minority groups) that sometimes lead to racist behavior (Entman & Rojecki, 2000). The concept of modern racism emerged from social scientists' observing the contradiction between white Americans' endorsement of racial equality in the abstract and their often-intense opposition to concrete policies designed to produce more equality. Entman (1990) states that modern racists express antagonism, resentment and anger toward blacks' interests. He posits that local television news and other forms of media promote modern racism even as (and particularly because) it delegitimizes old-fashioned racism.

As the stories about the Don Imus controversy began to accumulate the first week after the comments aired, it became evident that the emotional response patterns of audience members to the controversy were determined by their own cultural and ideological positions in society. Because of the charge of racism, the aspect of race and how it is socialized and legitimized in the society is an integral component in analyzing message decoding by the audience. Although framing studies typically are concerned with how people's opinions are affected by opposing ways of presenting, or framing, an issue or event, Gross and D'Ambrosio (2004) posit that different frames also lead to different patterns of emotional response by receivers of mediated messages. The researchers found that predispositions can mediate the effect of frames on opinion and that frames can alter the relationship between predispositions and emotions of audiences or readers.

As such, how news events and issues are packaged and presented by journalists can fundamentally affect how readers and viewers understand those events and issues and react to them. This framing effect is the result of news organizations producing stories that take an episodic rather than a thematic perspective toward the events they cover. Instead of explaining the general background and implications of issues, news reports emphasize the most recent and attention-getting developments (Price & Tewksbury, 1997), for example, "covering unemployment by focusing on vivid examples of people who have lost their jobs while failing to link unemployment to any broader social, economic, or political process. Social issues are thus treated mainly as discreet and isolated events" (p. 483).

Douglas (1995) asserts that this ambiguous perspective offered by the mainstream media when covering issues directly or indirectly related to race fans "mutual mistrust and resentment by sensationalizing racism" (p. 19). News coverage that does not include depth or profundity on such subject matter is at risk of ignoring the powerful role that institutional and systemic phenomena play in racial issues and the oppression of minority groups in American society.

Moreover, the media shift in coverage from the racist rhetoric of Don Imus to the ills and misogyny of the hip hop culture furthers the notion of the media's protection of a "privileged society" from ridicule while simultaneously demonizing the cultural expressions of a marginalized group and speaks to the ideological functions of contemporary American society. In all fairness, the eventual focus of the Imus controversy as a result of how the media would ultimately frame it was an aspect of hip hop that had been discussed and theorized previously. The debate over rap lyrics, the music that provides the perpetual framework of the hip hop culture, is an ongoing one that had been carried out on smaller media stages before.

According to Lorraine Ali in *Newsweek*, the Don Imus controversy "reopened the perennial debate over misogyny and offensive language in hip-hop" (April 26, 2007, n.p.). At issue in this instance is that the disparaging words came from the mouth of a white man on federally-regulated airways and that Imus had used what some may consider "in-group" language as socially acceptable commercial speech in mainstream arenas. Journalist and commentator Roland Martin (2007) noted that Don Imus made the fatal mistake that many do. Martin states in the article, "When you aren't part of a certain group, you can get in trouble for saying the wrong thing" (p. 80).

Once Imus "crossed the racist and sexist line" something had to be done. Imus was confronted by activists who challenged his sponsors and his networks. Sharpton, who is known as a "megaphone for the voiceless and an advocate for those in need" (National Action Network, 2007), led a coalition of public figures using activism and advocacy as a way to "represent" for marginalized citizens with a mission to get Imus off the air.

Framing News and Race

In the vein of discussing the media coverage in a critical and culturally inclusive way this chapter follows the approach of framing analysis critiqued by Durham (2008), who states that by "treating news frames as evidence of a system that defines what we know and how we know it, it is possible to consider the mass mediated process of framing as a social process that enables society to function" (p. 123). Further, the process of framing makes social interaction more likely because "as an exercise in construction of meaning, it codifies social experiences or voices into discrete units of social meanings," which are the frames. Durham posits that traditional studies that examine how news is selected are limited in their approach because they do not take into account that news information is subjective in nature and that the information that eventually becomes news, comes from diverse places and in different forms: "The diversity of this raw information often means that the news must be constructed according to schemes of interpretation and of relevance which are those of the bureaucratic institutions that are sources of the news or which process events" (p. 123).

Durham examines the underlying philosophical and ideological bases of news making as a rational process and interprets what journalism as a social practice actually means to questions of constructed reality, how it arrives at that meaning, and other implications for journalism. Further, the social power of journalism, according to Durham, lies precisely in the inclusion of certain voices in normative social discourse and the exclusion of others. As such, Durham considers a departure from traditional empirical analysis of framing, suggesting that more macro-level versions of framing analysis by researchers like Gitlin (1980), who focused on the frame as the site where dominant social power is produced, provides a basis for considering other nonempirical, or "interpretive" ways of knowing about social meaning, including concepts of framing.

To go beyond the previous considerations of what gets into the news and what gets left out, Durham uses Jameson's concept of ideologically discrete "social narratives" and proposes:

> All social meanings do not depend on their being included or excluded from an empirical meaning system or news frame. Conversely, while the literature on framing acknowledges the dichotomous nature of the framing process nowhere is attention paid to the social meanings that do not survive as frames … these meanings are important, especially as understanding them can tell us more about how framing happens within a holistic context. Instead of being included or excluded, Jameson proposes that it is possible for meanings to exist apart from an empirically ordered universe.
>
> (Durham, 2008, p. 127)

As the coverage of the Imus controversy basically shifted from that of an incident of disparaging remarks to a discussion on cultural issues within the African-American community, the ideological implications of that framing by the media takes on a dual meaning in relation to the discourse that followed. For one, the media served as a means of conceptualizing the topic. As traditional notions of framing suggests, journalists organize ideas so that audiences can make sense of them. In this case, the topic itself becomes valuable and essentially newsworthy because the criteria and functions of news value have been evaluated and critiqued by the media. Secondly, journalists validate the shift in focus following Imus' apology by adjusting their own focal point and directing the discourse to a one-dimensional discussion about the hip hop culture grounded more in philosophical and ideological notions that were more suited for interpretive functions of journalism.

Media Framing and Blame Shifting: "Who Can Say What?"

Using the Lexis Nexis database system, we retrieved 75 news stories concerning the Don Imus controversy and its aftermath produced over a two-week period (April 11–25, 2007). Many of the initial stories focused on the incident, reporting what was said and potential repercussions. Others were reports about activists calling for the firing of Don Imus and, in an apparent effort for media balance, other stories focused on the First Amendment rights of radio personalities. But when analyzing the media coverage of this issue it was immediately apparent that more time and focus was given to the themes of Imus' blame of the hip hop community for elevating the disparaging words he used to popular status and to the conceptualization of language and culture, specifically language associated by the media with hip hop music.

In fact, one of the more prominent angles that came to best represent the influence of media on public opinion during the Don Imus controversy was the influence of the hip hop culture on the language and culture of our society. For example, Don Imus' use of the racially tinged words "nappy-headed hos" is indicative of an obvious desensitization among segments of society when issues of race and racism are concerned. The cultural description of what "nappy" means is grounded in negative images of slavery, which would seemingly make outrage among African Americans understandable. But with the frequent use of misogynistic language and themes in hip hop music and the visual imagery that in many instances degrades women, media pundits argued that Imus' comments were no worse or, in some instances, more tame than what audiences hear from members of the hip hop community. Following Imus' firing, the media shifted its focus to center on hip hop culture and misogynistic language in song lyrics by rap artists.

One story published in the April 25, 2007 edition of the *Washington Post* examined the "misogyny and rap" debate that garnered steam from the Don Imus controversy. In the story the reporters announced that hip hop mogul Russell Simmons had called for a voluntary banning of "bitch," "ho," and the N-word from the lexicon as "extreme curse words" and also for a coalition of industry executives to "recommend guidelines for lyrical and visual standards." It was also reported that the NAACP had unveiled an initiative to halt racist and sexist imagery in the media and that the civil rights organization would honor C. DeLores Tucker, the late leader of the National Political Congress of Black Women, who "initiated a national crusade against gansta rap and took the recording industry to task for putting profits ahead of social responsibility" (n.p.). The conclusion of stories like this that focused heavily on the culture and repercussions of hip hop music and its negative effects on the culture is that systemic forces already prevalent in the community that Imus apparently offended by his comments were the "real" root of the issue and removed the originator of the controversy, Imus himself, from the argument about misogyny and race. *Today* contributor Mike Celizic (2007) quotes Imus as stating, "Those terms didn't originate in the white community. Those terms originated in the black community" (n.p.).

The example also illustrates that framing can be racialized and, as such, can be used to enhance a negative attitude among some whites who had "less sympathy" for those who felt that Imus' insult of the women on the Rutgers basketball team was racially charged. According to Edelman (1993), by selecting which aspects of an issue to include and emphasize, and which to ignore or downplay, a multitude of representations can be displayed: "Far from being stable, the social world is a chameleon, or, to suggest a better metaphor, a kaleidoscope of potential realities, any of which can be readily evoked by altering the ways in which observations are framed and categorized" (p. 232).

As the insistence by Imus and his supporters that blame should not just lie with him for his insult of the Rutgers' women's basketball team, but also the rap artists that have used lyrics in their music similar to those in his controversial statements, the media's focus on this aspect grew stronger. This framing of the event became the focal point and in many instances became the perfect scapegoat for Imus to become no more than a back drop for the story. Journalistic frames are used to elucidate how society perceives issues of the day. And, as framing shapes perceptions of the target issue, framing manipulations can make certain facets of the issue seem more important and/or prime the recipient to more readily access certain thoughts. Some journalists, including African Americans, expanded their rhetoric concerning the Imus controversy to include rap bashing. Columnist Leonard Pitts, Jr. (2007) wrote in his syndicated column:

> While it is fitting that Imus' slur has angered and energized the African-American community, one hopes we'll see the same in-dignation next time some idiot black rapper (paging Snoop Dogg) refers to black women in terms this raw or worse. Indeed, it's doubtful Imus would have even known the word "ho"—black slang for "whore"—had idiot black rappers not spent the last 20 years popularizing it.
>
> (n.p.)

Kansas City Star columnist Jason Whitlock (2007), who is also African American, also shifted blame from Imus to hip hop. He writes:

> We all know where the real battleground is ... we know that the gangsta rappers and their followers in the athletic world have far

bigger platforms to negatively define us than some old white man with a bad radio show.

(n.p.)

Some media outlets used "free speech" as a scapegoat and further pulled hip hop into the fray. In a news story titled, "Is Imus firing a turning point" (2007), NBC's *Today* host Matt Lauer in an interview asked Michele Moore, senior vice president of the National Urban League, "Is free speech a right of everyone except for white people?" Moore's response was matter of fact: "It (free speech) doesn't mean you can use the public airwaves, which is a privilege, to spread hate and to spread derogatory statements about women who have done the right thing" (n.p.). Activist Sharpton further stressed that position when commenting on his reason for wanting the shock jock removed from the airwaves. In a *New York Times* article, reporters Bill Carter and Louise Story reported that Sharpton's movement to force Imus out represented a larger agenda than racist words, quoting Sharpton, "This has never been about Don Imus … This is about the use of public airwaves for bigoted, racist speech" (Carter & Story, 2007, n.p.).

Even with the expressed concerns of Imus' use of public airways to make his controversial statements, the focus tended to stay on the influence of hip hop culture. *Washington Post* writers Teresa Wiltz and Darragh Johnson (2007) echoed what many journalists were focusing on—rap music under examination—stating the controversial debate "seems to be gathering renewed strength" (n.p.). NBC's *Today* contributor Mike Celizic argued that blacks and whites disagree on why Imus' comments were so offensive. He asks in his commentary on the topic, "Is there a double standard?" and "What gives?"(2007, n.p.).

The disagreement could be rooted in the history of the shock jock's use of derogatory statements about minorities and women in the past. According to public intellectual and cultural critic Michael Eric Dyson (2007), "This isn't the first time that Imus or his colleagues on his show have overstepped the boundaries of ethical sensitivity in speaking crudely of black folk, referring to respected and award-winning journalist Gwen Ifill as a 'cleaning lady' and *The New York Times*' sports columnist William Rhoden as a 'quota hire'" (p. 126). Both of these journalists are black.

This fact makes Imus' blame shift quite contradictory as his pattern of insulting black journalists, scholars and political figures is noted, but without reference to hip hop's role or influence. *Washington Post* columnist Michael Wilbon (2007) wrote about the controversial jock, "There's nothing rare about Imus' vile attacks. This is what he does as a matter of course. Imus and his studio cohorts have painted black people as convicts and muggers and worst of all, apes. Not only do they find it funny, they expect everybody else will as well" (n.p.). Most noted are his comments during a broadcast in 1995 about Ifill and Rhoden, but Wilbon states that Imus also sat by as an on-air colleague stated that African-American tennis stars Serena and Venus Williams would "be better off posing in National Geographic than Playboy" (*Washington Post*, April 11, 2007, p. E01).

It would actually take several days of uproar in the media over Imus' racist remarks and multiple apologies before Don Imus was fired by CBS Radio, his main employer. Following the firing, CBS president and Chief Executive Officer Leslie Moonves said, "There has been much discussion of the effect language like this has on our young people, particularly young women of color trying to make their way in this society" (Faber, 2007, n.p.).

On an episode of *The Oprah Winfrey Show* (2007), former NAACP president (and CBS board of directors member) Bruce Gordon said that Imus' behavior was "intolerable, and it would not be accepted. An extreme statement like his required an extreme response" (quoted on Oprah.com, April 16). The expressed satisfaction of many notable public figures with the firing of Don Imus seemed to have little effect on focus of media coverage concerning the issue. Imus was fired following his two-week suspension. During that time, major media outlets began to lead the charge in critiquing the role of hip hop in contemporary culture.

One of the first media giants to jump on the "blame-shifting band-wagon" was media mogul Oprah Winfrey, who hosted three town hall meeting-styled episodes of her show to discuss sexist, misogynistic language in hip hop culture. In this case, Winfrey bought into the notion that was perpetuated through the media's framing of Imus' remarks and his blame-shifting to the African-American community's alleged frequent use of that discourse. Winfrey's involvement is significant as her show is the highest-rated talk show in American history and serves a demographic that includes a more mainstream audience than most of her contemporaries. Her platform exposed individuals who may have had little to no involvement or cultural ties to the hip hop culture to an issue about this culture now deemed by the media as an important one.

The Oprah Winfrey Show's Town Hall: Hip Hop Under Attack

Oprah Winfrey chimed in on the discussion of race, language and hip hop, dedicating three episodes (April 12, April 16 and April 17, 2007 broadcasts) to examining racist remarks and widely used disparaging language in hip hop culture. Each episode was made up entirely of African-American guests. The initial broadcast on April 12, titled "Rutgers players speak out," dealt with the problematic issue of Don Imus naming the women "nappy-headed hos." The April 16 broadcast, "Response to Imus," focused on the April 4 controversy that eventually resulted in Imus' suspension and then his being fired. African-American poet Maya Angelou stated on the show, "Isn't it ironic—poetically ironic—that here we are with the chance to say, 'What comes next?'" (n.p.). (Angelou had also been the topic of some of Imus' negative remarks in the past.) This episode showcased African-American journalists and writers, including syndicated columnist Stanley Crouch; award-winning newspaper columnist Jason Whitlock; former editor-in-chief of *Essence* magazine Diane Weathers; and poet, author and former editor of *Essence* Asha Bandele. Also appearing were former president of the NAACP (and member of the CBS board) Bruce Gordon, along with activist Al Sharpton and two-time Grammy award-winning artist India Arie, who was introduced as representing a younger generation of women who have positive messages in their music. On this particular broadcast, Crouch said that because of the Imus controversy, the issue [denigration of women] is "getting the attention it deserves" (n.p.). The final episode titled, "A Hip Hop Town Hall," aired on April 17 following Imus' firing and featured a panel of experts, including: music mogul and entrepreneur Russell Simmons; executive vice president at Warner Music Group Kevin Liles; former NAACP CEO and current president/CEO of the Hip-Hop Summit Action Network Dr. Benjamin Chavis; and Grammy-winning *conscious* rapper Common (formerly Common Sense). Simmons, who is not a rapper but is recognized as one of the cultural creators of the hip hop industry, said on the April 17 episode, "I almost want to thank him [Imus] for creating this forum. It's a long time coming" (n.p.). On the same episode, Chavis stated that "hip-hop artists are not responsible for what Don Imus did … there's no way that Don Imus can blame hip-hop for what he did … We've got to make it better … by making society better." Chavis concluded that "there's too much poverty, there's too much injustice, and there's too much bad treatment of women in our society" (n.p.). Common had little criticism about hip hop culture noting that his earliest memories of hip hop were about "consciousness," and that "now as hip hop has evolved and grown up, our parents are expecting hip hop to be perfect and to be right" (*The Oprah Winfrey Show*, 2007, n.p.).

Least critical of Imus during the town hall special was African-American award-winning newspaper columnist Jason Whitlock from the *Kansas City Star*. Whitlock argued on the show that, "Our real problem is that we're not willing to accept responsibility for our role in this [problem]" (quoted on Oprah.com, April 16, 2007). Whitlock's examination of the negativity of hip hop culture further legitimizes that African Americans are not only divided when it comes to social issues that impact black men and women in America, but that a double standard exists in the black community. Whitlock goes on to explain his position by stating:

> We've allowed our kids to adopt a hip-hop culture that's been perverted and corrupted by prison values. They are defining our women in pop culture as bitches and hos. ... We are defining ourselves. Then, we get upset and want to hold Don Imus to a higher standard than we hold ourselves to. That is unacceptable.
>
> (quoted on Oprah.com, April 16, 2007)

To further illustrate the divide on this topic, *Chicago Tribune* columnist Clarence Page was quoted by Howard Kurtz in a *Washington Post* (2007) article titled "Imus, Duke & the media," stating:

> Imus' defenders argue that he shouldn't be punished while countless rap stars get away with using that word and much worse. That's a pretty feeble diversion from the question of why Imus felt compelled to use it against what he now admits was a thoroughly "inappropriate" target.
>
> (n.p.)

Washington Post writer Nekesa Mumbi Moody (2007) notes that the Imus controversy may be the catalyst that brings focus to offensive language in rap music: "Four months after outrage over Imus' sexist and racial comments led to intense scrutiny of rap's negative imagery, and as the genre's sales continue to plummet, some artists are publicly abandoning offensive language" (p. 1). That hope, shared by many in the hip hop community, is often coupled with a defense of the art form. Danyel Smith, editor-in-chief of *Vibe* magazine, said, "Rap gets a lot of blame, fairly and unfairly, for misogyny and violence, while people tend to forget American cinema, for the last 100 years, has explicit misogyny and explicit violence in Technicolor. Which frankly is what lot of rappers, gangsta and otherwise, are influenced by" (*Washington Post*, April 25, 2007, p. C01).

In American society, it can be argued that we operate under a double standard when it comes to race and language. As such, the blame shift seemed to create a defensive posture by those who "represented" the hip hop community and its culture. Martin's (2007) position that Imus made a mistake by engaging in language and dialogue considered "exclusive" to a particular culture was a sentiment resonated by the critics around the country. Author Cora Daniels (2007) was quoted in same *Ebony* article as Martin, stating, "where Imus erred was in not realizing the setting he was in, and by his 'trying to use bad behavior for bad behavior'" (p. 82).

Perhaps Winfrey's interest in the negative images reflective of hip hop culture is understandable considering the language and imagery that has become for some an unbearable, yet undeniable part of the culture. Her "town hall" approach to discussing this topic did contribute to national discourse, but offered no real solution to resolving America's or hip hop's problem with race. What it was successful at doing was validating the issue as worthy of focus on a national scale and not just within the black community. Winfrey's audience is mainstream and the fact that she dedicated three shows to this topic, to this type of audience, speaks to the effectiveness of Imus' ability to remove the blame away from him and shift the focus to the so-called root of the problem.

Conclusion

How the media covered the Don Imus controversy is more a lesson in how this powerful cultural industry effectively perpetuated dominant views that exist in society about a particular marginalized group and how one powerful player in the industry was able to shift the blame for his disparaging remarks to a segment of that marginalized group. The media's framing of the event would eventually fall in line with Imus' notion that the hip hop community should not just share, but take the blame for the misogyny and overt racism found in contemporary popular language and discourse. The ideological implications resonate here since both Imus and the corporate structure that supported him have historically benefited from the protection of social privilege extended to members of the dominant class in society. Ironically, the more powerful of these two entities, CBS Corporation, would have to part ways with Imus in order to maintain its status as major media conglomerate. *The New York Times* journalist Bill Carter (2007) reported that NBC News (which simulcast Imus' program on its cable news network MSNBC) first suspended Don Imus for two weeks, calling his comments "racist and abhorrent" (n.p.). The final decision for the company was to fire Imus for his comments, thus solidifying its position that taking a stand was economically, socially and culturally beneficial for it in the long run.

Further, with the media deciding to frame the coverage of the Imus controversy around hip hop and its troubles, many readers and viewers began to question the reason for the Imus backlash. The media had served their role as a constructor of reality for their audience and legitimized the notion that the hip hop community had a moral obligation in this situation as well. In response to the "What's the big deal?" question, *Time* writer James Poniewozik (2007) offers a legitimate explanation: "There was a racial element, a gender element and even a class element" (n.p.), three aspects that illustrated an "equal opportunity" insult by the radio personality and a fair argument for outrage. *Washington Post* columnist Eugene Robinson stated in a column titled, "Why Imus had to go," that "the aging shock jock's fall from undeserved grace raises some important questions about just who in our society is permitted to say just what. Wherever 'the line' delineating acceptable discourse might be, calling those young women from Rutgers University 'nappy-headed hos' is miles on the other side" (2007, n.p.).

But in an effort to restore his image, these arguments were countered by Imus using what Harvard University sociologist Orlando Patterson calls the classic appeal to the authentic self. Of his controversial comments, Imus said on an episode of the *Today* show (2007), "It was comedy. It wasn't a malicious rant. I wasn't angry. I wasn't drunk. I wasn't stating some sort of philosophy … I'm not a racist. And I've demonstrated that in my deeds and my works" (Duke, 2007, n.p.). Patterson states that individuals that appeal to the authentic self try to override bad behavior by pushing the notion that deep down you are a good person:

> It's kind of arrogance, if you ask me … this lack of honesty, this denial, could be the reason this unfortunate phenomenon of bilious public language keeps happening again and again and again. This time, the young female athletes of Rutgers are collateral damage, their courageous basketball season forever associated with the "nappy-headed ho" slur.
>
> (quoted by Duke, 2007, n.p.)

References

A hip-hop town hall (2007, April 17). *The Oprah Winfrey Show*. Retrieved June 21, 2007 from: http://www2.oprah.com/tows/slide/200704/20070417/slide_20070417_284_101.jhmtl.

Benoit, W. L. (1995). Exxon and the Valdez oil spill. In W. L. Benoit (Ed.), *Accounts, excuses, and apologies* (pp. 119–131). Albany, NY: State University of New York Press (SUNY Series in Speech Communication).

Benshoff, H. M. & Griffin, S. (2004). *America on film: Representing race, class, gender and sexuality at the movies*. Malden, MA: Blackwell Publishing.

Blaney, J. R. & Benoit, W. L. (2001). The theory of image restoration discourse. In J. R. Blaney & W. L. Benoit (Eds.), *The Clinton scandals and the politics of image restoration* (pp. 15–25). Westport, CT: Praeger Publishers (Praeger Series in Political Communication).

Carter, B. (2007, April 9). Imus suspended for 2 weeks over racial remark. *The New York Times*. Retrieved September 18, 2009 from: http://nytimes.com/2007/20/09/busiess/media/09cnd-imus.html.

Carter, B. & Story, L. (2007, April 12). NBC News drops Imus show over racial remark. *The New York Times*. Retrieved September 18, 2009 from: http://www.nytimes.com/2007/24/12/buisness/media/12dismiss.html.

Celizic, M. (2007, April 12). Blacks, whites disagree on "ho" comment: Blacks and whites disagree on why Imus's "ho" comment was so offensive. *Today Show*. Retrieved September 23, 2009 from: http://www.msnbc.msn.com/id/18054788/.

Daniels, C. (2007, July). I can but you can't. *Ebony*, 80–82.

Douglas, S. (1995). The framing of race. *Progressive*, *59*(12), 19.

Duke, L. (2007, April 11). What is revealed by a crack in the "good person" façade. *Washington Post*. Retrieved April 16, 2007 from: http://www.washingtonpost.com/wp-dyn/content/article/2007/04/10/AR2007041001836.

Durham, F. D. (2008). Breaching powerful boundaries: A postmodern critique of framing. In S. D. Reese, O. Gandy, & A. E. Grant (Eds.), *Framing public life: Perspectives on media and our understanding of the social world*. Mahwah, New Jersey: Lawrence Erlbaum Associates, Inc.

Dyson, M. E. (2007). *Know what I mean?* New York: Perseus Books Group.

Edelman, M. J. (1993). Contestable categories and public opinion. *Political Communication*, *10*(3), 231–242.

Entman, R. (1990). Modern racism and the images of blacks in local television news. *Critical Studies in Mass Communication*, *7*, 332–345.

Entman, R. M. (1993). Framing: Toward clarification of a fractured paradigm. *Journal of Communication*, *43*(4), 51–58.

Entman, R. & Rojecki, A. (2000). *The black image in the white mind: Media and race in America*. Chicago: University of Chicago Press.

Faber, J. (2007, April 12). CBS fires Don Imus over racial slur. *CBS News*. Retrieved September 15, 2009 from: http://www.cbsnews.com/stories/2007/04/12/national/main267523.shtml.

Gaines, J. (1986). White privilege and looking relations: Race and gender in feminist film theory. *Cultural Critique*, *4*, 59–79.

Gitlin, T. (1980). *The whole world is watching*. Berkeley, CA: University of California Press.

Griffin, R. J. & Dunwoody, S. (1997). Community structure and science framing of news about local environmental risks. *Science Communication*, *18*(4), 362–384.

Gross, K. & D'Ambrosio, L. (2004). Framing emotional response. *Political Psychology*, *25*(1), 1–29.

Haider-Markel, D. P., Delehanty, W., & Beverlin, M. (2007). Media framing and racial attitudes in the aftermath of Katrina. *Policy Studies Journal*, *35*(4), 587–605.

Hall, S. (1990). The whites of their eyes: Racist ideologies and the media. In Manuel Alvarado and John O. Thompson (Eds.), *The media reader*. UK: BFI.

hooks, b. (1994). *Outlaw culture: Resisting representations*. New York: Routledge.

Is Imus firing a turning point?: NBC News president Steve Capus, Al Sharpton and others share thoughts (2007, April 12). *Today Show*. Retrieved September 23, 2009 from: http://www.msbnc.msn.com/id/18072729/.

Kraeplin, C. (2008). Two tales of one city: How cultural perspective influenced the framing of a pre-civil rights story in Dallas. *American Journalism*, *25*(1), 73–98.

Kurtz, Howard. (2007, April 16). Imus, Duke & the Media. *Washington Post*. Retrieved June 30, 2007 from: http://www.washingtonpost.com/wpdyn/content/blog/2007/04/16/BL2007041600432_pf.html.

Lavelle, K. & Feagin, J. (2006). Hurricane Katrina: The race and class debate. *Monthly Review*, *58*(3). Retrieved from: http://www.monthlyreview.org/0706lavelle.htm.

London, S. (1993). How the media frames political issues. Retrieved from: http://www.scottlondon.com/reports/frames.html.

Martin, R. (2007, July). I can but you can't. *Ebony*, 80-82.

Mies, M. (1998). *Capitalism and accumulation on a world scale: Women in the international division of labour*. London and New York, NY: Zed Press.

Moody, N. M. (2007, April 3). Imus backlash has some rappers cleaning up their acts. *Houston Chronicle*. Retrieved from: http://www.chron.com/disp/story.mpl/headline/entertainment/5023161.html.

Morris, M. (2006). A moment of clarity? The American media and Hurricane Katrina. *Southern Quarterly*, *43*(3), 40–46.

National Action Network (2007). Retrieved from: http://www.nationalactionnetwork.net/.

Nelson, T. E., Oxley, Z. M., & Clawson, R. (1997). Toward a psychology of framing effects. *Political Behavior*, *19*(3), 221–246.

Noveck, J. (2007, April 9). Imus critics say apologies are hollow. *Washington Post*. Retrieved April 16, 2007 from: http://www.washingtonpost.com/wp-dyn/content/article/2007/04/09/AR2007040901054.

Peck, J. (1994). Talk about racism: Framing a popular discourse of race on Oprah Winfrey. *Cultural Critique*, *27*, 89–126.

Pitts, L. (2007, April 13). Firing of Imus removes leader of sorry band. *Miami Herald*. Retrieved June 1, 2007 from: http://www.miamiherald.com/285/v-print/story/72285.html.

Poindexter, P. M., Smith, L., & Heider, D. (2003). Race and ethnicity in local television news: Framing, story assignments, and source selection. *Journal of Broadcasting & Electronic Media*, *47*(4), 524–536.

Poniewozik, J. (2007, April 12). The Imus Fallout: Who can say what? *Time*. Retrieved September 23, 2009, from: http://www.time.com/time/printout/0,8816,1609490,00.html.

Price, V. & Tewksbury, D. (1997). News values and public opinion: A theoretical account of media priming and framing. *Progress in Communication Sciences*, *13*, 173–212.

Response to Imus (2007, April 16). *The Oprah Winfrey Show*. Retrieved June 21, 2007 from: http://www2.oprah.com/tows/slide/200704/20070416/slide_20070416_284_101.jhmtl.

Richardson, J. D. & Lancendorfer, K. M. (2004). Framing affirmative action: The influence of race on newspaper editorial responses to the University of Michigan cases. *Harvard International Journal of Press/Politics*, *9*(4), 74–94.

Robinson, E. (2007, April 13). Why Imus had to go. *Washington Post*. Retrieved April 16, 2007 from:http://www.washingtonpost.com/wpdyn/content/article/2007/04/12/AR2007041201825_pf.htm.

Rutgers players speak out (2007, April 12). *The Oprah Winfrey Show*. Retrieved June 21, 2007 from: http://www2.oprah.com/tows/slide/200704/20070412/slide_20070412_350_102.jhmtl.

Watson, J. (2007). Representing realities: An overview of news framing. *Keio Communication Review*, *29*, 107–131.

Whitlock, J. (2007, April 11). Imus isn't the real bad guy. *The Kansas City Star*. Retrieved from: http://www.kansascity.com/2007/04/11/1904516/imus-isnt-the-real-bad-guy.html.

Wilbon, M. (2007, April 11). Out of Imus's bigotry, a zero tolerance for hate. *Washington Post*. Retrieved April 16, 2007 from: http://www.washingtonpost.com/wpdyn/content/article/2007/04/10/AR2007041001891_pf.htm.

Williams, D. E. & Olaniran, B. (1998). Expanding the crisis planning function: Introducing elements of risk communication to crisis communication practice. *Public Relations Review*, *24*(3), 387.

Wiltz, T. and Johnson, D. (2007, April 25). The Imus Test: Rap lyrics undergo examination. *Washington Post*. Retrieved September 23, 2009 from: http://www.washingtonpost.com/wpdyn/content/article/2007/04/24/AR2007042402496.html.

Discussion Questions

1. What do you recall about the Don Imus remark about the Rutgers' women's basketball team? How does this chapter's assessment of the controversy fall in line with your thoughts about the remarks?

2. Compare the initial newspaper coverage of *The New York Times* with that of another national newspaper (such as *Washington Post, Los Angeles Times, Atlanta Journal Constitution, Chicago Times, Miami Herald*, or others). Then localize the coverage to the newspaper in your town or state. Once you have made those comparisons, try to locate news printed in an African-American publication and contrast the difference in how the same story was reported. Are there

obvious differences in how the story was told? Is the focus different based on race? Is the focus on hip hop?

3. If news organizations are expected to have a point of view, does that expectation impact objective news reporting and framing of issues in the media? In your analysis of Question 2, what point of view is expressed in the news coverage you analyzed? Is it obvious, subtle, or difficult to determine? Explain your answer and provide examples to support your position.

4. Do you think Imus' apology was sincere? Why or why not?

5. What were the issues Imus faced following his disparaging comments?

6. How could Imus take responsibility for his actions? What do you recommend someone do in this situation that would be acceptable to African Americans? To all races? To women?

Chapter Assignments

1. Point out any words, certain facts or treatments of the coverage you found to determine if "race framing" or "blame shifting" has taken place.

2. Select two news stories from the incident that you found particularly compelling or disturbing. Describe the journalists … male, female, African American, white? Do you think the reporter's gender and/or race made a difference in the reporting of the story? If so, describe how you think the reporter could have better told the story without regard to race.

3. What impact do you think Oprah's three-day coverage of hip hop had on viewing audiences? Did her assessment of hip hop culture reflect your views of hip hop? Did it affect your thoughts about how minorities are portrayed in music, videos, on television or any other medium?

4. How do you decide where to place blame for Imus' comments? Did the media influence your thoughts in some way? If so, how?

Additional Sources

View excerpts of *The Oprah Winfrey Show* about the Imus controversy: http://www.oprah.com/oprahshow/Response-to-Imus/4.

View other television coverage of the controversy on YouTube: http://www.youtube.com/watch?v=25-tfvogqAE.

CHAPTER 10

Recoding New Orleans

News, Race, Representation and Spike Lee's *When the Levees Broke*

CHRISTOPHER P. CAMPBELL AND KIM M. LEDUFF

On September 2, 2005, the national 9 p.m. *Prime News Tonight* newscast on CNN's Headline News cable network opened much like coverage of Hurricane Katrina by other TV networks in the early days after the storm. Co-anchor Erica Hill: "We begin tonight with the latest for you from New Orleans, a city drowning in chaos and at this point on the brink of exploding. And there the sun has set on another day of desperate anarchy." Co-anchor Mike Galanos continues: "Hurricane victims will spend the next several hours fighting to stay alive amidst the turmoil and hope tomorrow will bring some relief. An atmosphere of lawlessness is settling over New Orleans as snipers freely open fire on police and rescue crews. And desperate hospital workers moved patients up to higher floors to escape looters. But officials say 4,200 National Guard troops will be deployed in the next three days." As the audience is shown footage of people—virtually all of them black—stranded by the storm near the New Orleans Convention Center, a series of subtitles reads, "KATRINA: THE DEVASTATION," "SNIPERS FIRING ON POLICE & RESCUE CREWS IN NEW ORLEANS," "TENS OF THOUSANDS OF PEOPLE ON STREETS IN NEW ORLEANS," "NEW ORLEANS DESPARATION." As the broadcast continues, the audience hears that looters had overturned rescue boats, that teenage boys had raped young girls and that "chaos ruled."

The coverage was compelling, and the 24-hour news networks' Katrina coverage attracted some of their largest viewing audiences ever. CNN saw a 39 percent increase in viewership during the quarter that followed Hurricane Katrina; likewise, ratings for the Fox News Channel were up 31 percent (Learmonth, 2005). The coverage was also highly inaccurate, as was coverage by non-television news media in Katrina's aftermath. For instance, the *Financial Times* of London reported on September 5 that "girls and boys (in the New Orleans Convention Center) were raped in the dark and had their throats cut and bodies were stuffed in the kitchens while looters and madmen exchanged fire with weapons they had looted" (quoted in Thevenot, 2006, p. 3). The local *Times-Picayune*, which later won a Pulitzer Prize for its coverage of the storm, reported 30 or 40 bodies had been stuffed in a freezer at the New Orleans Convention Center, including a "7-year-old with her throat cut" (Thevenot, 2006, p. 1).

None of this, of course, turned out to be true. No snipers fired at rescue crews. No looters invaded hospitals. Nobody overturned any rescue boats. No children were raped in the Convention Center. No bodies were piled into a freezer. No seven-year old had her throat cut. Some news organizations later filed reports about the inaccuracy, including the *Times-Picayune*, *The Los Angeles Times* and *The New York Times* (Thevenot, 2006). Others—including the cable news networks—never bothered.

While we are bothered that national television news organizations would be indifferent about the accuracy of their reports, our concern here is with network coverage that reinforced blatant racial stereotypes. News coverage in the aftermath of Hurricane Katrina was filled with coded representations of African Americans consistent with the reprehensible images of another era. Unfortunately, those representations are not so far removed from those that Americans see on their local TV newscasts night after night. The coverage of Hurricane Katrina led us to wonder: What is it about the news process that allows for such blatant misrepresentations? Could news organizations have presented a more accurate and thoughtful portrait of the residents of New Orleans who were stranded in the city?

After viewing *When the Levees Broke: A Requiem in Four Acts*, the 2006 documentary produced for HBO by filmmaker Spike Lee—a film in which New Orleans' stranded residents were represented as a diverse, complex and sometimes heroic lot—we were troubled by the difference between his representation of New Orleans and the representations that we saw in the late summer of 2005. The purpose of this chapter is to contrast the racial codes and mythmaking that surfaced in mainstream news coverage in the early days after Hurricane Katrina with the racial coding in Spike Lee's

When the Levees Broke. We'll argue that daily journalism might be improved by approaching stories in the more thoughtful, complicated—but still *compelling*—manner that Lee's documentary reflects. We do, of course, realize that there are considerable differences between daily news and documentary production; we'll argue, however, that—at least in terms of racial coding—news organizations could learn something from Lee's sense of race and class in America.

The sensational national newscasts in the early days after Hurricane Katrina were consistent with daily television journalism's penchant for enticing viewers by focusing on the criminal activities—real or imagined—of underclass African Americans in urban communities. Newsrooms by all accounts tend to remain the domain of white men, who may or may not be sensitive to the racial stereotyping that has marked American news coverage throughout its history. The dominant representations (and stereotypes) of African Americans that surfaced in the initial network coverage of Hurricane Katrina endure on local television newscasts, representations that have been documented in numerous studies (e.g., Brown, LeDuff, & Campbell, 2005; Campbell, 1995, 1998; Dixon, 2004; Dixon & Linz, 2000; Entman, 1990, 1992, 1994; Entman & Rojecki, 2000; Gilliam & Iyengar, 2000; Gray, 1991; LeDuff, 2009; Pease, 1989; Poindexter, Smith, & Heider, 2003; Romer et al., 1998). A 2005 examination of local television newscasts' mythological representations of race concluded, "Audiences ... continue to see the distorted 21st century versions of the 'Birth of a Nation' stereotypes that were unacceptable in 1915 and are simply shocking to see in 2005" (Brown, LeDuff, & Campbell, 2005, p. 35).

One explanation for journalism's failed representation of African-American life can be found in a body of research known as Critical Race Theory (CRT). Yosso (2002) explains that "CRT is a framework that can address the racism, sexism, and classism embedded in entertainment media. CRT draws from and extends a broad literature base in law, sociology, history, ethnic studies and women's studies" (p. 3). Laurence Parker and Marvin Lynn (2002) characterize Critical Race Theory as incorporating three main goals:

> a) to present storytelling and narratives as valid approaches through which to examine race and racism in law and society;
> b) to argue for the eradication of racial subjugation while simultaneously recognizing that race is a social construct; and
> c) to draw important relationships between race and other axes of domination.
>
> (p. 10)

The theory also allows researchers to examine race by acknowledging the inherent privilege of "whiteness" and analyzing race from a perspective that recognizes that privilege. Mahoney (1995) explains that "part of white privilege, is not seeing all we (white people) have and all we do, and not seeing how what we do appears to those defined as other" (p. 306). She continues, "This country is both highly segregated and based on the concept of whiteness as 'normal.' It is therefore hard for white folks to see whiteness both when we interact with people who are not socially defined as white and when we interact with other white people, when race doesn't seem to be involved" (p. 306). In examining the coverage of Hurricane Katrina, it is important to consider that white journalists may not factor in their own race or ethnicity and how their experience may subconsciously impact the way they frame stories.

That also might explain the difference in the representations found in Spike Lee's *When the Levees Broke*. The four-hour documentary he produced for HBO about Hurricane Katrina's impact in New Orleans first aired in August of 2006, about one year after Katrina struck the Gulf Coast. The film was generally hailed by critics, who praised it as an innovative and exhaustive account of the storm's impact on New Orleans and the failed response of public officials. *New York Times* film critic Stephen Holden, for instance, wrote:

> A powerful chorus of witnesses and talking heads that cuts across racial and class lines was assembled for the four-hour film … Although seeds of hope are woven into this tapestry of rage, sorrow and disbelief, the inability of government at almost every level to act quickly and decisively leaves you aghast at what amounts to a collective failure of will.
>
> (Holden, 2006)

Like many of Lee's dramatic films, *When the Levees Broke*, a documentary, bridges the issue of not only racism, but classism, with unusual perspective. While the national media's "parachute journalism" style of coverage limited voices and perspectives, Lee's approach allowed more voices and varying perspectives to be heard. Lee's approach to addressing racism in his films has been examined by a number of critical cultural scholars. Winn (2001) argues that Lee does not avoid controversial material in his films "and often incorporates other black voices that also speak to racial inequality" (p. 456). Rowland and Strain (1994) note, "Lee's film (*Do the Right Thing*) illustrates how stories may be used to confront society's 'dirty little secrets.' A dirty secret is a theme too unpleasant or impolitic to be discussed in public" (p. 220). Hurricane Katrina exposed a number of "dirty little secrets" not only in New Orleans but in America. While news coverage only looked at the effects, Lee examined the heart of the matter: the societal inequities that existed before Katrina even struck. There are a number of lessons that can be learned through critical examination of this documentary.

Codes in Media Texts

The heart of this chapter will be textual analyses of, first, CNN's *Prime News Tonight* September 2, 2005 coverage of New Orleans after the city flooded in the early days after Hurricane Katrina. The program is billed as "the only national 9 p.m. newscast," and the September 2 coverage was consistent with what national television audiences were seeing around the clock after the New Orleans levee system failed. Second, we will analyze three segments of Spike Lee's *When the Levees Broke*. Again, the authors are aware of the significant differences between daily news and documentary production; however, our interest is in the differences between the language—both aural and visual—that was used in the two representations of the catastrophe.

These analyses will include both denotative and connotative "readings" that are premised on the work of cultural studies researchers who have identified means of analysis that allow us to explore the codes of media texts by beginning at the denotative level and moving on to the connotative and the mythic. For instance, Stuart Hall has described "decoding" media texts through three levels of analysis. The first step is to describe the denotative or "preferred" meaning—that which was intended by the producer—and is followed by connotative ("negotiated" and/or "oppositional") readings of the same message. Hall explains:

> The domains of "preferred readings" have the whole social order imbedded in them as a set of meanings, practices and beliefs; the everyday knowledge of social structures, of "how things work for all practical purposes in this culture," the rank order of power and interest and the structure of legitimations, limits and sanctions.
>
> (1982, p. 134)

Similarly, Fiske and Hartley (1978) describe three levels of codes to be found in television messages. Like Hall's "preferred reading," the first order is the denotative message and "the sign is self contained" (p. 41). Like Hall's "negotiated reading," the second order calls for the connotative reading of the message, including its potential for myth-making. In this analysis, Fiske and Hartley include the impact of television production techniques to connote meanings: "Camera angle, lighting and background music [and] frequency of cutting are examples" (p. 45).

What Hall would describe as a "negotiated" reading of the stories allows for analysis beyond the meaning intended by the team of journalists who produced them. According to Hall, such a reading requires a recognition of the "dominant ideology" that is at work and how that ideology is "shot through with contradictions" (p. 137). Hall writes, "Negotiated codes operate through what we might call particular or situated logics: and these logics are sustained by their differential and unequal relation to the discourses and logics of power" (p. 137). For Hall, the denotative, common-sense meanings of the stories are less significant than the connotative, interpretive readings. Fiske and Hartley (1978) say this second level of analysis allows us to identify the potential of the message to create cultural myths.

Hall describes "oppositional" readings of media messages in which a viewer

> detotalizes the message in the preferred code in order to retotalize the message within some alternative framework of reference. … One of the most significant political moments … is the point when events which are normally signified and decoded in a negotiated way begin to be given an oppositional reading. Here the "politics of signification"—the struggle in discourse—is joined.
>
> (1982, p. 138)

Similarly, Fiske and Hartley describe the highest level of analysis of television messages as that which recognizes the "mythology" or "ideology" that hides in the coding of media messages: "This, the third order of signification, reflects the broad principles by which a culture organizes and interprets the reality with which it has to cope" (p. 46). It is at this level that we will make the case that CNN's coverage of Hurricane Katrina reified dominant, stereotypical newsroom codes of African Americans, in stark contrast to the more thoughtful and complicated coding found in *When the Levees Broke*.

CNN's New Orleans: "An Atmosphere of Lawlessness"

The September 2, 2005 edition of *Prime News Tonight* that aired on the CNN Headline News cable network was much like other network coverage that aired in the aftermath of Hurricane Katrina. The program was dominated by images of black New Orleanians stranded near the city's convention center and the Louisiana Superdome. Anchors and reporters provided a fearful account of a city that had been overwhelmed by criminal activity. It included a plea from Mayor Ray Nagin, who issued "a desperate SOS."

At the "preferred" level of meaning, the coverage was designed to tell a story of chaos and lawlessness that erupted as water from a failed levee system inundated the city. Journalists relied on police and government sources (as well as reports from other news organizations) to confirm their accounts. The magnitude of the event—arguably the greatest natural disaster in American history—called for round-the-clock coverage by the 24-hour news networks.

That the frenzied accounts of criminal activity were later found to be inaccurate was generally attributed to 1) rumors that surfaced in the horror that engulfed the convention center and Superdome, where thousands of stranded New Orleanians had sought shelter only to find little public aide and 2) confirmation by the city's mayor and police chief, themselves caught up in the frenzy and frantically trying to appeal for federal assistance. (New Orleans) *Times-Picayune* reporter Brian Thevenot later admitted, "Many if not most of the alarmist reports of violence were false, or at least could not be verified" (2006, p. 2).

Perhaps the inaccuracy of the reports is understandable. Journalists were working in extraordinary conditions, and local public officials, beleaguered and frustrated by the lack of a federal response, were eager to corroborate horrendous accounts of pathological behavior. And there was at least some truth to the reports of widespread crime: Stores were definitely looted after the flood, and TV news cameras captured looters in action. On a denotative level, the "common sense" of the coverage reflected the journalists' willingness to believe that New Orleans had indeed been overrun by violent crime. The language used by the *Prime News Tonight* anchors is indicative of that willingness. During the hour-long program, they reported that New Orleans was consumed "by an atmosphere of lawlessness," that it "was on the brink of exploding," that "looters had overturned rescue boats," that "snipers had fired on rescue helicopters" and that "chaos ruled." The show included sources—police officers and stranded evacuees—who said that "teenage boys were raping young girls," that "neighborhoods were overrun by thugs" and that "carjackings and shootings were rampant."

Visually, the "B-role" that viewers watched during the program didn't support the hysteria of the language of the anchors or their sources. Yes, things looked grim, but the footage primarily included shots that showed hundreds of people—most of them black—stranded and waiting for help.

The blanketed body of a dead victim who remained for days in a wheel chair was shown repeatedly. The visual language established a sense of desperation—little food and water was available—but it was not the chaotic and criminal desperation that the anchors were using to describe the city's problems.

On a connotative level—what Hall (1982) would describe as a "negotiated" or "oppositional" reading—the *Prime News Tonight* newscast works to reinforce stereotypical racial codes that are all too familiar to Americans who watch local television newscasts. As multiple studies of local TV journalism have found, local newscasts—obsessed with covering violent crime in underclass black communities (but not interested in reporting on the historical, political, social and economic roots of that crime)—routinely represent African Americans as sub-human. Campbell (1995) found that "local news ignores life outside of middle-American/ dominant culture parameters [and] contributes to an understanding of minority cultures as less significant, as marginal" (p. 132). He argues,

> When journalists attempt to cover life in minority communities but neglect and dismiss the attitudes and perceptions of people of color, they compound that sense of marginality. When the news sustains stereotypical notions about nonwhite Americans as less-than-human, as immature, as savage, as derelicts, it feeds an understanding of minorities as different, as "other," as dangerous.
>
> (p. 132)

The journalists working for CNN, by the nature of the profession, are former local television newscasters who learned journalism by covering violent crimes in the American cities where they worked. When the levees flooded New Orleans, the event—like the violent crimes that lead so many local TV newscasts—became an opportunity to do on a national level what television journalists have been doing on the local level for decades: expose presumed pathologically violent African Americans in the urban underclass.

Visually, the newscast shows us that thousands of black New Orleanians are stranded. But as those images roll by, we're bombarded with language about lawlessness, chaos, snipers, looters, thugs, rapes, carjackings. The language is not about the fact that tens of thousands of people were stranded and that the federal government had yet to mount a response to the disaster. Indeed, the news reports framed the call for federal help as a need to quell the violence rather than to provide basic necessities to the thousands of people who had fled their homes as water filled the streets.

Some of the television journalism out of New Orleans did focus on the dire conditions in which the stranded residents were living. But the dominant message of CNN's Headline News coverage—as well as much of the other national coverage of the disaster—was on the violent crime that had erupted in the city. Though the journalists had not fully confirmed the reports of "lawlessness," that was the message that dominated the newscast. The coding in the coverage is not far removed from the coding in coverage of violent crime that Americans in large cities routinely see on their local newscasts. Black crime suspects are depicted in mug shots and in "perp walks" (staged events in which violent crime suspects— perpetrators—are paraded before local TV news cameras). Local police are called upon to explain the dastardly nature of the crime that the suspect committed. Never is there a presumption of innocence, and rarely do local television journalists bother to follow up on the treatment of the suspect in the justice system. Additionally, journalists rarely provide audiences with any kind of explanation of the existence of violent crime in impoverished urban communities. Stories that might offer audiences some insight into the problem—stories about substance abuse, about the underground economy of the drug trade, about historical and institutional racism, about substandard public schools, about gun laws—are not even considered as part of the daily news routine, especially in local television newsrooms.

When New Orleans flooded and thousands of the cities' black citizens were stranded without adequate shelter and resources, CNN's Headline News journalists—like many others whose coverage was frightfully inac- curate in the days after the storm—represented those citizens as lawless, as violent, as inhuman. Rather than approaching the story in an accurate, explanatory and insightful manner, the September 2 *Prime News Tonight* coverage bordered on hysteria and served to reinforce stereotypical and mythical representations of African Americans. Rather than focusing on the failure of the government to adequately respond to the needs of the flood's victims, the crisis in New Orleans was depicted as one that was caused by the criminal behavior of the city's black population.

Spike Lee's New Orleans

In *When the Levees Broke: A Requiem in Four Acts*, the montage of black voices, white voices, middle class, rich and poor voices and the intersection of local, national and international news coverage allows viewers to piece together a complicated puzzle of events surrounding Hurricane Katrina and the failure of the New Orleans levee system. But there were specific instances in the documentary where Spike Lee offered significant context where CNN and other national media organizations failed to do so.

Blahniks, Broadway and Balls

The national media suggested from the beginning that people didn't get the help they needed initially because some level of government essentially dropped the ball. Lee incorporated "the blame game" that took place among local, state and federal officials in his documentary as well. In Act II, CNN reporter Soledad O'Brien appears in an extreme close-up with strong criticism of the government in general. "It was baffling," she says of the government reaction. "They were so out of touch with reality." O'Brien was on the scene in New Orleans and reflects on the conditions at the Convention Center. Lee uses CNN footage to show O'Brien in a live shot (shot shortly after the hurricane) standing next to a dead body covered with a blanket. She explains in her interview with Lee that three days later she returned to the same spot only to find the man's body still sitting in the middle of a public street. She suggests that it was an indication of the lack of attention given by government to the dire situation in New Orleans in the days after Katrina.

Cultural scholar Michael Eric Dyson then explains to Lee that while FEMA director Michael Brown was given the brunt of the criticism in the media, he was actually a scapegoat. Dyson suggests that a number of other federal officials were to blame. President Bush, for example, claimed he was uninformed about what was happening in New Orleans. Dyson further explains that as the events unfolded Vice President Dick Cheney was fly fishing, White House assistant Karl Rove was nowhere to be found, Homeland Security chief Michael Chertoff was in Atlanta at a meeting about disease, and Secretary of State Condoleeza Rice was shopping for shoes, attending a Broadway play and playing tennis. Dyson notes, "Blahniks (footwear), Broadway and balls were more important than black people."

But Lee shows that not everyone agrees that the federal government alone was to blame, and local and state leaders also contributed to the failed response to the disaster. Lee interviews former Louisiana State Representative Karen Carter, who argues that Mayor C. Ray Nagin was to blame. She says, "He is the first line of defense. There was a plan in place— I'm not sure he'd ever read it before." But not all of the locals shared her view, and Lee follows Carter's charges with a number of New Orleans residents (of multiple races and classes) essentially defending why they voted for Nagin and explaining that they understood the difficult and unusual task that Nagin had to contend with.

The viewer then hears from Nagin firsthand as it sees images of him in the days following Hurricane Katrina. Nagin defends himself, suggesting that no American city's leader has been faced with a city 80 percent under water and without communication or electrical power. He then makes reference to New York Mayor Rudy Giuliani's leadership after the World Trade Center was attacked on 9/11. Nagin says, "I'm not trying to be Rudy. I don't get the Giuliani pass." Lee cuts to WWL Radio news reporter Garland Robinette, who recounts the calls Nagin made into the radio station as the city flooded. The audience hears Nagin in full rage, describing the ominous situation in New Orleans over the radio air waves: "I need buses, I need troops, … get every Greyhound in the country and get their asses to New Orleans … Excuse my French everybody in America, but I am pissed!" Robinette commends Nagin, arguing that while everyone was trying to be politically and racially correct, only Nagin had the guts to speak out.

Louisiana Governor Kathleen Blanco is then interviewed and explains, "The slow response was a puzzle to me. As Governor I threw every asset that I had against the storm." But Nagin then suggests that for the governor the situation became a power struggle. Lee carefully crafts the inner workings of the blame game from a first hand perspective. We hear state and local officials offer their individual perspective. In an article in a London newspaper, Lee was asked why federal officials weren't interviewed in the documentary. He explained, "They are conspicuous by their absence." He said that nearly all of them declined (*Financial Times*, 12/2/06, p. 46).

We hear national leaders and media figures comment on the failures of federal officials. But this is where national media coverage of the situation ended. In national news coverage after the storm, the primary message about New Orleans was one of chaos. While national audiences had context when judging federal officials, they may not have had much context when judging Louisiana's governor and the mayor of New Orleans. As a result, to those unfamiliar with Nagin and Blanco, the picture of each created in national media had the potential to conjure stereotype in the minds of viewers. As a black male, Nagin was portrayed as an incompetent city official who lost control (especially when national media played the recording of him cussing on the airwaves over and over again). As a woman, Kathleen Blanco became a poster child of sorts representing the age-old stereotypical belief that women can't handle responsibility in government.

But through the documentary Lee explored the possibility that the problems among government officials extended beyond the events surrounding Katrina. In the documentary, Nagin takes the viewer back to the first meeting he had with President Bush and Governor Blanco.

He says that as they sat around a table he "cut to the chase" by saying, "Mr. President if you and the governor don't get on the same page this is gonna embarrass the nation." He says that the president then met with the governor in private. Bush came out of the meeting and told Nagin that he and Blanco had a difficult time coming to an agreement but that he gave her two options and she told him she needed time to think about it. The governor attempts to defend herself in an interview, saying, "It wasn't as though I asked the president for 24 hours to make a decision."

Lee then backtracks through the voices of local newspaper reporters who explain that both Nagin and Blanco are Democrats. During the last gubernatorial election (pre-Katrina) Nagin publicly backed Republican candidate Bobby Jindal, a Republican and friend of the Bush Administration. Since then there has been animosity between the two. This exchange allows context that the national media missed. It is important because it suggests that just as politicians play politics in any other city or state around the country, New Orleans and Louisiana are no different. Lee allows audiences the opportunity to recognize that the failure to react was not necessarily about race, but about politics. To further drive this important point home, former New Orleans Mayor Marc Morial ends the segment in an interview saying, "I don't care what the political relationship is between the mayor and the governor. Political B.S. has to be put aside!"

In an interview in *Newsweek* (August 21, 2006) Lee explains, "One important thing to come out of this is you could be next. You are living on the San Andreas Fault, or in a flood zone, or where tornadoes hit. These are natural disasters" (p. 94). The film's analysis of the post-Katrina leadership crisis had the benefit of hindsight, but it does provide a model for news organizations to find alternative perspectives that are useful in explaining the complexities of a crisis. Rather than falling back on stereotypical notions and standard sources of information, the coverage (and its impact on audiences' perceptions) would surely have been different.

Transforming the Jericho Road

> Most of Katrina's victims were black, but Lee hasn't made a racial polemic. Some viewers will be surprised to find that Lee views the tragedy as a national betrayal rooted in class not skin color. To him, what the victimized share most is that they had very little to begin with and were left with nothing.
>
> (*Newsweek*, August 21, 2006, p. 96)

In Lee's interview with cultural critic Dyson, Dyson recalls Martin Luther King, Jr. when he spoke of the Jericho Road in the Bible: When you see a beggar along the road and you give him money, that's charity and that's good. But eventually one must ask why that man can't get off the Jericho Road. What got him there? And sometimes it means that you have to transform the Jericho Road. New Orleans, for Dyson, is that Jericho Road. The situation that Katrina exposed in New Orleans didn't happen overnight. As Dyson explains, "People have made money from keeping an underclass in New Orleans." Calvin MacDonald, an engineering professor from Tulane University who was one of the locals who Lee used throughout the film, explained that crime was largely out of control in New Orleans before Katrina. He says that black males were killing black males at an alarming rate, the school system was one of the worst in the nation, the poverty rate was higher than that of any other major city in the nation and wages for laborers and professionals were well below national averages.

State Representative Karen Carter opines, "African-American crime on African Americans—particularly young black men—is a direct result of the education system … If you don't give them the opportunity to better themselves and in turn their families, it's a vicious cycle." Mayor Nagin and Carter agree on this point. He tells Lee, "The education system is killing the city. Young brothers are dropping out (dying) at 14, 15, 16 (years old) and getting involved in activities we wish they never would."

A myriad of voices—city council members, local news reporters, residents—describe the problems with the New Orleans Public Schools: a 60 percent dropout rate; state revenue so low that there was far too little support for public schools; the school system could not produce an accurate financial report for the past five years; the system was so corrupt and out of control pre-Katrina that the superintendent allowed the FBI to have an agent stationed at school board headquarters.

These statements are juxtaposed with a clip from CNN's Nancy Grace admonishing the residents of New Orleans based on reports of a double murder that took place shortly after residents were allowed back into the city. She suggests that the people of New Orleans have learned nothing after all they've been through. Grace, like so many other national journalists, just doesn't seem to get it. After Katrina, the national media latched onto stories about crime in New Orleans, suggesting that post-Katrina crime was worse than ever. But through the documentary Lee looks at the roots of the city's crime problem. He suggests that the reality is that crime, whether pre- or post-Katrina, is the direct result of something much deeper that has existed in New Orleans for decades. By offering context, a light is shed on a problem that exists not only in New Orleans, but in major cities around the country.

He also looks to the future for some of those displaced and the future of the city if better opportunities are not made available. Lee incorporates a local TV news story about a black woman from New Orleans named Cathy Phipps. Phipps was evacuated to Utah and separated from her son and daughter who were sent to Texas. She decided to bring them to Utah where the community embraced her. She was given a home, a job, better schools for her children and a positive outlook on life that she didn't have in New Orleans. In the piece Phipps says, "Looks like I went through this hurricane and made it to heaven!"

Lee clearly set out in his documentary to expose significant social issues that were at work in New Orleans before the storm. Denotatively, the film can be read as Lee as a provocateur. But beyond the provocation, the film works at the connotative level as a contrast to mainstream news coverage of Hurricane Katrina and its aftermath. Daily news tends to focus on the negative effects without looking at societal forces that cause those events. The residents of New Orleans responsible for committing crime before or after Katrina did not develop in a vacuum. Lee's film—working at multiple levels—does look to the past for lessons learned in hopes of creating a better future. The lessons of Katrina are useful in examining problems across impoverished parts of the country—but these lessons can't be learned from news organizations that don't scratch beyond the surface to find them.

The New Orleans Diaspora

Near the end of Act II, the audience sees a four-minute sequence in which a series of New Orleanians discuss their exodus from the city. As Terrence Blanchard's haunting musical score—a take on the classic "St. James Infirmary Blues"—plays in the background, they tell the stories of their departures, by plane or bus, to cities across the United States. This sequence, like the entire documentary, refrains from the hysteria that daily television journalism tends to conjure. The montage of evacuees features people who have been interviewed earlier in the film—white, black, poor, middle-class, male, female—telling the stories of their exits from the city at the hands of public officials. When they discover they are about to be flown to San Antonio, a white couple describes their efforts to reach family and friends to see if they can find someone who knows somebody who lives there. An African-American man discusses a trip that begins in Tennessee but takes him to Alabama, Florida, Louisiana and back to Alabama. Two men—one white, one black—describe their shock at being sent to Utah. A white man expresses his fear about being loaded onto a bus bound for Dallas and describes his successful effort to get off the bus at a rest area near Shreveport, Louisiana. Several discuss their separation from members of their family. An airport official defends the government's efforts to get people out of New Orleans, and "back to civilization," without concern for their ultimate destinations. An African-American woman says, "With the evacuation scattering my family all over the United States, I felt like it was an ancient memory, as if we had been on the auction block."

Lee then interviews cultural critic Dyson, who says a comparison of the New Orleans diaspora to the historical dispersal of slaves from ships is anything but "hyperbolic," an accusation he had faced from critics who said Dyson had engaged in racial rhetoric. "The fact is," says Dyson, "is that they *were* treating them like slaves. Families were being separated. People lost sight, lost sound, lost sense of their loved ones." The volume on Blanchard's musical score then rises, as Lee shows a powerful series of still photographs taken at shelters—domed sports complexes, gymnasiums, military bases—that show evacuated New Orleanians living dignified lives in remarkably trying circumstances. A close-up shot shows a toddler sucking his thumb as he sleeps on a cot. A mother feeds her baby. A family huddles on makeshift bedding on a gym floor. Children play jump rope. A young boy holds a puppy. The sequence ends with a series of photos that show people waiting in lines, where their sorrow—and the summer heat—is apparent. Lee's version of the New Orleans natives who lost their homes—a diverse group of people who survived extraordinary circumstances with dignity and compassion—contrasts dramatically with the images that Americans saw on television in the early days after Katrina, where those same citizens were portrayed as lawless savages, not victims of a government that had failed to respond to the largest disaster any American city has seen.

In *When the Levees Broke,* Lee clearly set out to provide audiences with a different sense of the impact of Hurricane Katrina on New Orleans than they were offered in the news coverage that followed the storm. A denotative or "preferred" reading of the film would acknowledge Lee's attempt to play his typical role as a voice of resistance. But beyond his role as a controversial film-maker, Lee has created a film that functions as an alternative form of journalism. His selection of sources to tell stories—some public officials, but just as many New Orleans locals who would never surface in mainstream news coverage—provides a much broader and more accurate perception of the event and of New Orleans. The power of both the aural and visual language of the film offer television and multimedia journalists a lesson in storytelling that could result in less myth-making and more accurate, useful coverage of daily events.

Conclusion

As we said early in this chapter, we understand the difference between daily journalism and the production of a documentary film. Daily journalism is a deadline-driven enterprise, and television news crews and anchors work under extreme pressure. Time limits on TV news often preclude thoughtful discussions of complicated issues. News organizations are also under increasing pressures from the corporate conglomerates that own them to build bigger audiences so that they can demand more money from their advertisers. Documentary producers have the luxury of time—both in the length of the stories they tell and in their efforts to track down reliable sources and useful experts. And Spike Lee had the support of the HBO cable network, so he didn't face the pressure that TV news organizations face from bean-counting executives.

And we also acknowledge that there was a lot of great daily journalism in the wake of Hurricane Katrina. The Pulitzer Prizes won by *The Times-Picayune* and the (Biloxi) *Sun Herald* were well deserved. The Peabody Awards handed out to CNN, NBC and local TV stations from New Orleans and Biloxi recognized the bravery of television journalists who produced remarkable stories about the storm's impact and the ineptitude of the government's response to the catastrophe.

But our concern is with the racist coding of New Orleans that television news audiences saw after Katrina. More than that, we are concerned about a news industry that does not seem particularly bothered by the fact that it reproduced horrendous stereotypes and that the routines of daily television journalism and how news is defined are so rarely questioned by journalists themselves. Is it possible for daily news programs to provide audiences with something beyond the shallow representations of daily events that currently define the news? Is it possible for 24-hour news networks to attract audiences by providing insightful and thoughtful coverage rather than repeating ad infinitum the day's most sensational headlines? Is it possible for TV news to tell stories that provide audiences with a more complex understanding of race and racism?

Years after Hurricane Katrina, much of the city of New Orleans remains in ruins. Some of the city's neighborhoods, including the tourist-friendly French Quarter, were spared from the flooding and quickly rebounded. But the vast majority of the city was under water for weeks, and many of those neighborhoods remained largely uninhabited. Many of the city's residents never returned. More than half of the city's homes were destroyed or heavily damaged. Public officials were slow to develop a plan for the city's recovery, and billions of dollars in federal funds that were supposed to be directed to the city were misspent or unspent. Outside of the region, daily journalism moved on. The primary story coming out of New Orleans in the years after the storm? That crime was on the rise. CNN's Anderson Cooper, viewed as a hero for his brave reporting from New Orleans shortly after Katrina, revisited the city two years later, and he titled the segment during his *360 Degrees* program "Murder City U.S.A.: 24 Hours in New Orleans." When the Pulitzer Prize finalists were announced in 2007, no news organizations were being cited for their continuing coverage of the disaster (Strupp, 2007). The American journalism industry had determined that the story of New Orleans' recovery was no longer newsworthy, and that the displacement of thousands of poor people—most of them black—no longer merited the attention that the alleged criminal activity in the flooded city deserved.

We believe that Spike Lee's *When the Levees Broke* is an example of compelling televisual storytelling that provides unusual insight into a complicated story and that recasts the catastrophe in New Orleans as a story of an underdog population that behaved heroically in the face of enormous government ineptitude. That's a story that is continuing today, and we believe it is a story that TV news audiences—if given the opportunity—would watch. We believe that Lee's film provides newsrooms with a new model for news coverage of daily events (like hurricanes and violent crimes), a model that allows for journalists to consider stories in the context of a broader cultural, economic, political and social history. For that to happen, television journalists would need to redefine their craft and to reconsider their approach to the entire news process. We sadly admit that that's not going to happen anytime soon. We also admit that the analysis in this chapter has its limitations. We have examined only a small piece of the network coverage that followed Katrina, and Lee's film is deserving of a much more comprehensive analysis. Our intention here is to raise important issues regarding racial coding in the news and to provide some questions for journalists, journalism students and journalism educators to consider.

Ron Dellums, the mayor of Oakland, California, once said, "Katrina was a metaphor for everything wrong in urban America. What Katrina did was expose the stark reality of the vulnerability of urban life" (quoted in Prince, 2006). It could also be argued that the network news coverage of the early days of the disaster was a metaphor for everything wrong with American journalism, and that Katrina exposed the stark reality that daily journalism is consumed by racism and is ill equipped to provide audiences with the kinds of complex and useful information that citizens in a healthy democracy need to make informed political decisions and to engender intelligent public policy. Spike Lee's *When the Levees Broke* gave audiences (and journalists) a taste of storytelling that resisted dominant, racist coding and that complicated rather than simplified the story of Hurricane Katrina, an event that will have an impact on the Gulf Coast region for years to come.

References

Brown, R., LeDuff, K., & Campbell, C. (2005). Rebirth of a nation: Race, myth and the news 2005. Paper presented at the convention of the Association for Education in Journalism and Mass Communication, San Antonio, August.

Campbell, C. P. (1995). *Race, myth and the news*. Thousand Oaks, CA: Sage Publications.

Campbell, C. P. (1998). Beyond employment diversity: Rethinking contemporary racist news representations. In Y. R. Kamalipour and R. Carilli (Eds.), *Cultural diversity and the U.S. media* (pp. 51–64). Buffalo, NY: State University of New York Press.

Dixon, T. (2004). Racialized portrayals of reporters and criminals on local television news. In R. A. Lind (Ed.), *Race/gender/media: Considering diversity across audiences content and producers* (pp. 132–145). Boston: Pearson.

Dixon, L . & Linz, D. (2000). Overrepresentation and underrepresentation of African Americans and Latinos as lawbreakers on television news. *Journal of Communication, 50* (2, Spring), 131–154.

Entman, R. M. (1990). Modern racism and the images of blacks in local television news. *Critical Studies in Mass Communication, 7*(4), 332–345.

Entman, R. M. (1992). Blacks in the news: Television, modern racism and cultural change. *Journalism Quarterly, 69*(2), 341–361.

Entman, R. M. (1994). African Americans according to TV news. *Media Studies Journal, 8* (3, Summer), 29–38.

Entman, R. M. & Rojecki, A. (2000). *The black image in the white mind: Media and race in America*. Chicago: University of Chicago Press.

Fiske, J. & Hartley, J. (1978). *Reading television*. London: Methuen & Co.

Gilliam, Jr., F. D. & Iyengar, S. (2000). Prime suspects: The influence of local television news on the viewing public. *American Journal of Political Science; 44* (3, July) 560–574.

Gray, H. (1991). Television, black Americans, and the American dream. In R. K. Avery & D. Eason (Eds.), *Critical perspectives on media and society* (pp. 294–305). New York: Guilford.

Hall, S. (1982). Encoding/decoding. In S. Hall, D. Hobson, A. Lowe, & P. Wills (Eds.), *Culture, media, language* (pp. 128–138). London: Hutchinson.

Heider, D. (2000). *White news: Why local news programs don't cover people of color*. Mahwah, NJ: Lawrence Erlbaum & Associates.

Holden, S. (2006, August 1). "When the Levees Broke": Spike Lee's tales from a broken city. *The New York Times*. Retrieved December 12, 2006 from: http://movies2.nytimes.com/2006/08/21/arts/television/21leve.html?n=Top%2fReference%2fTimes%20Topics%2fPeople%2fH%2f Holden%2c%20Stephen.

Learmonth, M. (Sept. 27, 2005). Ratings flood for Fox, CNN. *Variety.com*. Retrieved Jan. 25, 2006, from: http://www.variety.com/article/VR1117929812.html?categoryid=1275&cs=1.

LeDuff, K. (2009). *Tales of two cities: How race and crime intersect on local TV news*. Saarbrücken, Germany: Lambert Academic Publishing.

Mahoney, M. (1995). Racial construction and women as differentiated actors. In R. Delgado and J. Stefancic (Eds.), *Critical white studies: Looking behind the mirror* (pp. 305–309). Philadelphia; Temple University Press.

Parker, Laurence & Lynn, Marvin. (2002). What's race got to do with it? Critical Race Theory's conflicts with and connections to qualitative research. *Methodology and Epistomology, 8*(1), 7–22.

Pease, E. C. (1989). Kerner plus 20: Minority news coverage in the Columbus Dispatch. *Newspaper Research Journal, 10*(3), 17–38.

Poindexter, P. M., Smith, L., & Heider, D. (2003). Race and ethnicity in local television news: Framing, story assignments, and source selections. *Journal of Broadcasting & Electronic Media, 47*(4), 524–536.

Prince, R. (Nov. 6, 2006). A mayor-elect says media misread election. *Journalisms*. Retrieved Feb. 27, 2007 from: http://www.maynardije.org/columns/dickprince/061115_prince/.

Romer, D., Jamieson, Kathleen H., & de Coteau, Nicole J. (1998). The treatment of persons of color in local television news: Ethnic blame discourse or realistic group conflict? *Communication Research, 25* (3, June), 286–305.

Rowland, R. & Strain, R. (1994). Social function polysemy and narrative dramatic form: A case study of *Do the Right Thing*. *Communication Quarterly, 42*(3), 213–228.

Strupp, J. (March 14, 2007). List of leaked Pulitzer finalists expanded! *Editor and Publisher*. Retrieved March 15, 2007, from: http://w3556011ww.editorandpublisher.com/eandp/news/article_display.jsp?vnu_content_id=100.

Thevenot, B. (2006). Myth-making in New Orleans. *American Journalism Review*, December/January 2006. Retrieved March 9, 2006 from: http://www.ajr.org/Article.asp?id=3998.

Winn, J. E. (2001). Challenges and compromises in Spike Lee's *Malcolm X*. *Critical Studies in Media Communication*, 18(4), pp. 452–465.

Yosso, Tara J. (2002). Critical race media literacy: Challenging deficit discourse about Chicanas/os. *Journal of Popular Film and Television, 30* (1, Spring), 52–75.

Discussion Questions

1. Do you recall viewing news coverage of New Orleans in the days following Hurricane Katrina? Does this chapter's description of CNN's coverage appear consistent with the coverage that you viewed? When you viewed the coverage, did you consider the racial implications? Do you believe that CNN's journalists considered the racial implications of their coverage? Do you believe that television journalists often consider the racial coding in the stories they produce about violent crime?

2. How does the "coding" of African Americans in *When the Levees Break* differ from that in typical local TV news crime coverage?

3. Wildfires in California have caused people to have to evacuate and in some cases lose their homes, but the population being affected is very different from the one affected by Hurricane Katrina in New Orleans. Is there a difference in the way the national news covers the stories?

4. Since Hurricane Katrina there have been other natural disasters in the world including the 2004 tsunami and the earthquake in Haiti in 2010. How did the coverage of these natural disasters compare to the coverage of Katrina?

5. In the years following Katrina, news of the recovery in New Orleans began to fade, especially in the national news. The same happens for every disaster when new and breaking news stories rise to prominence. Why are follow-up stories important to communities trying to recover? How do these stories give voice to the voiceless?

Assignments

1. View Spike Lee's *When the Levees Broke*. First, write a summary of the documentary that explains the film's primary messages. Second, select two scenes from the film that you found particularly compelling. Describe those scenes, then describe your response; that is, describe what you found compelling.

2. There have been other documentaries done about Katrina. *Trouble the Water* was a documentary that included one New Orleans family's experience during and after Katrina. Watch the documentary and closely examine the images and depictions of the main characters. Is this positive? Does it offer useful insight by allowing audiences access to a lifestyle and experience that they may not know or understand? Or, does it do more harm than good by reiterating stereotypes of African Americans?

3. Search on-line and find at least two recent (published in the last year) follow-up stories about the recovery process in New Orleans post Katrina. Answer the following questions about each story:

   a. Was the story published by a major media organization? Which one? Is it based in Louisiana? (If not, where?)
   b. Would you classify the news angle as positive or negative? Why?
   c. What impression does the story give you about the status of life in New Orleans today?
   d. What sources are incorporated in the story? Are they diverse?
   e. Does the story seem objective or biased? Why?

Useful Tools on the Web

- The Real Media Ethics Web site includes a discussion of race and disaster coverage: http://realmediaethics.com/category/natural-disaster-journalism/.
- The Web site for the Dart Center for Journalism and Trauma includes advice on covering disasters: http://dartcenter.org/.

CHAPTER 11

Localizing Terror, Creating Fear in Post 9/11 Local TV News

KIM M. LEDUFF

As the war on terror continued and the focus shifted from Iraq to Afghanistan, American citizens expressed mixed feelings about it. Of course there are many opinions when it comes to the war on terror, but time has also allowed many to forget the sense of fear that existed in this country when America was under attack on September 11, 2001. There are occasional reminders in the news of why we are at war. But national and local news outlets don't cover terrorism with the same fervor that they did immediately following the attacks in New York and Washington D.C. on September 11, 2001. Truth be told, this may not be such a bad thing. Immediately following the attacks of September 11, 2001, the media often created an unwarranted sense of urgency and fear in audiences. The coverage wasn't always event driven. At times news outlets would ponder the "what ifs." What if there was another attack on U.S. soil? What if terrorists were living among us? The possibilities were endless and so was the potential to create anxiety and fear in the hearts and minds of American viewers.

The data examined in this chapter was collected at a time when America was consumed by the terrorist attacks and the possibility of waging war on those believed to be responsible. On March 20, 2003, President George W. Bush officially declared war on Iraq. According to the BBC News, "U.S. cruise missiles and bombs were dropped on Iraq's capital city,

Baghdad. They were targeting Saddam Hussein, his sons, key members of his leadership and government buildings" (BBC, 2003). As the war on terror began, American audiences often were often reminded by both local and national news media that there was the possibility that more attacks might occur on American soil. Local TV news stations across the country thought it might be useful to look into possible terrorist connections in their respective cities. This study is a case study of one such report in Indianapolis, Indiana. A series of reports on one local station exemplified how the local news media perpetuated unnecessary and unwarranted fear in viewers.

Media Frames

A study of how local media framed terrorism is important because it serves as an example of the power mass media have to shape the perceptions of audiences. Framing analysis is a useful theory when examining how storytelling can affect viewers. Entman (1993) says that "to frame is to select some aspect of a perceived reality and make them more salient in communicating text in such a way as to promote a particular problem definition, causal interpretation, moral evaluation, or treatment recommendation for the item described" (p. 52). Iyengar (1991) defines two types of frames: episodic frames that tend to be more dramatic and visually interesting and thematic frames that offer context, background and analysis in the news story (pp. 15–16).

Weaver (2007) notes that framing may also be referred to as second level agenda setting: "Both are more concerned with how issues or other objects (people groups, organizations, countries, etc.) are depicted in the media than with which issues or objects are more or less prominently reported" (p. 145). Severin and Tankard (2001) also note that "Much of the power of framing comes from its ability to define the terms of a debate without the audience realizing it is taking place" (p. 27). This becomes especially dangerous when race or ethnicity of a particular group is identified as a danger in news. Most people don't experience terrorism personally on a daily basis. What they know about is usually what they learn from watching the news. Post 9/11 this has been common in coverage of Arab people living in the U.S. The American Muslim Voice Foundation reports that even six years after 9/11:

> There is a rising tide of Islamaphobia, intensified by the war in Iraq and U.S. government measures at home. Americans' attitudes about Islam and Muslims are fuelled mainly by political statements and media reports that focus almost solely on the negative image

of Islam and Muslims. The vilification of Islam and Muslims has been relentless among segments of the media and political classes since 9/11.

(Ghazali, 2007)

While a great deal of mass communication research has focused on the treatment of African Americans and Latinos over the years, research regarding the depiction of Arab people was virtually nonexistent prior to the event of 9/11 and appears to have peaked post 9/11. Definitions of racism still apply when looking at how this group has been portrayed in the media. Gilliam and Iyengar (2000) define "new racism" as being closely tied to conservative beliefs in modern society:

The new racism is thought to be symbolic, subtle, covert, hidden, and underground. Although the meaning and measurement of the new racism has varied widely from study to study and has been the basis of much controversy, there is a general agreement that racial attitudes have become increasingly tied to support for traditional American values.

(p. 566)

In the case of Arabs (ethnic minorities in the U.S.) and Muslims (religious minorities in the U.S.), they are depicted as the antithesis of what is considered traditionally American in the mass media. This is especially true since the terrorist attacks.

The Cultural Indicators Project is a good place to begin looking into the impact of TV news images on audiences. The work of George Gerbner and his colleagues (1969), "Cultivation Research," explored violence on television and found that the more people watched television, the more violent they believed the world to be. Gerbner and Gross (1976) found that "television cultivates opinions about social reality which heavy viewers will learn from being disproportionately exposed to them: victims, like criminals, must learn their proper roles and televised violence may perform the teaching function all too well" (p. 45). Cultivation theory suggests that heavy television viewing cultivates beliefs about the real world in individual audience members. The theory is approached with certain basic assumptions: television is a storyteller, all programming reinforces common themes, and viewers are unselective when watching programming (Gerbner & Gross, 1976). As a result, Gerbner and his camp suggest that mainstreaming occurs, meaning that because television messages are similar, they override any political or social beliefs causing commonality of perspective among viewers.

Hawkins and Pingree (1981) re-analyzed the work of Gerbner and his colleagues and suggest that whether individuals are heavy or light viewers is not as telling as analyzing the type of content they select and what they believe to be true in their real world experiences (p. 300). They offer five steps involved in the process of constructing social reality: information processing, critical awareness of media messages, direct exposure and experience, social-structural influences, and active (rather than passive) audience members. Similarly, Entman (1994) argues that "over time, the specific realities depicted in single stories may accumulate to form a summary message that distorts social reality. Each in a series of news stories may be accurate, yet the combination may yield false cognitions within audiences" (pp. 509–510). According to Delgado and Stefancic (2001), "Society constructs the social world through a series of tacit agreements mediated by images, pictures, tales, and scripts. Much of what we believe is ridiculous, self-serving, cruel, but not perceived to be so at the time. Attacking embedded preconceptions that marginalize others or conceal their humanity is a legitimate function of all fiction" (p. 42).

Terrorists in Indiana

This chapter is an attempt to identify specific elements of news stories that evoke both positive and negative interpretations from viewers. Visual and auditory cues were examined in the stories individually and in combination. When looking at a news story, most viewers first process the message at the denotative level. This, according to Berger (1998), means "taking terms literally (including images, sounds, objects, or other forms of communication)" (p. 85). Hall (1982) explains that this is the meaning as intended by the producer. But rarely is the message decoded exactly as intended by the audience. This is where the connotative reading comes in. Connotation is defined by Berger (1998) as "the cultural meanings attached to a term—and by extension, an image, a figure in text, or even a text" (p. 84). In this research there were specific elements that I looked for in the story as I made both denotative and connotative interpretations. I looked for stereotypical images of Middle Eastern people. Functioning as the critical viewer also enabled me to piece together stories as they were told and to make interpretations.

Semiotic analysis allows critical researchers to analyze both words and visuals on a number of levels. For the purposes of this study I examine both denotative and connotative readings. Barthes (1972) refers to denotation as the first level of signification or words and images described in literal terms, whereas the connotative reading is an interpretation of what is signified. The connotative reading is where the researcher attempted to identify possible interpretations in the minds of viewers. This differs from *quantitative research*—like content analysis and survey research—that attempts to use mathematical methods to prove theories and hypotheses. *Qualitative research* is not governed by a single theory, but is more or less critical theory (Lazarsfeld, 1941). The analysis presented in this research, much like the work of Campbell (1995) and Heider (2000), is an effort to contribute to an on-going conversation about race and news among critical scholars. The goal is to identify intricate details of the news story that convey larger meanings.

Wolfe (1992) acknowledges that there is some question about this type of analysis as it relates to media texts. Some insist "the meaning of media texts is found not in the texts themselves, but rather in audience activity in relation to them" (p. 261). The criticism is that without audience analysis the interpretation of the text is deemed meaningless. For the purposes of this study the texts alone will be analyzed because, as Wolfe (1992) points out, "an approach to mass media texts derived from certain literary-critical, film, theoretical, and communication perspectives can account for identifiable textual elements that arguably enunciate meanings such texts may be said to convey" (p. 262). The researcher functions as a critical viewer and therefore is arguably capable of offering an analysis of the text which might be representative of the message as interpreted by other viewers.

A series of reports on WTHR-TV in Indianapolis in 2003 focused on Muslim student groups on major university campuses in Indiana. Angie Moreschi, a white female reporter, conducted the "investigative" reports. The series began with coverage of possible connections to al-Qaeda at Indiana University in Bloomington, Indiana. The story began with the anchor lead-in: "For the past three months the eyewitness news investigators looked into terrorist threat level in Indiana and tonight Angie Moreschi uncovers evidence of a link between Bloomington and an al-Qaeda sleeper cell." She reports: "The FBI won't say who is under surveillance and why. But the eyewitness news investigators have learned one reason why authorities might be so interested." In a reporter stand-up in front of the Islamic Center on the campus of Indiana University in Bloomington, the reporter explains that a prayer leader by the name of Juma el Desari is the reason for concern. Apparently, he is linked to an al-Qaeda sleeper cell in New York that was exposed shortly after 9/11.

The reporter explains that the Indiana FBI would not talk about the investigation. Tom Fuentes (a white male) of the Indiana FBI, however, confirmed in a sound bite that Juma was part of the cell. The group known as the Lackawanna Six was trained in Afghanistan. The Lackawanna Six defense attorney, Rodney Personius, then explains Juma's relationship to the group: "Juma was basically brought on the scene to close the deal. Mr. Juma would focus on the idea that you've led a bad life, now it's time to cleanse your soul. The only way you can do it is to attend this religious Jihad like training in Afghanistan."

The reporter then goes to the neighborhood where Juma reportedly spent time in New York. Juma is described as emotional and charismatic. The video is file footage of an Afghan terrorist training camp. The report then turns back to Bloomington, Indiana, where leaders at the Bloomington Mosque were asked if they knew of this connection. The reporter speaks to two men, one who appears to be a white Muslim and the other who looks more Middle Eastern. The white one, Nathan Ainsley, who is identified as the former president of the student organization, speaks first: "It wouldn't be surprising. Muslims are known to live in Iowa, Illinois, Indiana. Muslims live in the Midwest. It wouldn't be surprising. But, like, none of us know this guy."

The reporter asks, "Did Juma have discussions here similar to those in Lackawanna? Did he recruit anyone here to attend the al-Qaeda camp?" She then explains that after their interview, mosque leader Nathan Ainsley did not return her calls. She also says that the man featured in the interview, Amr Sabry, refused to talk on camera again. He told her in a phone interview that Juma was a paid employee of the Mosque and the audience hears segments of his phone interview: "He never did anything as far as I know except for once … There was an informal discussion, he said something about the Taliban talking about how good they were and he was kind of sympathetic. Another person disagreed with Juma, yelled at him and they got into an argument."

Sabry would not say if Juma talked to him or why he left. The reporter explained that after 9/11 he went to Afghanistan to fight for the Taliban and was now in custody as an enemy combatant and being held at Guantanamo Bay. The reporter explained that Juma also reportedly spent time on the campus of Purdue University and there will be follow up there in another story. The anchor ends the package by noting: "Earlier this year a major al-Qaeda operative captured indicated an attack on the heartland specifically targeting gas stations for fuel tankers. The FBI put out an alert, so heartland states like Indiana are on the radar."

To critically analyze this story, first it is important to remember that this was a year and a half after the 9/11 attacks and America was entering the war on terror. This was indeed a scary time in America. It is also essential to refer back to the literature on framing. Papacharissi and Oliveira (2008) say that "applying frames to a crisis situation such as a terrorist attack may serve as a strategy with which to identify main causes and responsible agents, make moral judgments, and finally to suggest policy responses to the event" (p. 54). In this case all these elements were present, but the fact remains that this was essentially a "what if" story rather than a story grounded in factual evidence.

On the denotative level this story is simply the news media speculating about the potential for terrorist organizations to strike in Indiana. The reporter simply talks to people on a local college campus about possible connections to al-Qaeda. In light of the fact that universities tend to be diverse environments where students come from around the world for educational purposes, there may be some logic in thinking of universities as a potential point of entry to the U.S. for those with ill intentions.

But on the connotative level stories like this one strike fear in viewers where there may not be reason for it. The story begins by saying the FBI is conducting investigations of possible connections between Indiana and al-Qaeda sleeper cells. The fact that the FBI is involved suggests to viewers that this must be serious. But the point is that the reporter takes it upon herself to investigate the universities—she says the FBI won't identify where they are investigating. But the fact that this is news and news is supposed to be factual likely causes audiences to unconsciously put a great deal of belief into the possibility that dangerous people might be lurking on college campuses in Indiana.

This message is also dangerous for people who are part of the ethnic or religious groups identified as "the enemy" in this piece. The story doesn't make it clear that many students affiliated with the Muslim student centers may have no connection to or don't share the beliefs of those who are responsible for violent acts. The suggestion that members of these organizations are on college campuses and that they want to target the Midwest are presented as fact in this story, with little or no context.

Another danger was the imagery that was implicit in this story. The placement of a Muslim man who appears to be white may cause audiences to believe that they are in even greater danger because some times (as in this story) the enemy "looks just like us" (Americans). It is also interesting to note that even in this case, of the two men, the reporter chooses to use sound bites of the Muslim who looks white as the authoritative voice and places the darker of the two in a position as one who has something to hide. The combination of imagery, language and the story frame suggest to audiences that the threat level for those in Indiana may be higher than the reality. But this was only the first part of the series. In the next part, an effort was made to put things into context for audiences who might not understand the complexity of Muslim religious beliefs.

Fear of Wahabbism

The follow-up story by the same reporter, Angie Moreschi, begins with footage from 9/11 and sounds of people screaming. She begins: "The kind of hate for America that produces this kind of terror has its roots in a radical form of terror known as Wahabbism." In a graphic, an image of the Koran floats over images of people running in the streets and fire burning. The word *Wahabbism* fades into the image. The next shot is of the two men featured in the previous day's story from the Bloomington Muslim Center. The more Middle Eastern-looking of the two, Amr Sabry, says: "It's a mystery, nobody admits to being a part of it. It's a derogatory term." The other, Ainsley, adds, "It's got a negative connotation. If you call someone a Wahabbi, you're calling them a fundamentalist." The audience sees video of the two praying as the reporter explains that the overwhelming majority of Muslims do not promote violence as a practice of their religion. Ainsley tells her, "I don't know anyone who ever has those kinds of points of view who would even consider doing anything violent." The next part of the package recaps what was covered the day before about Juma. The story then turns to the Greater Lafayette Islamic Center at Purdue University.

The reporter talks to a student, Ebadatullah Shahrani, who says he remembers a Juma at the center: "I do remember an Imam that came here a couple years ago that didn't know very much English. He would give talks in Arabic and there would be a translator." Shahrani says that the center functions under Salafi influence. Another graphic similar to the one prior appears and the word *Salafi* fades into the graphic. The reporter explains that it is a less controversial term used to describe Wahabbism. Shahrani explains that there is support for violence of some sorts. He says that during the Iraq war there were prayers for the killing of American soldiers in Iraq on the campus of Purdue. Tom Fuentes of the FBI appears again, noting that the bureau is concerned about when talk amongst Muslim students will become action.

Once again it is important to look at what was likely intended (the denotative reading) as opposed to what the images, words and frames connote. First of all, this second part of the story offered more context—but not without stereotypical implications. First of all, the screams and fire that were part of the presentation of Wahabbism suggest to audiences that this aspect of the Muslim religion is dangerous and threatening. This is especially true for American audiences who have little to no understanding of the religion or the term being presented and, more than likely, little to no direct contact with Muslim people. Papacharissi and Oliveira (2008) remind us that "frames present a central part of how individuals cognitively comprehend and file events, and as such are an important determinant of how a news story is told, especially in times of conflicting accounts and factual uncertainty" (p. 53). In light of September 11, it is no wonder the religion is presented in this story as dangerous and shrouded in secrecy. It is also likely that this piece only reinforces negative perceptions in American minds about Muslims and Middle Eastern people who were virtually non-existent in American media prior to the events of 9/11.

Once again, the reporter features the white-looking Muslim as opposed to the more Middle Eastern-looking men first. And as in the first piece, the Arab-looking men come across as secretive, when the first suggests that no one would admit to being involved in the religion and the second says that they do believe in violence. The white-looking Muslim says he doesn't know anyone who holds those beliefs. One might ask, which of the three is perceived by the audience as being most credible? Which men are perceived as most dangerous? The story clearly places the two darker skinned men in the position of withholding information. While the white Muslim claims not to know anyone who holds the violent Wahabbi beliefs, one can't help but wonder if he is being truthful or falling under the influence of what is depicted as a dangerous religion. The images and words suggest to audiences the danger of a religion capable of "brainwashing" someone who appears white and American to lie to and potentially hurt his own people. This is yet another stereotype that viewers see more and more of since the declaration of war on Iraq—the depiction of Muslim people as negative and lurking in the shadows of mainstream culture, waiting to strike.

The story reaffirms the danger for those living in close proximity to these universities when a student from the Purdue Muslim student center reports that there were students on campus praying that American soldiers would be harmed in Iraq, and the FBI agent confirms that his organization is concerned. This sounds threatening to American audiences. Should we be scared? In a column following the events of 9/11, syndicated columnist Leonard Pitts made a valid point that this story forgets. He cautioned, "Take it as a reminder: The enemy is not Arab people or the Muslim religion. The enemy is fanaticism, extremism, intolerance, hate. The madmen who commandeered these planes don't represent the followers of Islam any more than the madmen who blow up abortion clinics represent followers of Christ" (9/12/01).

Framing the Unknown

It is unfortunate that Arabs and Muslims are minority groups that rose to prominence in U.S. news in a negative and dangerous light after the September 11 attacks in 2001. Delgado and Stefancic (2001) note that "the differential racialization thesis maintains that each disfavored group in this country has been racialized in its own individual way and according to the needs of the majority group at particular times in its history" (p. 69). It is clear that in an effort to build support for "the war on terror," mainstream society and news media have found a new minority group to pit audiences against. While the stereotypes of other minority groups have long and deeply entrenched histories, the stereotypes of Middle Easterners and Muslims began to truly shape through media frames since 9/11. Ethnic minorities such as Afghans, Iraqis, Iranians and others were lumped under one label, not by ethnicity but crime—terrorism. The same can be said for Muslims regardless of sect (Sunni, Shia, etc.) or school of thought (Hanafi, Maliki, Wahabbi, etc.). American audiences and, in many cases, American reporters are not familiar enough with these groups to have an under-standing of the underlying complexity of the situation.

This study examines only one example, in one city, of local news attempting to localize a national and international news story and simplify it in a way to make it palatable for American audiences. The only problem is that, in the process, journalists stereotype and make assumptions that are dangerous for audiences and for those who are part of the groups being singled out as potential terrorists. *Cultivation* and *Construction of Social Reality* theories suggest that media have a "mainstreaming" effect. This means that when audiences are repeatedly exposed to similar messages about a particular issue they develop an over-arching believe about the issue. It is not difficult to imagine the over-arching image that many Americans have about Muslims and people of Middle Eastern descent based on the coverage in both the local and national media that wrongly equates all members of these groups with terrorism. It is an unfair and potentially dangerous depiction.

Blondheim and Liebes (2003) called the media coverage following the September 11 attacks a "disaster marathon." This was true not only of the coverage that immediately followed the events but also the coverage that came along after every attempted bombing or suspected terrorist incident that has occurred since September 11, 2001. The color-coded terror threats slide back and forth from yellow… to orange … to red … and back again. But what does that really mean for Americans? Is it creating reasonable awareness in dangerous times or is it just another way for the media to heighten fear and anxiety amongst viewers? The answer is debatable.

It is important to note that in the years since this data was collected there have been no terrorist attacks on the campuses of Indiana or Purdue (nor in the state of Indiana for that matter). An attempted attack was thwarted on Christmas Day 2009 on a plane headed for Detroit, and once again the media jumped on board questioning airplane security and the future safety of air travel in America and abroad. There have been many lessons learned by the media post 9/11, but it does not appear that they are any less likely to ponder the "what ifs" even when those stories are weak on facts and are approached with less than objective frames.

References

Barthes, R. (1972). *Mythologies.* (A. Lavers, Trans.) New York: Hill and Wang.

Berger, A. (1998). *Seeing is believing.* Mountain View, CA: Mayfield Publishing.

Blondheim, M. & Liebes, T. (2003). From disaster marathon to media event: Live television's performance on September 11, 2001 and September 11, 2002. *Crisis Communication. Lessons from September, 11,* 185–197.

Campbell, C. (1995). *Race, myth and the news.* Thousand Oaks, CA: Sage.

Delgado, R. & Stefancic, J. (1997). *Critical white studies: Looking behind the mirror.* Philadelphia: Temple University Press.

Delgado, R. & Stefancic, J. (2001). *Critical race theory: An introduction.* New York: New York University Press.

Doob, A. & McDonald, G. (1979). Television viewing and fear of victimization: Is the relationship causal? *Journal of Personality and Social Psychology, 37,* 170–179.

Entman, R. (1993). Framing: Toward clarification of a fractured paradigm. *Journal of Communication, 43,* 51–68.

Entman, R. (1994). African Americans according to TV news. *Media Studies Journal, 8* (3, Summer), 29–38.

Gerbner, G. (1969). Toward cultural indicators: The analysis of mass mediated message systems. *Communication Review, 17,* 137–148.

Gerbner, G. & Gross, L. (1976). Living with television: The violence profile. *Journal of Communication, 26*(2), 173–199.

Ghazali, Abdus Sattar (2007). American Muslims 6 years after 9/11. *American Muslim Voice.* Retrieved June 2009 from: http://www.amuslimvoice.org/html/body_six_years_after.html.

Gilliam Jr., Franklin D. & Iyengar, S. (2000). Prime suspects: The influence of local television news on the viewing public. *American Journal of Political Science, 44* (3, July), 560–574.

Hall, Stuart. (1982). Encoding/decoding. In S. Hall, D. Hobson, A. Lowe, & P. Willis (Eds.), *Culture, media, language.* London: Hutchinson.

Hawkins, R. & Pingree, S. (1981). Television's influence on social reality. In National Institute of Mental Health (Ed.), *Television and behavior: Ten years of scientific progress and implications for the eighties. Vol. 2: Technical review* (pp. 224–247). Rockville, MD: National Institutes of Health.

Heider, Don. (2000). *White news: Why local news programs don't cover people of color.* New Jersey: London: Lawrence Erlbaum & Associates.

How did the war start? *BBC.* Retrieved December 2006 from: http://news.bbc.co.uk/cbbcnews/hi/find_out/guides/world/iraq/newsid_2181000/2181249.stm.

Iyengar, S. (1991). *Is anyone responsible? How television frames political issues.* Illinois: University of Chicago Press.

Lazarsfeld, P. (Ed.) (1941). *Radio research.* New York: Arno Press.

Papacharissi, Z. & Oliveira, M. (2008). News frames terrorism: A comparative analysis of frames employed in terrorism coverage in U.S. and U.K. newspapers. *The International Journal of Press and Politics, 13*(1), 52–74.

Pitts, L. (2001, September 12). We'll go forward from this moment. *The Miami Herald.* Retrieved January 23, 2010 from: http://www.miamiherald.com/living/ columnists/leonard-pitts/v-print/story/374188.html.

Severin, J. S. & Tankard, Jr., J. (2001). Scientific method. Ch. 2 in *Communication theories: Origins, methods, and uses in the mass media* (5th ed., pp. 25–46). New York: Longman.

Weaver, D. (2007). Thoughts on agenda setting, framing and priming. *Journal of Communication, 57,* 142–147.

Wolfe, A. (1992). Who's gotta have it? The ownership of meaning and mass media texts. *Critical Studies in Mass Communication, 9,* 261–276.

Discussion Questions

1. There are many misconceptions about Middle Eastern people in the U.S. Often the terms Arab and Muslim are used interchangeably. Why is this problematic?

2. Other than the negative images seen in the news, can you think of other images of people of Middle Eastern descent in other places in the mass media? Entertainment? Sports? Others?

3. Do you remember where you were on September 11, 2001? What did you think of the media coverage surrounding the events? Is "disaster marathon" a good way of describing it? Why?

4. Middle Eastern men are often depicted as terrorists in the news. But what is the image of Middle Eastern women often portrayed in the media?

Assignments

1. Is there a Muslim student association on your campus? Plan a visit to the center or have a representative come to class and discuss some of the common misrepresentations of Muslim people in the mass media.

2. Newspaper columnist Leonard Pitts won a Pulitzer Prize in 2004, but received a great deal of attention for his raw and emotional columns in the days following 9/11. Find his September 12, 2001 column, "We'll go forward from this moment" and his September 13, 2001 column "Hatred is unworthy of us" and discuss some of the points he makes about America and how he anticipated we would recover from September 11. Describe his concerns. Were his predictions true?

3. Sometimes it is helpful to see ourselves through the eyes of others. How do you think Muslim people might view Americans and Christians? Do they lump together American and Christian values? What might they believe about the way American women

are treated? Do they see American soldiers as allies? Do some research on-line and see what you find.

For Further Study

Ali-Karamali, Sumbul. (2008). *The Muslim Next Door: The Qur'an, the Media, and That Veil Thing.* White Cloud Press.

American Muslim Voice: http://www.amuslimvoice.org/html/body_six_years_after.html.
(A Web site dedicated to helping Americans understand the life and culture of Muslims living in America.)

Moore, Michael (2004). *Fahrenheit 9/11.*
(This documentary was made by controversial social critic Michael Moore and offers a unique take on the events surrounding September 11 and the war on terror declared by President George Bush.)

Miami Herald columnist Leonard Pitts; 9/11 column: http://www.miamiherald.com/2001/09/12/374188/sept-12-2001-well-go-forward-from.html.
For a different perspective on the war on terror, view the Arab news organizations English-language site at http://english.aljazeera.net/.

CHAPTER 12

Race and Objectivity

Toward a Critical Approach to News Consumption

CHERYL D. JENKINS AND DONYALE R. GRIFFIN PADGETT

> Objectivity is a false god. We are human beings and we screw up
> or have flaws that are hidden from us. But fairness and balance are
> possible. Not stereotyping people we write about is possible. We
> can be skeptical without being cynical ...
> (Ken Auletta, *New Yorker* columnist, 2010, n.p.)

To the average American journalist, following the hallowed tenet of
objectivity in news reporting is as much a priority as making sure every
fact is correct. Impartiality and detachment from news stories are taught
as the ultimate goals of good news reporting. But with the history of
American journalism filled with examples of disturbing representations of
people and communities of color and the use of stereotypes and more
subtle myths reflected in routine coverage by local television journalists,
this foundational principle of journalism is weakening in stature and is
possibly an unrealistic and ineffectual achievement in the practice of
journalism. In this past decade alone, national coverage of stories with a
racial angle like Hurricane Katrina, the Don Imus controversy, Barack
Obama's presidential candidacy and even the Virginia Tech shootings,
have provided unique opportunities for journalists to add interpretation,
clarification and insight into stories that have sparked national dialogues
about race.

Unfortunately, media coverage of these significant news events and the media's questionable handling of the issues that specifically relate to race in this country became as great a problem as the issues themselves. Scholars like Dates and Barlow (1990), Campbell (1995), and Wilson, Gutierrez, and Chao (2003) have already surmised that traditional mainstream news media serve up a view of the world that may not be representative of American pluralism and that diverse views about issues that affect our lives are often absent in traditional mainstream storytelling. So, just as individual case studies in this book have pointed out obvious bias in news framing as it relates to stories dealing with race and the misrepresentation of marginalized groups, this chapter addresses the notion that how journalists are trained to report stories may be problematic in itself.

Problematizing Objectivity

The basis of contemporary traditional journalism calls for reporters to report in an unbiased and objective way, reporting free of interpretation. However, claiming to be objective or unbiased is virtually impossible because we all carry perceptions of the world that stem from our own personal experience. Nowhere is this more evidenced than in the Hurricane Katrina controversy with the reporting of photo captions by two different Associated Press photographers released on August 30, 2005 of two families (one black and one white) wading through the contaminated waters with food and other goods. The black man was identified with the caption "A young black man walks through chest deep flood water after looting a grocery store in New Orleans," while the white family was depicted as, "Two residents wade through chest-deep water after finding bread and soda from a local grocery store" (Haider-Markel, Delehanty, & Beverlin, 2007, p. 590). When asked why he labeled the black family as "looters," the photographer said he was simply reporting what he saw through *his* eyes. Reporting on this story and other similar stories is problematic in a general sense because organizing news stories involve subjective decision-making (i.e. deciding the angle, selecting the sources, deciding page placement) and there are limitations that are at play that involve bias before the content is disseminated to the viewers and readers.

But more specifically for our discussion in this chapter, when covering complex topics that involve issues of race, ethnicity and culture in general, we argue that taking an interpretive approach to news coverage can provide "a truthful, comprehensive, and intelligent account of the day's events in a context which gives them meaning" (Davies, 2005, p. 208). The benefits of news being reported and interpreted for clarity, value and cultural significance may be a more useful need in journalism than just repeating facts that have no intrinsic meaning or value to everyday citizens. This is not to say that a more interpretive form of journalism is free of balance or fairness. Nor do we advocate for the *opposite* of objectivity, which is subjectivity. On the contrary, interpretive journalism is not about putting oneself in the story; it's about looking at the news through the eyes of those who are being covered—those who are a part *of* the story. This could be done by explaining news developments in the context within which they are created, which lends itself to more analysis that goes beyond traditional reporting.

As a framework, objectivity is concerned with descriptive reporting. It uses a more straightforward description of events, in which reporters focus on facts and leave the interpretation of the event to the reader (Patterson, 2006). In his book *We the People*, Patterson (2006) argued that descriptive reporting is being upstaged by interpretive approaches that include a more in-depth analysis of stories. This is characterized by specific reporting styles that may include summarizing broad findings, providing explanations for complex stories, discussions of meaning or significance of the news, using unattributed statements and including reporter's opinions—the latter of which occurs mainly in editorial writing (Craig, 2006, p. 7).

Particularly as the media cover events of national importance, cultural significance, and with lasting effects, it becomes even more important to entertain the notion of a more critical read of those issues through an interpretive lens. Coverage of issues and events that have gained national attention like the Don Imus controversy, Hurricane Katrina, immigration and the like include a context with interpretation that allows consumers of media a broader view of the issues. In the case of Don Imus' gross misstep on the airwaves in which he referred to black women on the Rutgers University basketball team as "nappy-headed hos," Imus defended his choice of words using the justification that hip hop's own artists demean black women. His became a story about passing the blame instead of a story about the implications of a patriarchal society that seems to turn a blind eye to the objectification of black women. In an interview, Imus said, black rappers "call them worse names than I ever did" (Associated Press, 2007). A more interpretive approach to that story could have opened up the dialogue on the historical assault on black women in this country and the white male patriarchy that provides excuses for this behavior.

Also problematic in traditional journalistic coverage of stories is the over-emphasis of news stories that focus on crime by blacks and other non-whites that reflect what Stuart Hall (1982) calls the "preferred meanings" of the dominant white society. Citing a longitudinal study by Stabile

(2006), Byerly and Wilson (2009) argue that the criminalization of African Americans by the news media has been a staple of the news industry since the 1800s. Stabile recommends that journalists "need to break out of the crime news frame altogether, and seek the causes and solutions to such deeply entrenched social problems in places other than the criminal justice system, and offer perspectives that do not merely reproduce the logic of racialized [culture]" (Stabile, 2006, quoted in Byerly & Wilson, 2009, p. 215).

In addition, the effects of technological advancements made in multi-media platforms are at issue. With so much access to information via various technological innovations, media audiences are getting inundated with "stuff" that has no real meaning or context. These advancements have led to greater access for those who may otherwise have limited media consumption; but, unless the information is put into proper, intellectual perspective, clarity is difficult to achieve. With the public getting news from such an array of alternative news sources, (i.e. blogs, radio talk shows, cable news programming, social networking sites, etc.), it is imperative that reporting styles provide more depth in order to help consumers of news make sense of views expressed across these non-traditional forms of media. Otherwise, as Patterson (2006) argued, we are left with news that is "soft" and more like "infotainment" than information we can rely on.

As diverse issues and topics become progressively more common and as news story ideas and technological advancement in news dissemination allow a more diverse audience access to news and information, the rules of the newsroom and the idea of "real" objectivity in reporting and editing becomes a difficult tenet to navigate. However, the fact that a story itself involves diverse people is not enough. We need stories that are told by people with diverse backgrounds to expand the scope of coverage.

Revisiting Objectivity: A Tale of Two Students of Journalism

The authors of this chapter had relatively different experiences in their journalism training as undergraduates. For instance, one was trained in a minority scholarship program in the Midwest—a program that had been established by local media outlets that recognized that the field needed more diversity. In contrast, the other was trained in a more traditional journalism academic program and eventually worked for a newspaper owned by a major media conglomerate recognized as a leader in diversifying newsrooms and news content.

One was taught that objectivity was not the goal to strive for. Instead, students were asked to recognize the diverse perspectives with which the news is understood and report within the context of those who were being covered. It was also important to recognize that news was generally told through the eyes of the mainstream population, leaving much to stereotypical images, myths of people of color and often void of the perspectives of marginalized groups. This shaped not only the way she witnessed news on television and interpreted news in print, but also the way she understood the real story behind what was shown or printed.

The other's training was not specifically focused on issues of diversity, but on the structured or traditional guidelines and tenets of journalism. Her first introduction to covering news with aspects of multicultural concern actually came during her time as a working journalist. She was employed by a newspaper that was involved in a larger effort by its parent company to make news more "inclusive." She became engrossed with efforts of "mainstreaming" news stories to meet diversity requirements and was also involved in training sessions and seminars on diversity issues. Although these efforts by a major media company were unique at the time, the overall attempt for a more diverse news product did not trickle down to the paper for which she was a reporter. It became apparent that "just meeting the mainstreaming" requirements for a news story (add a black perspective and/or mug shot) was satisfactory for diversity requirements. This experience was actually helpful in her understanding of the difficulty in making news more diverse, insightful and inclusive in most mainstream newspapers. Many in the media see a dichotomous solution to making news more diverse while also remaining fair, balanced, and objective. But more critical discussions about the influence of personal world views or perspectives on news gathering have raised a legitimate concern about the role of traditional tenets in journalism.

Media scholars summarize objectivity as the "rules that mainstream journalists follow in attempting to arrive at the best obtainable version of the truth" (Brooks et al., 2002, p. 16). The idea of objectivity is to report stories without interpretation from the journalist. News organizations expect reporters to adhere to this idea that was created with the assumption that reporters inherently remove their emotions or personal perspectives from reporting the story. This concept has been and, according to the researchers, "still is accepted as a working credo by most American journalists, students, and teachers of journalism" (p. 16).

But such notions of this increasingly less transparent tenet of the traditional journalism process have become less ideal in popular media production and consumption, and many arguments against its achievement and usefulness have appeared in research on news gathering. As early as the 1960s, researchers (March & Simon, 1967; Tuchman, 1972) argued that in many instances objectivity can be seen as a strategic ritual protecting reporters from the risks of their trade and their critics. Tuchman (1972) observed:

> Newspapermen believe they may mitigate such continual pressures as deadlines, possible libel suits, and anticipated reprimands of superiors by being able to claim that their work is "objective." He (reporter) can claim objectivity by citing procedures he has followed which exemplify the formal attributes of a news story or a newspaper. For instance, the newsman can suggest that he quoted other people instead of offering his own opinions.
>
> (p. 660)

In this regard, Tuchman supports sociology scholar Everett Hughes' (1964) contention that occupations develop ritualized procedures to protect themselves from blame. Following the formal journalistic process of news story building, reporters are able to claim to have participated in the "strategic function" of objectivity (i.e. interviewed sources from two sides of an issue) and have thus successfully met the requirement of that tenet.

Tuchman's study coincided with the push by media scholars and members of the Kerner Commission (1968) for more diverse thought in the news business, and it provides a historical framework for arguments against and critiques of the traditional journalistic process. Historically, news standards and guidelines are defined and redefined depending on the era in which the "rules of news" are being discussed. Hume (1996) stated that even in the most respected newsrooms, traditional standards of verification, objectivity, and relevance have become more elusive. As such, contemporary arguments that challenge the idea of objectivity in journalism seem to have fewer cynics. As Mindich (1998) wrote, "Lately 'objectivity' has come under fire, a casualty of a bitter battle over the future of journalism … even though it was the central tenet in American journalism for much of this century (20th century), 'objectivity' has no biographer, no historian, no soothsayer" (p. 1).

Further, the contemporary arguments that challenge objectivity also have historical precedence. According to Davies (2005), journalists' faith in objectivity began to weaken between the years of 1945 and 1960 following several significant events in American history, including the Civil Rights Movement and Senator Joseph R. McCarthy's anti-Communist crusade. Following World War II, there was actually a "renewed emphasis on interpretation" of news information that illustrated how those within the journalism profession saw the shortcomings of objectivity. Davies argued, "Reporters found that just-the-facts journalism was ill suited for explaining the complex news about McCarthy and school desegregation" (p. 206). Critics of journalism during this time also called for changes in journalistic practices and "assailed objectivity directly" and by the 1960s, reporters were much more willing to include interpretive elements in news stories (p. 206).

Davies stated that complex news issues that dealt with economics and industry following World War II "seemed to demand a higher quality of news writing … editors and publishers believed that they had a responsibility to make such important information understandable to the public" (p. 206). News was more complex and readers needed to understand the complexities of the issues surrounding the economic conditions of the country. Davies cites journalism educator Frederic E. Merwin's definition of interpretation, who said that "interpretation is news writing that explained the 'how' and 'why' of news events." He continued:

> Interpretation means clarification, integration, and logical generalization. It merges background, present, and likely future. It always must be considered as a reporting not only of the bud that has just broken through the ground but also with the roots underneath which forced the bud out into the air.
>
> (p. 206)

Critics of objectivity saw the use of interpretive reporting as more significant than the "impossible" and sometimes "undesirable" use of objective journalism. As a result, the Associated Press announced that it would "step up its use of interpretive reporting" in the early 1940s, but as a companion to objectivity. Not surprisingly, the use of interpretive reporting was not without controversy. Davies (2005) stated that many editors during this period could not agree on the definition of interpretation with some believing it was "an objective accounting of events with additional background" and others believing it was "including the writer's definition of what a given development or statement may mean." Although debatable, editors ultimately agreed that there was an increased need for interpretive reporting "to bring depth and perspective to daily journalism" (p. 206).

This is particularly true in contemporary journalism in which the American news media serve an evolving demographic that is more brown, black and international than even two decades ago. Unfortunately, the news industry itself reflects limited understanding of that change, which is problematic if we are to have true interpretation of complex news issues that affect our society. A key recommendation from the Kerner Commission Report published 40 years ago states that more diverse voices in the news workforce play a major role in "identifying events, issues, and perspectives of those within their demographic communities" (quoted in Byerly & Wilson, 2009, p. 213). As such, diversity in our newsrooms is a major component in moving towards a more critical and interpretive account of news events.

Diversity and News Interpretation

The ultimate role of journalism is to provide information that should give people the ability to make intelligent decisions about their daily lives and about things that will affect them. That information needs to be synthesized in a way that's understandable in order to carry out that function. In order for this more interpretive form of journalism to be useful, there needs to be a continued push to have multiple perspectives providing the context for the information given in our news.

Each journalist is a product of his or her environment, so that diverse perspective will inherently come into play in their interpretation of complex topics; newsrooms that have fewer diverse voices have fewer diverse perspectives about what constitute news anyway. In fact, many scholars link the inadequacy of minority coverage to the lack of minority journalists and executives in mainstream newsrooms (Bramlett-Solomon, 1993; Dates & Barlow, 1990; Entman & Rojecki, 2000; Heider, 2000; Nishikawa et al., 2009). Moreover, what one thinks is news says as much about him/her as it does the story that one covers. Who writes and reports the news stories matters. Further, one's view of news will also reflect one's background, community and sense of audience (Scanlan, 2000). This assertion is also significant in the argument for a more interpretive form of journalism and re-evaluation of the almost century-old rule of journalism that requires news reporters to simply relate the facts of news truthfully and comprehensively without the conscious manipulation from social or cultural influence.

Unfortunately, despite the call for a more diverse news industry and coverage of minority issues by the Kerner Commission, there has been slow progress in the employment of minority journalists (Dates & Barlow, 1990; Nishikawa et al., 2009; Weaver & Wilhoit, 1991, 1996). According to a 2008 survey by the American Society of Newspaper Editors (ASNE), which monitors employment in the print industry, 13.5 percent of the 52,600 full-time journalists were people of color. This is a slight change from a decade ago when only 12 percent of the full-time journalists in newsrooms were racial minorities. According to Byerly and Wilson (2009), most of those journalists of color were concentrated in large urban areas, leaving small towns and rural communities—many of which are witnessing increases in people of color—with "woefully white reporting staffs" (p. 213). This overwhelming whiteness in most print newsrooms is also reflected in the broadcast industry. Consider network news' failure to use women and people of color as experts, even on issues related to gender and race. According to a study by Howard (2002), about 92 percent of all American sources on the big three U.S. network news shows in early 2000 were white and about 85 percent were male.

Lehrman (2002) asserted that many diversity pitfalls reflect a narrowness of vision. Some editors rely on cultural events to tell the story of a varied population, instead of incorporating people from a range of backgrounds into all stories, "be they about businesses, churches, growth debates, or what-have-you." He continues:

> You might call it the "all festivals, all the time" syndrome. Then there's "seen one (name the ethnicity or gender), seen 'em all"— a tendency by reporters to rely on one person to represent the opinions of an entire community. This is not only an unreasonable expectation, but we often select the wrong person. We also can make poor assumptions: that all white people are of Western European descent; that all Midwesterners are conservative, white and heterosexual. No wonder readers and listeners accuse us of inaccuracy.
>
> (p. 45)

In addition, Byerly and Wilson (2009) noted the Kerner Commission's contention that racial and ethnic minority reporters have always had a major role to play in identifying events, issues, and perspectives of those within their demographic communities: "Kerner commissioners envisioned the non-white journalist as key to the agenda-setting process for news organizations, as well as the mentors for white editors, news producers, journalists, photographers, and others in the production of news" (p. 213). So, a more diverse newsroom becomes a significant factor in incorporating more inclusive views within news topics that affect various cultural entities.

Applying an Interpretive Approach

The Don Imus controversy and the aftermath of Hurricane Katrina are two recent examples of media events in which coverage could have included a more interpretive approach to news reporting in order to provide a clearer perspective on a complex issue like race. They are obviously not the only two news events where an interpretive approach would be valuable, but were selected by the authors as examples to illustrate the usefulness of such an approach on complex news topics. The American news media have traditionally had a hard time covering issues that are concerned with class and race, issues that ultimately require diverse and critical perspectives. Reporting from a "narrow range" of proven topics on such issues, the news media, according to Entman (1990), may be "helping to encourage and legitimize modern racism by inadvertently reinforcing impressions of minorities as threatening, overly demanding, and undeserving" (p. 335). This is particularly the case when media organizations produce stories that take an "episodic" rather than a "thematic" perspective towards issues that are culturally sensitive. Instead of explaining the general background and implications of issues, news reports emphasize on the most recent and attention-getting developments, lacking a more comprehensive and intelligent discussion about how the topic may affect society.

Interpreting Don Imus

It's important to note that these two controversial incidents offer significantly different perspectives about the usefulness of interpretive journalism in synthesizing topics that deal with a complex issue like race. In the case of Don Imus, there were two issues that tend to undergird the complexity of the incident. The first issue centers around the use of pejorative language in the American culture in general and why that language seems to be acceptable coming from certain segments of the population and not others. Language itself is such an integral aspect of social construction and in-depth discourse on its significance in our culture could have possibly limited the "who's to blame" coverage and sparked the discussion on the impact of language and how it works in society.

Second, the news media tended to follow the seemingly natural tendency to generalize the foundational and cultural aspects of the "hip hop culture" by interchanging it with "black culture." For example, *Today* show contributor Mike Celizic (2007) quoted Imus as stating (in response to the controversy), "Those terms didn't originate in the white community. Those terms originated in the black community" (n.p.). Although the artistry and fan base of hip hop tends to be predominately African American and Hispanic, there are aspects of black culture that are not inherently hip hop. As such, to blame the perpetuation of derogatory and misogynistic language on the "black community" is problematic.

Coverage of the Don Imus controversy started out as an episodic account of a flamboyant and notorious radio shock jock's ghastly attempt at humor by referring to members of the 2007 Rutgers' women's basketball team as "nappy-headed hos." What eventually ensued were repeated protests by civil rights groups denouncing the remarks and calls for the firing of Imus for his insensitive and racially tinged words. The media followed the incident closely and highlighted the progress of both sides of the issue. On one side was Imus and his "first amendment" and "free speech" supporters, and on the other side, civil rights groups and activists bemoaning the use of federally regulated airwaves to spread derogatory and inappropriate language and commentary. Imus was ultimately fired for his actions, but that aspect of the news event took a backseat to a more popular angle in the story. Following Imus' firing, the media shifted its focus to center on the hip hop culture and misogynistic language in song lyrics by rap artists.

The origins of this angle actually stemmed from Imus himself as his "blame" of the hip hop community for the use of similar derogatory terms gained support from individuals across the country. As a result, some journalists, including African Americans, expanded their rhetoric concerning the Imus controversy to include rap bashing and moved the focus away from the initial outcry of racist, sexist remarks from Imus. The controversy is cleverly redirected to a now mediated discourse on the use of inappropriate language in the hip hop culture—a culture which consists of a large number of minority artists and fans. In this vein, the media begins to perpetuate the seemingly ongoing debate about misogyny and offensive language in rap music, the nucleus of artistic expression in the hip hop culture.

A more interpretive approach to the coverage of the Imus controversy would have included a critical explanation of language and race and how historically they share a role in social construction. The two constructs are also important in understanding the anger among some members of the African-American community for Imus' use of such language as a way of being humorous. His position in American society and the connotation of the language he used circumvents humor for those who have suffered physically, socially, politically and economically at the hands of the dominant power structure of society of which Imus is a part. *Times*' columnist James Poniewozik (2007) notes in a column titled, "The Imus Fallout—Who can say what":

Imus uses jokes to establish his power … He's hardly the only humorist to do that. But making jokes about difference—race, gender, sexual orientation, the whole list—is ultimately about power. You need to purchase the right to do it through some form of vulnerability, especially if you happen to be a rich, famous white man.

(n.p.)

Furthering this point, Imus' use of the racially tinged words "nappy-headed" is indicative of an obvious desensitization among segments of society when issues of race and racism are concerned. The cultural description of what "nappy" means is grounded in negative images of slavery. It is also parallel to a view about the impact of racial imagery on a culture held by critical theorist David Milner (1996), who stated that the psychological dimension in racism is important in constructing an ideology which "rationalizes maltreatment by the creation of different (and lesser) beings … and generates a gallery of stereotypes of suitable hate objects—justifying hostile attitudes" (p. 260). In Milner's view, there is acceptance of negative connotations of an "oppressed group" by that "oppressed group" because majority values have been internalized, "including the picture of them and their place in society" (p. 260). "Nappy," in reference to the hair texture of those from African descent, gains its negative connotation by the association of hair texture with standards of beauty that, in American culture, are guided by Eurocentric values.

Some attempts were made by the mainstream media to create dialogue about the sensitive issues surrounding the Don Imus controversy. In fact, the majority of "news" articles examined for this discussion were in the form of commentary and editorials that addressed the racial and misogynistic angles that were obviously at play here. Talk shows, like Oprah Winfrey's, and bloggers also joined in the discussion, bringing in "experts" and members of the hip hop community to address concerns about the type of language Imus was vilified for using. But, even in those formats, the commentary begins with the notion that Imus' behavior is rooted in other, more "deviant" aspects of culture. With a focus almost entirely framed around blame and consequences, critical dialogue about why the language has such deep-rooted negative connotations were mainly used for background, if at all. Columnists, in particular, had the opportunity to synthesize issues of race and gender in relation to hegemonic structures in American society like the billion-dollar media conglomerates that cash in on the contentious music's popularity. Poniewozik's (2007) piece took a backhanded look at the more critical aspect of the Imus issue, but leaves the discussion void by immediately returning to the aspect of blame. He begins:

The line was as damning as anything for what it suggested about Imus' thought process: a 66-year-old white male country-music fan rummaging in his subconscious for something to suggest that some young black women looked scary, and coming up with a reference to African-American hair and a random piece of rap slang. (Maybe because older, male media honchos are more conscious of—and thus fixated on—race than gender, much of the coverage of Imus ignored the sexual part of the slur on a show with a locker-room vibe and a mostly male guest list. If Imus had said "niggas" rather than "hos," would his bosses have waited as long to act?)

(n.p.)

And concluded:

So who gets to say "ho," in an age when *Pimp My Ride* is an innocent car show and *It's Hard Out Here for a Pimp* is an Oscar-winning song? As even Essence Carlson, one of the Rutgers students Imus insulted, acknowledged at a press conference, black rap artists labeled young black women as "hos" long before Imus did.

(n.p.)

The position of media scholars Price and Tewksbury (1997) on the shortcomings of news media and its coverage of complex issues holds true in our analysis of the coverage of the Don Imus controversy. In regard to the ultimate framing of this issue following a shift in coverage that focused on language and who may or may not have a right to use it, the media provided very little context or background on the role of language in culture, the ideology of cultural signifiers or the influence of culture on the connotation of words and concepts. According to the scholars, the framing effect used by contemporary news media is the result of news organizations producing stories that take an episodic rather than a thematic perspective toward the events they cover. They stated, "Instead of explaining the general background and implications of issues, news reports emphasize on the most recent and attention-getting developments" (p. 173).

Further, news coverage that does not include depth or complexity on sensitive, yet culturally relevant subject matter, is at risk of ignoring the powerful role that institutional, systemic and cultural phenomena play in racial (as well as gender) issues and the oppression of minority groups in American society. With the Imus controversy, if blame is the decisive angle, then media consumers should be provided with enough "intelligent" information to understand the complexities of all the issues at play and to ultimately understand why "blame" is necessary.

Interpreting Hurricane Katrina

For many, Hurricane Katrina is a vivid reminder of the federal government's failed response to a domestic case of natural disaster (Griffin, Jenkins, & Allison, 2008). While the media played a significant role in defining the key elements of this tragic event, this institution "was harshly criticized for its depiction of minorities ... as passive victims ... rarely shown in positions of expertise" (Voorhees, Vick, & Perkins, 2007, p. 415). Our critique of the mass media's coverage of Hurricane Katrina must be tempered with the recognition that through its intense coverage of this tragic event, the media "became a lifeline for suffering communities" (Voorhees, Vick, & Perkins, 2007, p. 416). The media provided a lens through which we could see first hand the horrors of residents trapped in flooded houses, on rooftops and neighboring bridges, in college dorms, and eventually in the New Orleans Superdome. But because of the vital role that media outlets play during crisis events, the mainstream media (particularly television) was further criticized for failing to focus on the underlying problems of systemic racism and geographic poverty that served as a breeding ground for this kind of crisis. As Livingstone (1998) pointed out, for many who witness crisis events, television becomes a primary source of information because it is often the primary means through which the masses interpret those events.

Much research has focused on the specifics of the opportunities missed by the American media in their coverage of Katrina, which included depictions of rampant crime and lawlessness, loss of government control and utter chaos in the Superdome and on the streets of New Orleans (Haider-Markel, Delehanty, & Beverlin, 2007; Prah, 2005; Tierny, Bevc, & Kuligowski, 2006). Voorhees, Vick, and Perkins (2007) argued that while disparities with regard to race and class were clearly visible in the news coverage of Katrina, "almost no mention of this disparity surfaced in the mainstream media" (p. 416). This is significant when we consider that, according to Gilens (1996), the ways in which the media stresses certain issues over others influences what the public takes away from events that are covered. In their study of Katrina coverage by mainstream media, Voorhees et al. (2007) characterized the following backlash:

> National Public Radio's On the Media (2005) reported that media critics faulted the mainstream media for ignoring issues of race in the face of obvious ethnic disparity; according to media critic Jack Shafer (of NPR): "nearly every rescued person, temporary resident

of the Superdome, looter or loiterer on the high ground, of the freeway seen on TV was black, with no questions about race asked or answered.

(p. 419)

In our analysis of mainstream news coverage of Hurricane Katrina, we agree with Sommers et al. (2006) and their assertion that "much of the media controversy to emerge in the aftermath of Katrina focused on issues of language" (p. 40). Receiving national attention were debates over the use of "refugee" versus "evacuee", use of the term "looters" and issues of "blame." In the controversy we mention earlier in this chapter over the term "looters," taking a more interpretive approach to coverage helps us to explore the real detriment of this kind of coverage. Huddy and Feldman (2006) note that this kind of racial framing not only had the potential to stir the pot of negativity among blacks about the government's botched response, but it may have also caused some whites to become desensitized to the sufferings of the victims of the Hurricane, who were predominantly black and poor.

While there was strong debate on the national front about definitions of the word "refugee" used to describe victims of the Hurricane, it took firm words of protest by Rev. Jesse Jackson and Al Sharpton to cease using "refugee" and begin using "evacuee" or "victim" to describe those left without homes. As Sommers et al. (2006) noted, the outcry also prompted President Bush to denounce use of the word. Even amidst the protest, the mainstream media missed an opportunity to use a more interpretive frame to debunk the negative connotations associated with the use of this term, particularly in a country as developed as the United States, to describe its own people.

Finally, the issue of "blame" sparked much debate on the national front. However, this issue was mostly relegated to a tit-for-tat finger-pointing squabble between public officials and government agencies. A more interpretive frame could have sparked an in-depth discussion on *why* the recovery effort took so long to get organized and why, ultimately, it left hundreds of the region's poor and African Americans "uncollected in the streets, on porches, hospitals, nursing homes, in electric wheelchairs, and in collapsed houses" (Giroux, 2006, p. 173). Giroux blamed it on a bio-political social agenda in which "individuals are no longer viewed as citizens but are now seen as inmates, stripped of everything, including their right to live" (p. 179).

Ultimately, particularly in the case of Hurricane Katrina, while the media provided crystal clear images of the tragedies of the event itself, it failed to bring into clarity the underlying factors that motivated such a negligent effort to recover those who were left to make sense of the devastation of this crisis event. What this and the case of Don Imus demonstrate is the need for the public to be more critical consumers of the news. In these and other cases, the mainstream media has an opportunity through an expanded range of interpretations of events, to increase our "ability to develop original and critical understandings" of the events themselves (Porto, 2007, p. 312).

Concluding Thoughts

The task of remaining objective in reporting is daunting and has been called into question by many media scholars. For example, Scanlan (2000) stated that news judgment is often a subjective process and is one that reflects the interests, prejudices and mind-sets of reporters and editors. According to Lehrman (2002), the best defense for this is for reporters to acknowledge their frame of reference and correct for it by asking them to consider how the elements of race, class, gender, generation, geography and other factors influence interpretations of news events. This notion also underscores the need for diversity in the news business, which ultimately pushes us to look more critically at traditional notions of objectivity and its continued function in a more diverse newsroom.

Further, threats to objectivity in contemporary media seem more substantial. Mindich (1998) stated that "the practice has come under scrutiny from those who point out that it too often reflects a world dominated by white men and that it too often serves the status quo" (p. 4). He notes that a female writer for the *New York Times* felt that one of the chief problems at the paper was its "white male voice ... seldom reflecting America's diversity;" and an African-American female writer for the *Washington Post* stated that "blacks must struggle daily with this notion of objectivity," a notion she equates with a white voice (p. 4).

As we move further into the twenty-first century, we must recognize that objectivity limits the ability of the reporter to discuss critically issues that can have detrimental effects on his/her community, culture, or country. Michael Schudson wrote in *Discovering the News*, "Journalists came to believe in objectivity, to the extent that they did, because they wanted to, needed to, were forced by ordinary human aspiration to seek escape from their own deep convictions of doubt and drift" (as cited in Brooks et al., 2004, p. 12). But as newsrooms continue to meet the demands of diversity and more minorities become a part of the mainstream news media, the traditional journalistic values may no longer fit into the business of news dissemination.

Historically, these values rose from a different view of society held by those who enjoyed a more monopolistic control of news information during the late nineteenth and early twentieth centuries. According to Doug McGill (2004), author of the McGill Report and former reporter with the *New York Times*, the rise of the famous "inverted pyramid" form of newspaper writing and other traditional tenets of journalism during this period were linked directly to publishers' growing belief that what readers—especially busy, educated, upscale readers—wanted was "just the facts." But, McGill notes that in that vein of "he said/she said" reporting "the norm of objectivity often has allowed serious social wrongs to continue unabated, while reporters misguidedly pursue the goal of 'balanced' coverage" (McGill, 2004, n.p.). As with missteps in coverage of issues like Hurricane Katrina or Don Imus, the notion of a "traditional" media that follows formulaic structures in news gathering does more to limit the understanding of social issues in society than to help.

Ultimately, it is not enough to say that we advocate an interpretive approach alone. We must also provide a diversity of interpretations that include underrepresented groups, and more importantly, groups that are directly affected by the events we cover. Research in this area must begin to include alternative news outlets in the discussion of interpreting complex events, including ethnic media in order to provide expanded options for coverage. Reporting by ethnic newspapers was key in the cases of both Don Imus and Hurricane Katrina not only because they provided an alternative perspective, but because that perspective pushed critical issues into the discussion that were important to a more diverse population of people. With newspapers in the early twenty-first century folding regularly and citizens turning to alternative sources of media for a more in-depth level of engagement with the day's issues, mainstream media will find its relevance in helping to articulate beyond the "who," "what," "where," and "when," and move toward a more critical discussion of the "why" and "how" certain events shape our lives in such complex ways.

References

Associated Press. (2007, April 13). Rap lyrics take a hit after Imus controversy. Retrieved March 12, 2010 from: http://abclocal.go.com/wpvi/story?section=news/entertainment&id=5208034.

Auletta, K. Who does a journalist work for? The Annual Red Smith Lecture at Notre Dame University. Retrieved January 7, 2010 from: http://www.kenauletta.com/notredame.html.

Bramlett-Solomon, S. (1993). Job appeal and job satisfaction among Hispanic and Black journalists. *Mass Communication Review, 20*, 202–211.

Brooks, B., Kennedy, G., Moen, D. R., & Ranly, D. (2002). The nature of news. In The Missouri Group, *News reporting and writing* (7th ed.). Boston/New York: Bedford/St. Martin's.

Brooks, B., Kennedy, G., Moen, D. R., & Ranly, D. (2004). The nature of news. In The Missouri Group, *Telling the story: The convergence of print, broadcast and online media* (2nd ed.). Boston/New York: Bedford/St. Martin's.

Byerly, C. & Wilson, C. (2009). Journalism as Kerner turns 40: Its multicultural problems and possibilities, *The Howard Journal of Communications, 20,* 209–221.

Campbell, C. (1995). *Race, myth and the news.* Thousand Oaks, CA: Sage.

Celizic, M. (2007, April 12). Blacks, whites disagree on "ho" comment: Blacks and whites disagree on why Imus's "ho" comment was so offensive. *Today.* Retrieved September 23, 2009, from: http://www.msnbc.msn.com/id/18054788/.

Craig, D. A. (2006). The ethics of interpretation and analysis in journalistic writing. Paper presented at the International Communication Association Conference, Dresden, Germany.

Dates, J. L. & Barlow, W. (1990). *Split image: African Americans in the mass media.* Washington, D.C.: Howard University Press.

Davies, D. (2005). The challenges of civil rights and Joseph McCarthy. In S. R. Knowlton & K. L. Freeman (Eds.), *Fair & balanced: A history of journalistic objectivity* (pp. 206–220). Northport, AL: Vision Press.

Entman, R. (1990). Modern racism and the images of blacks in local television news. *Critical Studies in Mass Communication, 7,* 332–345.

Entman, R. M. & Rojecki, A. (2000). *The Black image in the White mind: Media and race in America.* Chicago, IL: The University of Chicago Press.

Giroux, H. A. (2006). Reading Hurricane Katrina: Race, class and the biopolitics of disposability. *College Literature, 33*(3), 171–196.

Gilens, M. (1996). Race and poverty in America: Public misperceptions and the American news media. *Public Opinion Quarterly, 60*(4), 515–541.

Griffin, D. R., Jenkins, C. D. & Allison, D. (2008). *Framing "race" in Hurricane Katrina: Invisibility and disposability.* Paper presented at the annual meeting of the National Communication Association, San Diego, CA.

Haider-Markel, D. P, Delehanty, W. & Beverlin, M. (2007). Media framing and racial attitudes in the aftermath of Katrina. *Policy Studies Journal, 35*(4), 587–605.

Hall, S. (1982). Encoding/decoding. In S. Hall, D. Hobson, A. Lowe, & P. Wills (Eds.), *Culture, media, language* (pp. 128–138). London: Hutchinson.

Heider, D. (2000). *White news: Why local news programs don't cover people of color.* Mahwah, NJ: Lawrence Erlbaum Associates.

Howard, I. (2002, May/June). Power sources: On party, gender, race and class, TV news looks to the most powerful groups. Retrieved from: http://www.fair.org/index.php?page=1109 .

Huddy, L. & Feldman, S. (2006). Worlds apart: Blacks and Whites react to Hurricane Katrina. *Du Bois Review, 3*(1), 97–113.

Hughes, E. (1964). *Men and their work.* Glencoe, IL: Free Press.

Hume, E. (1996). The new paradigm for news. *Annals of the American Academy of Political and Social Science, 546,* The Media and Politics, 141–153.

Lehrman, S. (2002). Good cause still needs questioning. *Quill, 90*(6), 44–46.

Livingstone, S. M. (1998). *Making sense of television: The psychology of audience interpretation.* London and New York: Routledge.

March, J. G. & Simon, H. A. (1967). *Organizations.* New York: Wiley.

McGill, D. (2004). The fading mystique of an objective press. Message posted to http://www.mcgillreport.org/objectivity.htm.

Milner, D. (1996). Children and racism: Beyond the value of dolls ... In W. P. Robinson (Ed.), *Social groups and identities: Developing the legacy of Henri Tajfel* (International Series in Social Psychology, pp. 249–269). Jordon Hill, Oxford: Butterworth-Heinemann.

Mindich, D. T. Z. (1998). *Just the facts: How "objectivity" came to define American journalism.* New York: New York University Press.

Nishikawa, K. A., Towner, T. L., Clawson, R. A., & Waltenburg, E. N. (2009). Interviewing the interviewers: Journalistic norms and racial diversity in the newsroom. *The Howard Journal of Communications, 20,* 242–259.

Patterson, T. E. (2006). *We the people: A concise introduction to American politics.* New York: McGraw-Hill.

Poniewozik, J. (2007, April 12). The Imus Fallout: Who can say what? *TIME*. Retrieved September 23, 2009, from: http://www.time.com/time/printout/0,8816,1609490,00.html.

Porto, M. P. (2007). Frame diversity and citizen competence: Towards a critical approach to news quality. *Critical Studies in Media Communication, 24*(4), 303–321.

Prah, P. M. (2005). Disaster preparedness. *CQ Researcher, 15*, 981–1004.

Price, V. & Tewksbury, D. (1997). News values and public opinion: A theoretical account of media priming and framing. *Progress in Communication Sciences, 13*, 173–212.

Scanlan, C. (2000). News thinking in a changing word. In C. Scanlan (Ed.), *Reporting and writing: Basics for the 21st century*. New York: Oxford University Press.

Sommers, S. R., Apfelbaum, E. P., Dukes, K. N., Toosi, N., & Wang, E. J. (2006). Race and media coverage of Hurricane Katrina: Analysis, implications and future research questions. *Analysis of Social Issues and Public Policy, 6*(1), 39–55.

Tierny, K. Bevc, C., & Kuligowski, E. (2006). Metaphors matter: Disaster myths, media frames, and their consequences in Hurricane Katrina. *The Annals of the American Academy of Political and Social Science, 604*, 57–81.

Tuchman, G. (1972). Objectivity as strategic ritual: An examination of newsmen's notions of objectivity. *The American Journal of Sociology, 77*(4), 660–679.

Voorhees, C. C. W., Vick, J., & Perkins, D. D. (2007). "Came hell and high water": The intersection of Hurricane Katrina, the news media, race and poverty. *Journal of Community & Applied Social Psychology, 17*, 415–429.

Weaver, D. & Wilhoit, G. (1991). *The American journalist: A portrait of U.S. news people and their work*. Bloomington, IN: Indiana University Press.

Weaver, D. H. & Wilhoit, G. C. (1996). *The American journalist in the 1990s: U.S. news people at the end of an era*. Mahwah, NJ: Lawrence Erlbaum Associates.

Who's on the news? Study shows network news sources skew white, male & elite (2001). Retrieved January 7, 2010 from http://www.fair.org/index.php?page=1865.

Wilson, C., Gutierrez, F., & Chao, L. M. (2003). *Racism, sexism and the media*. Thousand Oaks, CA: Sage Publications.

Discussion Questions

1. Discuss your understanding of the journalistic tenet of objectivity. How does this chapter's assessment of objectivity fall in line with your thoughts/understanding of it?

2. Compare coverage of a news story from a major national newspaper (*New York Times, Washington Post, Los Angeles Times, Chicago Times*, or others) with coverage of the same news story on a major network news broadcast (NBC Nightly News, ABC News, CBS News, Fox News, or others). Contrast the difference in how the same story was reported in each medium. Are there obvious differences in how the story was told? Is there more depth or explanation in one or the other?

3. What point of view is expressed in the news coverage you analyzed? Is it obvious, subtle, or difficult to determine? Explain your answer and provide examples to support your position.

4. Do you think news stories can be completely unbiased? Why or why not?

5. How has the Internet affected the way news stories are told?

Assignments

1. Point out any words, certain facts or treatments of the coverage of a current news story to determine if there is bias in the story.
2. Select two news stories from a newspaper that you found particularly compelling or disturbing. Describe the journalists … Was the journalist male, female, African American, Caucasian or an identifiable race? Do you think the reporter's gender and/or race made a difference in the reporting of the story? If so, describe how you think the reporter could have better told the story without regard to race.
3. From the news stories you selected, select a concept or aspect that can be further explained or explicated (i.e. racism, stereotypes, language) and provide additional background material to explain what the concept means in a broader context.

For Further Study

Journalism historian and scholar Michael Schudson is an excellent source for reviewing the debate over objectivity and other journalistic tenets. His work includes *Discovering the News: A Social History of American Newspapers* (1981) and *The Good Citizen: A History of American Civic Life* (1998).

An excellent resource for examining the role of journalism in a democratic society is: *The Elements of Journalism: What Newspeople Should Know and the Public Should Expect,* by Bill Kovach and Tom Rosenstiel (2001).

Afterword

Rethinking the News: How American Journalism Can Improve Coverage of Race and Racism

On his last day on the job as the dean of the faculty at the Poynter Institute for Media Studies, Keith Woods, a veteran journalist who led the institute's diversity training for many years, outlined his ideas for improving journalistic coverage of diverse communities. First, he described the four "evergreens":

- Hire a diverse staff.
- Diversify your source base.
- Learn—and keep learning—about the people in your community.
- Tell great stories.

He then offered five more "notions," which he described as "a mix of time-tested wisdom and new-realities thinking." They follow:

1. Set priorities. Recognize that you serve everyone—but especially the most vulnerable communities—by sticking to two core principles: Hold the powerful accountable. Give voice to the voiceless.
2. Talk to the community: Tell people what you can do with your resources and what you can't; seek their help in getting their news to you and your news to them.
3. Pursue the ordinary: There is a cruel irony that often reveals itself as organizations position themselves as champions of the forgotten

and downtrodden. The picture we paint tends to be a one-dimensional portrait of people who are only forgotten and down-trodden and in need of help. We miss their ordinariness. They become frozen in permanent pathology. We miss the normal parts of their lives that make them laugh, love, cry, rejoice.

4. Be strategic about platforms. Recognize that every platform—traditional or brand new—includes and excludes. Be thoughtful about who you're trying to reach with your news and where you're most likely to reach them. Some groups use Facebook more than Myspace and Myspace more than Twitter, e-mail more than texting, on-line more than radio, etc. Keep current on these differences through research and feedback.

5. Separate these two ideas: A) Covering communities is core to your democratic mission. B) Covering people better could get them to use your product more. Too often, journalists conflate mission and money. That means that if (B) turns out not to be true, it negates the need to do (A). If your primary mission is to have an informed public so that they can make the best decisions, then your first responsibility is to be sure that whoever is watching/reading/listening/clicking is getting the most complete story about themselves and everybody else.

We believe this is great advice. The simple truth is that good coverage of diverse communities is often a matter of effectively practicing the most basic tenets of journalism. But we also realize that many news organizations produce coverage—like much of what was analyzed in this book—that strays from these basic tenets. One of our primary concerns is that newsrooms aren't especially eager to embrace new ways to cover the news. Journalists tend to get defensive when they are challenged on their approaches. A telling anecdote: when asked for a definition of news, the legendary ABC News anchor David Brinkley offered this terse, oft-quoted response: "News is what I say it is." Most journalists are comfortable with the routines that they believe have worked effectively for decades. They are typically uncomfortable when challenged about those routines. When somebody in the community gets shot, journalists instinctively show up at the scene, interview the police and file a story. The event itself is the news. To suggest that news coverage might provide an audience with a broader perspective—for instance, why the violent crime rate is so high in impoverished communities—is dismissed. News is a deadline-driven process, and journalists are comfortable with their daily routines.

Woods' advice is sound, pragmatic counsel to news organizations that are willing to consider modest changes to their approach to covering diversity. We wish that more news organizations would heed his advice, as it doesn't really challenge journalists to reconsider their efforts in any dramatic way. But while we believe that news organizations should heed the relatively un-intrusive recommendations that Woods describes, we also believe that the profession should consider broader and more significant changes to newsroom routines if journalism is to wholly fulfill its mission to cover all communities and their full complexity. Among the suggestions that surfaced in various chapters of this book:

- Instead of focusing on the crime-of-the-day, news organizations should consider providing coverage that provides audiences with some sense of *context* for crime. We've heard this phrased as covering "crime" instead of "crimes." We wonder: Can news organizations tell compelling stories about the way in which poverty drives criminal behavior in impoverished communities? About how drug and alcohol abuse affect that behavior? About the relationship between failed public school systems and crime in the communities that those schools serve? About how the legacy of American racism still affects opportunities for people who live in difficult economic circumstances? We believe that these are questions that could lead to interesting, useful stories that would tell audiences much more about their communities than the violent crimes that are routinely covered as daily evidence of pathological behavior in poor communities.
- Keith Woods' first piece of advice to newsroom managers is to hire a diverse staff. While this is good advice, it may not by itself dramatically change coverage of diverse communities. A diverse staff—or any staff that is motivated to think differently about how the organization approaches its coverage—needs to be encouraged to think more broadly about coverage and to think more *thematically* then *episodically*. That is, journalists should routinely consider the broader context for daily events, especially when it comes to issues of race. First, journalists need to think twice before reinforcing stereotypes about people of color that emphasize extremes—either dire failure or spectacular success. Minority communities are much more diverse than that. Second, many journalists seem to believe that the election of President Barack Obama means that we are living in a "post-racial" America. There is plenty of evidence to demonstrate that that is simply not the case. Racism and its legacy continue to have a powerful impact on American economics, education, criminal justice, politics and public policy. Journalists should be covering that impact and providing context by telling stories that put human faces on the issues.

- News organizations need to pay attention to where audiences are turning for "news." As audiences turn to the internet, blogs or the entertainment industry, news organizations need to consider the potential to draw readers and viewers to compelling multimedia storytelling and interactive media that can provide a broader understanding of race. Currently, news organization Web sites routinely host on-line debates among anonymous audience members that are largely unedited and unmonitored, and they routinely reflect racist attitudes. That dialogue might serve a useful function if the debate is guided and anonymity is limited. Additionally, television journalists should consider adopting new approaches, including long-form and documentary-styled storytelling that provides perspective about the day's issues through compelling stories about individuals and communities affected by those issues.

- The Black Press and other ethnic media fill an important void for minority communities. Economic downturns typically have a more devastating effect on impoverished communities, and the Black Press and other ethnic media will struggle in weak economies. Media companies should consider investing in ethnic media, and not just for altruistic reasons. As American minorities become the majority population in the U.S. in the first half of the twentieth century, the need for strong ethnic media will be more important than ever. Mainstream news organizations would do well to pay attention to the ethnic media and provide coverage of the vital issues that are identified by media that serve minority communities.

- As media organizations become more politicized (for instance, television's Fox News), the chances for overtly or subtly racist journalistic representations become more likely. That is, discussions about race will tend to reflect the political biases of the news organizations; rather than real dialogue, race baiting and racial coding could dominate coverage. News organizations should attempt to provide coverage that encourages thoughtful debate on complicated notions related to race and racism. When news organizations reflect the splintering of public opinion—whether through political or regional biases—they are limiting the opportunity for audiences to consider alternative representations and understandings of the multicultural world in which they live.

- Several chapters in this book cite the work of Critical Race Theorists who examine the impact of white privilege on society. Rather than focusing on people of color as "others," these theorists shift the discussion to how "whiteness" works in American culture.

News organizations—especially at the leadership level—continue to be the domain of white males who tend not to recognize the privileges that they have historically enjoyed as members of a dominant, hegemonic cultural system. As issues with a racial component surface in the news—shock jock Don Imus' widely publicized controversial statements, for example—news organizations often appear ill-equipped to deal with the full complexity of the issue. White journalists, especially those in leadership positions, need to be especially aware of their privileged position in American society and open to interpretations of events that may conflict with their view of the world.

· Journalistic conventions—especially those typically practiced in television news operations—can contribute to racial coding that reinforces the attitudes behind contemporary racism. Most problematic are the routine local TV news stories that provide only cursory information and little context, especially when there are complicated historical, social, economic and political factors at work. But this isn't just an issue for local television news organizations. Major daily newspapers and network television news operations seem to provide less and less explanatory journalism, in favor of simple stories that can be easily pursued. When it comes to the issue of racial representation, that kind of coverage too often relies on stereotypical notions that do little to provide audiences with a real sense of understanding. While the process of documentary-making requires a very different approach to story-telling, daily journalism could, at least occasionally, utilize its resources to provide more in-depth coverage of issues that have a racial component instead of relying on the typical racial codes that often inform that coverage. We grow increasingly concerned as media companies continue to squeeze newsrooms and cut staffs to increase profits, rather than investing in journalistic endeavors that could potentially expand the audiences they seek to attract.

· Much of the analysis in this book has focused on the underrepresentation and misrepresentation of African Americans in the news. We have touched on problematic coverage of Latino, Arab and Asian Americans, and we remain deeply concerned about those and other representations. Coverage of American Indians and issues that affect Indian Country, for instance, is largely absent from mainstream journalism. Audiences need not only more coverage of diverse communities, they need coverage that will provide them with a broader sense of the challenges that are faced in a country whose future will be increasingly multicultural.

- Chapter 12 of this book recommends that news organizations consider a fairly dramatic shift regarding "objectivity" as the most fundamental notion of American journalism. Many journalists and scholars have observed that the notion of objectivity is a dubious one. Virtually every decision a journalist makes is subjective, from the questions posed to a source to the words and pictures that are selected to tell stories. "Objectivity" is often something that journalists hide behind when defending coverage that is actually unbalanced, unfair and (our primary concern) racist. Newsrooms would do well to consider more interpretive coverage, especially when it comes to stories about minority communities that have been badly misrepresented throughout the history of American journalism.

Several chapters in this book identified approaches that we believe offer a glimmer of hope for a future in which journalism does provide audiences with more insight about the multicultural world in which Americans live. There are plenty of good examples of journalism that has done just that: Network television coverage of the Civil Rights movement in the South, for instance, changed forever American public policy on legalized racial oppression. And we still see occasional stories about crime, poverty, immigration and other issues that give us the sense that some news organizations have not fully abdicated their role in giving voice to the voiceless. For instance, while we were generally critical of the mainstream media coverage of New Orleans shortly after Hurricane Katrina, we have seen remarkable coverage at both the local and national level that provides audiences with a better sense of the challenges faced by the city before and after Katrina. But we also consider that kind of coverage to be an anomaly. Far too often, when it comes to matters of race, we see routine and uninspired journalism that is not going to help the country deal with the myriad of issues faced by the world's most culturally diverse population.

We don't expect to see the kind of dramatic changes in newsroom routines that we are recommending, at least not in the near future. In fact, as news organizations fight for survival in a media world that is being controlled by fewer and fewer large companies, the likelihood for improved journalism diminishes. Media conglomerates looking for quick profits will continue to drain newsroom resources rather than increase them. Until strong, informed coverage of race and multiculturalism is proven to be profitable, we doubt that there will be any new investment in that coverage. We do have some hope, albeit long term. Younger Americans tend to be more comfortable with cultural diversity, and as they move into the news industry and into leadership positions, they will bring different sensibilities to the newsroom. The challenge for future generations of journalists will be to break down conventions and routines that have dictated coverage that for decades has under-represented or misrepresented people and communities of color.

About the Authors

Christopher P. Campbell is director and professor in the School of Mass Communication and Journalism at the University of Southern Mississippi. He has written a number of articles and book chapters about media and diversity. He earned his Ph.D. at USM in 1993. His dissertation research was published in 1995 as *Race, Myth and the News* (Sage Publications).

Kim M. LeDuff is assistant director and associate professor in the School of Mass Communication and Journalism at the University of Southern Mississippi. She earned her Ph.D. at Indiana University in 2007. Her dissertation research was published in 2009 as *A Tale of Two Cities: How Race and Crime Intersect on Local Television News* (Lambert Publishing).

Cheryl D. Jenkins is an assistant professor in the School of Mass Communication and Journalism at the University of Southern Mississippi. She earned her Ph.D. at Howard University in 2002. Her dissertation examined coverage of the 2000 presidential election by the Black Press.

Rockell A. Brown is an assistant professor in the School of Communication at Texas Southern University, where she has chaired the university's Intercultural Communication Conference since 2007. She earned her Ph.D. at Wayne State University in 2003. Her dissertation examined African-American newspaper coverage of the AIDS crisis; some of that research is included in Chapter 6 of this book.

About the Co-Authors

Reynaldo Anderson is an assistant professor in the Department of Teacher Education at Harris-Stowe State University.

Hazel James Cole is an assistant professor in the Department of Communication at McNeese State University.

Robin Cecala is a doctoral student in the School of Mass Communication and Journalism at the University of Southern Mississippi.

Donyale R. Griffin Padgett is an assistant professor in the Department of Communication at Wayne State University.

Jason Thompson is an assistant professor in the Department of Speech Communication Arts and Sciences at Brooklyn College-CUNY.

Index